D0323414

Vishnu in Hollywood

The Changing Image of the American Male

David I. Grossvogel

791.43
G878

The Scarecrow Press, Inc.
Lanham, Maryland, and London
2000

Alverno College Library
Milwaukee, WI

SCARECROW PRESS, INC.

Published in the United States of America
by Scarecrow Press, Inc.
4720 Boston Way, Lanham, Maryland 20706
www.scarecrowpress.com

4 Pleydell Gardens, Folkestone
Kent CT20 2DN, England

Copyright © 2000 by David I. Grossvogel

All rights reserved. No part of this publication may be reproduced,
stored in a retrieval system, or transmitted in any form or by any
means, electronic, mechanical, photocopying, recording, or otherwise,
without the prior permission of the publisher.

British Library Cataloguing in Publication Information Available

Library of Congress Cataloging-in-Publication Data

Grossvogel, David I., 1925–
   Vishnu in Hollywood : the changing image of the American male / David I.
Grossvogel.   p. cm.
   Includes bibliographical references and index.
   ISBN 0-8108-3767-6 (cloth : alk. paper)
   1. Men in motion pictures. 2. Motion picture actors and actresses—United
States—Biography.   3. Male actors—United States—Biography. I. Title.
PN1995.9.M46 G76 2000
791.43'652041—dc21   99-088551

♾️™ The paper used in this publication meets the minimum requirements of
American National Standard for Information Sciences—Permanence of
Paper for Printed Library Materials, ANSI/NISO Z39.48–1992.
Manufactured in the United States of America.

"Whenever order, justice, and morals are in danger," says Vishnu, "I come down to earth and take human shape." These descents of Vishnu are known in Hindu mythology as avatars: Vishnu does not actually become the shape he takes but, rather, strengthens and encourages his devotees through the power of the form he contrives. There are generally thought to be ten avatars of Vishnu, but some believe that his incarnations are without number and that it may happen that an unsuspected figure turns out opportunely to be a hitherto unrecognized avatar.

Kalki, the tenth avatar, is yet to come. Kalki will appear riding on a white horse or might be that horse itself. But when it occurs, it will finally destroy this impure world.

Contents

Acknowledgments

The following authorizations to quote are herewith acknowledged: Raymond Chandler, *The Big Sleep,* copyright 1975 by Alfred A. Knopf, Inc.; Donald Deschner, *The Films of Cary Grant,* copyright 1973 by the Carol Publishing Group, and Donald Deschner, *The Films of Spencer Tracy,* copyright 1968 by the Carol Publishing Group; Joseph McBride and Michael Wilmington, *John Ford,* copyright 1975 by Da Capo Press, and Frank Capra, *The Name above the Title,* copyright 1971 by Da Capo Press; Joseph Gelmis, *The Film Director as Superstar,* copyright 1970 by Doubleday and Co., and James Cagney, *Cagney by Cagney,* copyright 1976 by Doubleday and Co.; Sanche de Gramont, *The French,* copyright 1969 by G. P. Putnam; Edgar Morin, *The Stars,* copyright 1960 by Grove/Atlantic, Inc., and Stig Björkman, *Woody Allen on Woody Allen,* copyright 1995 by Grove/Atlantic, Inc.; Charles Chaplin, *My Autobiography,* copyright 1964 by Simon and Schuster; David Dalton, *James Dean: The Mutant King,* copyright 1974 by Straight Arrow Books; Irving Shulman, *Valentino,* copyright 1967 by Trident Press; John Kreidl, *Nicholas Ray,* copyright 1977 by Twayne Publishers; Paul Warshow, *The Immediate Experience,* copyright 1962 by Paul Warshow; Anne Edwards, *A Remarkable Woman: A Biography of Katharine Hepburn,* copyright 1985 by William Morrow and Co.

For assistance in using Cornell Cinema's remarkable archives, permission to draw from them, and help in guiding me through them, I extend grateful thanks to Mary Fessenden. I am thankful as well to Don Fredericksen for sharing with me his extensive and scholarly knowledge of film criticism, as well as for the many, many years we screened pictures together.

I am also grateful to the wonderful people at Scarecrow Press with whom I was associated and to copyeditor Elisabeth Graves for making the production part of the process such a pleasant and rewarding experience.

No book has a single author. But when the book is about cinema, about the way we were, about the way we are now, about men (and women too), it derives from a public domain so vast that all who prolonged a pleasurable evening at the movies into an even more pleasurable evening discussing them deserve thanks for contributing to its eventual birth. I would like to remember here at least three people who were willing to extend the discussion into an actual reading of the manuscript: Miriam Brody, Isaac Kramnick, and, as usual, my wife Jill.

Introduction

Since Molly Haskell's *From Reverence to Rape* (1974), film analysis has become an important province of feminist criticism in this country. In addition to the works cited in this study, works by Teresa de Lauretis (*Alice Doesn't,* 1982), Annette Kuhn (*Women's Pictures,* 1994), E. Ann Kaplan (*Women and Film,* 1983), Kaja Silverman (*The Subject of Semiotics,* 1983), Mary Ann Doane (*The Desire to Desire,* 1987), Judith Mayne (*Kino and the Woman Question,* 1989); *The Woman at the Keyhole,* 1990), Susan Jeffords (*Hard Bodies,* 1994), as well as the numerous voices in the editions of Steven Cohan and Ina Rae Hark (*Screening the Male,* 1993) or Pat Kirkham and Janet Thumim (*You Tarzan,* 1993; *Me Jane,* 1995), have been a few of those that, whether written on women, psychoanalysis, or semiotics, have used the film as a springboard. These authors and many others have also written scores of articles, finding a voice in journals like *Camera Obscura* and special issues of standard periodicals such as *Film Reader, Screen,* or *Wide Angle,* which link the concerns of feminism and film theory.

The questioning of domination subtends most contemporary analysis, whether in literature, social studies, or the arts.[1] Thus, to the extent that men enter into serious studies of films, they are primarily the implicit point of view (now made explicit) that accounts for the shaping of the motion picture, from the perspective of its scripts, its use of actors (and of course actresses), the form of its editing, the assumptions of its distribution and reception: in short, feminist criticism attends to men as an assumed and normative centrality that must be deconstructed by pointing out the distortions that result from it.[2] When these men are the ones who made Hollywood films, the entire industry is in-

dicted: Mayne writes that "classical Hollywood cinema has become the
norm against which all other alternative film practices are measured.
Films which do not engage the classical Hollywood cinema are by and
large relegated to irrelevance" (*Kino and the Woman Question*, p. 3).
The corollary is that alongside the "alternative" motion picture, it is in
fact classical Hollywood cinema that is irrelevant—interesting only as a
locus of derelictions.[3]

The sophistication of these critics requires an equally sophisticated
viewer to properly read the motion picture as distortion or as viable alternative. Marie-Claire Ropars echoes this familiar positioning in modern criticism, warning away the spectators from what they might think
they see, distinguishing between the film as "inquiry" rather than as a
"given": thanks to montage, the spectator pays attention to a process
rather than to the result of that process, understanding the film as "a
production of meaning . . . , not in the reproduction of appearances"
("Fonction de la métaphore dans 'Octobre' d'Eisenstein," p. 126).

"Classical Hollywood" never worried about these questions: it may
have been insensitive (and there are those like Heidi Dawidoff who
argue that this was simply not the case), but if it was, its insensitivity reflected the audience's. That is why, by the end of the Second World
War, two out of three Americans went to the movies at least once a
week and enjoyed what they were seeing. Few other industries listened more closely to what their customers wanted. Sociologists question the critic's right to identify "spectators," yet the film industry had
no trouble spotting them for the better part of a century. Not only was
the motion picture crafted with the greatest possible number of spectators in mind, but the people who made movies (nearly exclusively
men, as feminist criticism has not failed to point out) listened very carefully to their representative spectators and for a long time gave them
the closest possible approximation of their desires. When the film had
been written, rewritten, shot, reshot, argued, and reargued, it was
shown to preview audiences who were asked what they thought of it
before it was finally released. Much as it pains those who argue by exception, moviemakers were able to assume that their products would
find ready recognition and acceptance, and the figures (their bottom-
line interest) show they were right most of the time. So when the question is asked, "What average spectator do you have in mind?" The answer is, "The spectator, male or female, who responded millions of
times over to certain images of him- or herself—whether as projections
of that spectator's most intimate dreams or most repressed anger."

That being said, the author who attempts a cultural history of the male Hollywood star still has the problem of locating stars who were representative of a type during a given period so as not to be accused of selecting personal favorites, whether stars or motion pictures. For the thirties, when records of such matters began to be kept accurately, we have chosen the top box office draws—the stars that spectators paid to see in greatest numbers. These were not always men: in the second half of the thirties, children (Shirley Temple and Mickey Rooney in particular) dominate the charts. In the next decade, Abbot and Costello rise to the top with surprising frequency. Furthermore, the biggest box office draws during the 1930s are often women (who make up 50 percent of the lists, as opposed, for example, to 10 percent during the seventies): in 1932, the three most popular stars are Marie Dressler, Janet Gaynor, and Joan Crawford. Thus, the films that concern us, the very popular vehicles built around an everyday, contemporary, and therefore recognizable male figure with whom the spectator could readily identify, may not necessarily be the top drawers in any given year. Clark Gable remains through the thirties among the male stars with the greatest appeal. He eclipses Charles Boyer, who shares with Valentino only the appeal of the exotic but who retains, nevertheless, sufficient allure to be cast opposite the most alluring female leads. In 1931, *Little Caesar* is a top box office hit, but because his did not fully conform to male (or even female) phantasms, Edward G. Robinson's popularity never equaled that of the film. On the other hand, the somewhat less successful *Public Enemy* released at about the same time helped make James Cagney a top earner by 1935 because Cagney was much closer to the projection of the male spectator.

The Philadelphia Story was one of the more popular pictures of 1942, and in it, Cary Grant wins Katharine Hepburn over James Stewart, a perennial favorite who was rewarded with an Oscar that year. But because Cary Grant was something of an acquired taste (less obviously exotic than Charles Boyer but still someone whose charm was foreign), it took some fifteen years for him to emerge as a top money earner, even though he always remained high on the list of favorite screen males.

In 1940, two years before making *Woman of the Year,* Spencer Tracy was the second biggest box office attraction, and three years before making *The Big Sleep,* Humphrey Bogart was number seven: both would be enduring icons throughout the decade. In 1941, Gary Cooper, who has been among top-ranked males since 1936, stars in

Meet John Doe, and his box office appeal places him immediately behind the ever popular Clark Gable, who is second (both are behind Abbott and Costello). John Wayne's popularity was most likely the steadiest during this period: he appears on the roster of top-rated male stars more than any other. In contrast to these, Marlon Brando and James Dean appear in the next decade (the mid-1950s) as projections of the young's restlessness and assertiveness: their early portrayals of young rebels mirror a rift in the social fabric that extends to movie audiences. Consequently, Brando and Dean will not reach box office heights, but there can be no question that they are the screen incarnations of a substantial part of the population.

That division of the audience either accounts for or coincides with the end of the studio system: stars are more and more absorbed by their screen characters instead of representing them. This may make for better movies, but excellence of characterization stresses individuality over unanimity. In the seventies, Dustin Hoffman, Jack Nicholson, and Woody Allen will climb into box office prominence, even though their appeal is now to an admittedly fragmented audience. Nicholson is the most widely recognizable of the three, and as such maintains star quality; but even in him, facelessness testifies to the importance of characterization. On the other hand, it takes large city audiences to respond to the specific neuroses of Woody Allen.[4]

There are those who will argue that the idealized stars who enacted largely their own personas have not disappeared, that they endure in Arnold Schwarzenegger, Sylvester Stallone, or Harrison Ford (who, according to his own observations, always plays himself). Indeed, there are many recognizable names and faces even today. The question is whether they are given vehicles that are equally recognizable—or are the worlds in which they evolve simply phantasmic creations too remote to afford the spectator even the possibility of romance that a genre like the Western once held out? The scope of the new screen adventure and the brutality it often entails may allow the spectator to rehearse hostilities or dreams of escape born of his own discontent, but such rehearsals are limited because, within the spectrum of suggested possibilities, he can only indulge brutality.

We have no more quarrel with sociologists who would like to break the spectator down into many components affected by economic or class factors than we do with feminist analysis that points to the distortion of the male point of view, or with semioticians who remind us that an auteur film can be enjoyed far more for the *way* the auteur speaks than for what he says: we are only saying that these questions do not concern mainline Hollywood moviemakers.[5] Accepting that the film was "a *masculine* subject of enunciation" (as de Lauretis [*Alice Doesn't,* p. 20] says of the Lévi-Strauss she is deconstructing), the success of "classical Hollywood films" suggests that if we read them in the same way their first spectators did, we will have a fair idea of the evolving picture of the male in this country during the century—even if we extend this reading beyond the time of Hollywood's heyday.

We thus use the masculine *he* in identifying the spectator, in the belief that the masculine screen image was usually the product of a symbiotic relation with the male part of the audience (when his appeal was directed more specifically to women, we will naturally specify a female spectator). But as the masculine figure relies in a postmodern period on more complex appeals than the immediately sexual, the spectator tends to become nongendered and the *he* is neutered.

Of course, there have been attempts to analyze scientifically just who went to movies. We have, among others, the studies of the U.S. Department of Labor and the CNRS (France's national center for scientific research), which record who spent how much on what kind of entertainment; and we have additionally all the audience analyses that began early on with W. M. Seabury's *The Public and the Motion Picture Industry* in 1926 and proliferated in the postwar era when people still went to movies in droves, like those by *Mass Communications* (1949), Gilbert Cohen-Séat (*Essais sur les principes d'une philosophie du cinéma,* 1946), the various works by Leo A. Handel (*Hollywood Looks at Its Audience,* 1950), Edgar Morin (and in particular his *Recherches sur le public cinématographique,* 1953), Gilbert Seldes's *The Great Audience* (1951) or Jacques Durand's *Le Cinéma et son public* (1958). What these studies show is that, at the height of film's popularity, the greatest number of movie spectators were young (those under twenty-four would tend to go over once a week, those under thirty-four just under that, and higher age groups patronized them with decreasing frequency); that out of nine economic categories, the highest number of spectators was furnished by the third-lowest group—mainly the working class; and that this naive and enthusiastic audience was more apt to respond naively and enthusiastically (Durand, p. 121).

Such analyses are of interest mainly to sociologists: it stands to reason that no critic was ever likely to indulge in effortless identifications, and movies were not made, until fairly recently, with critics in mind: they were made for the box office. By examining the more successful box of-

fice draws, those actors who most nearly embodied the image of someone to whose manner, look, outlook, actions, circumstances—or any
combination of these—the greatest number of spectators responded,
we can trace the changing nature of American men as Hollywood analyzed it and as it very likely was.

After the demise of the star, other factors contributed to the screen
image that corresponded to the imperatives of a different age. But until
that time, a great fresco unfolds that we can now usefully decipher
long after the average spectator deciphered it with pleasure and quite
effortlessly on any given night of the week. The specialized reader of
a motion picture sees it as a set of complex manipulations—a visual
medium into the making of which enter the subtleties of editing, camera work, and other aspects of an elaborate mise en scène. The spectators whose masses first ensured the success of motion pictures did
not know this (it is doubtful that even today's nonspecialized spectator
is very aware of this process); for them, a story was being told: there
were people and a plot. If we are to understand their image of a man
(as well as Hollywood's), we must read what they were reading rather
than focus on the covert ways in which that reading was achieved or
on the possible aberrations implicit in either the reading or the manip-
ulation. We are talking here about a cultural acceptance that allowed
the accurate interpretation of a plot and the ready identification of its
characters.

To look for the image of the American male in the kaleidoscope of images
provided by Hollywood over the years is to look at patterns of reflected
light composing designs that only approximate reality. We recognize that
even male stars who endured for a long time in their portrayal of everyday types were first of all stars, and the star's persona transcends the character he plays. However much the star might represent a character, the
star in his enactment displays a heroic dimension, born as he is of a divine parent (his stardom) and of a mortal one (his role). It is in that mortal part that the evolving picture of the American man must be sought,
even though the divine halo undoubtedly persists.

That mortal part is important as well because it is the flaw in the
screen's bigger-than-nature image: it is the part of the star the spectator is able to contaminate, the spectator's contribution to the reality of
an image. It allows at least partial kinship by resisting the otherwise
total assumption into the star's illusive empyrean. But even so, the
character portrayed by the star will never be simply a character be-

cause it will always be contained within the aura of the star. And a part of the star always plays himself in the role he enacts.

Because that mortal part is so important, we have eliminated from this constellation of archetypal males those stars who were primarily stars, whose performance tended to exclude any other, even though they kept vast audiences enthralled over very long periods of time. Thus, we preferred the voiceless William S. Hart to Bing Crosby because Bing was primarily a voice. We chose Jimmy Cagney or Gary Cooper over Fred Astaire because they could be less easily reduced to the charm of their dancing or their smile. And if we kept charmers like Rudolph Valentino, Charles Boyer, or even Clark Gable, it was because their charm came from a more dangerous inwardness: in them, the immediacy of sex appeal was replaced by more deeply submerged meanderings of sexual calling, and at those depths, Eros is much closer to Thanatos.

For the same reason, we felt the image of Charlie Chaplin came closer to reflecting a person than the indestructible Laurel and Hardy or the equally resilient Marx brothers. In the first, the comic mask is apt to slip and disclose hidden pain—the spectator may laugh at or admire the comic character who is instantly destroyed only in order to be made whole again nearly as instantly, but he cannot assimilate him; the blows that bounce off that character leave bloody marks on human flesh.

The comic figure is impaired: by definition, he suffers from a dysfunction. His comic vice is a kind of disease. If he is wholly defined by that disease, he is tragic. It is when we note his contrast or resistance to a Bergsonian imposition of automatisms ("du mécanique plaqué sur le vivant," something mechanical impressed on something living) that we read the contrast as "funny." Dustin Hoffman's *Rain Man* is a tragic figure when we see a man wholly imprisoned within the debilitating limitations of the idiot savant. When, however, the *savant* emerges from the *idiot,* the identifiable human being overcomes those limitations and casts them retrospectively in a comic light. Sometimes, the contrast is reduced to its simplest expression: the Three Stooges are like cartoon characters—the blows that rain down on them would exhaust a human being; their unremitting (more than human) resilience is their comic motor. We have slighted these knockabout comics, alongside their noncomic counterparts who, like Douglas Fairbanks, tended to remain themselves from film to film in roles whose restrictive focus allowed them to do so.

Though the spectator's self-recognition in a comic character may appear to be unlikely, the comic character is actually the one who comes closest to being "real" because the comic character is not, in fact, a character. We are drawn to the clown in our identification of some part of ourselves that we recognize in the clown's dilemma, but this does not mean that we accept what caused the dilemma (we may indeed see that as unlikely, completely alien, or merely symbolic). This recognition of ourselves within the clown makes of him one of the few characters that elicit our identification without the need of a fiction to assist in that identification. Over many years, Charlie Chaplin may have become "the little guy," but it was not the peculiarity of a fictional role that created the character: on screen, Chaplin was a "little guy" around whom the fictional world arranged itself and to whom the spectator responded through his sense of himself as a "little guy"—regardless of whether or not he could respond to Charlie's fictional world.

There was of course a time before stars were born. Created first was the celestial realm in which they would one day dwell and which would confer on them at their birth a substantial part of its aura. At the turn of the century, huge numbers of people were afforded an experience like none ever known before—a replication of life, images that moved: the motion pictures. Gerald Mast has noted that the "first film audiences were amazed to see that living, moving action could be projected on an inert screen by an inanimate machine" (*A Short History of the Movies*, pp. 35–36).

It is difficult for us, a century later, to understand the awesomeness of that experience, but it was in fact so amazing that, again in Mast's words, "the first films merely exploited [the spectators'] amazement" (p. 20). The simple act of recording the entrance of a train in a railway station could panic the audience and send it ducking. And a conjurer like Méliès used motion pictures to extend the magic he had formerly created onstage. The instant success and huge popularity of movies must be ascribed to that early magic—their appropriation and reproduction of motion.

Like all intensities, that sense of awesomeness was fated to last but for a while. Soon, the miracle of a train entering a station was dissipated in the darkened rooms of the nickelodeons, along with that of galloping horses and cars in hot pursuit. What had once been a miracle became eventually no more than a routine expectation, and the subjective response of earlier spectators was replaced by that of new sophisticates more interested in why those horses were galloping or what would happen to the cars in hot pursuit. Such questions presupposed an anthropomorphous answer: it was time for the star to appear.

Motion pictures did not create the idea of the star: theater stages were jewel cases for matinée idols and divas (meaning goddesses) long before Hollywood. But those flesh-and-blood creatures were different, in part because they were flesh and blood and allowed a kind of immediate appropriation that the illusion of the silver screen defeated. Those who came to see the greats of the stage were relatively few in numbers (at least when compared with the millions who, early on, filled the picture houses) and were more given to identification than to a sense of awe. At the start, the spectator in the theater possessed; in the motion picture house, he was possessed. Malraux says that a theater actor is a small head in a large hall whereas a movie actor is a large head in a small hall.[6] The "small head" onstage signifies an equivalency between spectator and actor. The overpowering head of the movie actor is the emblem of the domination of the spectator by the screen star. And Malraux's sense of a small room within which this domination occurs refers only to the intimacy of a spectator possessed because, in fact, the motion picture auditorium can easily be much larger than any theater without negating that intimacy.

The miraculous medium thus produced a miraculous creature—miraculous first because it moved and later because of how it moved and in what circumstances it moved. All mortal men can move, but that other man who moved on the screen moved differently, for his motion on the screen was first of all a feat of magic; furthermore, he moved more perfectly than mortals move and even moved in ways that they cannot emulate. The spectator could both see and dream that sublime motion, recognizing its supernaturalness while fantasizing its accomplishment.

The demiurges who were mainly creatures of motion became first the solitary figures whose fictional trajectory carried them along psychological paths that, at some level, were not unfamiliar to the spectator. Those were the cowboys and then, with less meaning, the swashbucklers, the adventurers, whose circumstances existed largely for the performance of heroic calisthenics.

Alongside these figures of a simple motion were those whose motion was more complicated—the great comics, vulnerable innocents into whose paths were thrown obstacles of a magnitude commensurate only with their uncanny ability to overcome them. The childlike nature of these seemingly defenseless heroes magnified their predicaments into an unjustifiable persecution that allowed the spectator to recognize the harassments and annoyances of his own life. For such a spectator, the comic's grace in surmounting those obstacles represented spiritual trials rather than simply the spirited acrobatics of the swashbuckler whose outcome was always a foregone conclusion.

Lustered by the magic of motion and its charisma, the screen persona remained magical even after the magic of motion evaporated. In describing the changing characteristics of the American man on the screen, we are articulating a history of American motion pictures shaped by evolving technologies of production and by cultural perceptions responding to economic and political change. The representation of the male, played out within the larger context of our cultural archetypes, changes as the context does. The confidence of a William S. Hart or a Gary Cooper that a wordless gaze can convey a fixed moral code and the ultimate power of a manly civilization over an effete and possibly corrupt urbanity shifts as we move to a postmodern valorizing of the spoken word and a recognition of that world's fragmentation— a valorizing and a fragmentation reproduced in the sophistication of film technologies from silents to sound, from black-and-white symbols to a technicolor overdefinition of surfaces, from a lens that keeps only the hero in clear focus to one that analyzes with equal acuity all parts of his world.

Technology changed the way in which we perceived our world: movie audiences began to expect rather than to marvel at the performance reflected on the screen, but that was later. The first stage of cinema was its ecstatic stage, when the screen image created pure creatures, cleansed of human imperfections—starting with physical imperfections: the stars were instances of beauty and, as such, objects of love.[7] Ecstasy is a state of grace that transcends normal understanding: because they are pure states, beatific and sexual visions are essentially similar. Tensed toward the unattainable, the movie spectator's attempt at an impossible union with the screen idol replicated the postures of Eros—love and desire: the motion picture house was becoming a house of worship.

Perhaps because men have defined as feminine the ideal of human beauty, and perhaps because women have been accessories in accepting that definition, the image of the star has usually been female, the love goddess whose face and body magnetized desire—the desire of men to possess and the desire of women to wield that sexual power.

In the words of Annette Kuhn, "A glamorous image of a woman (or an image of a glamorous woman) is peculiarly powerful in that . . . sexuality is desirable exactly to the extent that it is idealized and unattainable" (*The Power of the Image,* p. 12).[8] But the masculine stars were equal paragons, from the great profiles of yesteryear to the gorgeous hunks of today. And because stars of both sexes were preeminently erotic objects, their most natural fiction was the love story.

Thus, as man created these gods in his image, his first incarnations were the solitary figure on horseback, the tragicomic innocent, and Zeus as he appeared to Semele in his consuming sexuality. These were the paradisiacal days of motion pictures, when the projection of the spectator's dream was least deflected by self-consciousness or self-awareness, when Eden and id were not so very far apart—and when shrewdly intuitive moviemakers fashioned the male hero out of the larger fabric of cultural icons that had already provided the shape of our traditional mythologies, some of whose sources were deeply submerged below our conscious level.

NOTES

1. See, for example, Patricia Elliot (*From Mastery to Analysis: Theories of Gender in Psychoanalytic Feminism*), who is concerned with "the discourse of mastery, when the analyst's interpretations assume the status of truth" (p. 117); or Annette Kuhn (*The Power of the Image: Essays on Representation and Sexuality*), who detects in *The Big Sleep* a "threat posed to the law of patriarchy by the feminine" (p. 95).

2. Barry Richards notes, "Of femininity, there are two conceptions: femininity as interiorized oppression, and femininity as revealed essence. [The first is] the damaging imprint in the female psyche of patriarchal society. Its characteristics are passivity, self-effacement, irrationality, impulsiveness, sentimentality, and so on. In the second . . . it is the spontaneous, essential nature of women. . . . Of masculinity, there is but one predominant conception . . . : it is of masculinity as domineering and defensive, as the installation in the male psyche of the presumption of patriarchal power" (p. 160).

3. It is, for example, the exclusivity of the male gaze (see Ann Kaplan, *Women and Film,* chapter 1); meanwhile, for Laura Mulvey, the woman on the Hollywood screen is there to satisfy male voyeurism (in "Visual Pleasure and Narrative Cinema").

4. Woody Allen himself has said that he plays mainly in big cities and university campuses.

5. Consider by contrast the difficulties of sophisticated present-day analysis; in talking of Kristeva, Jacqueline Rose *(Sexuality in the Field of Vision)*, in quest of gender, runs into a veritable maze: "As soon as we try to draw out of that exposure [of the complacent identities of psychosexual life] an image of femininity which escapes the straightjacket of symbolic forms, we fall straight into that essentialism and primacy of the semiotic which is one of the most problematic" (p. 157).

6. Quoted in Edgar Morin, *The Stars,* p. 142.

7. Roland Barthes speaks of Garbo's face, "where the flesh gives rise to mystical feelings of perdition" *(Mythologies,* p. 56).

8. This renders somewhat problematic her thesis, according to which "to possess the image of a woman's sexuality [is] in some way to possess, to maintain a degree of control over, woman in general" (Kuhn, p. 11).

Part 1

When Stars Were Stars (1914-31)

1

The Exterminating Angel: William S. Hart and the Western

As in all other depictions by Hollywood of the American male, there are two images of the Western hero: the one presented by the surface, and an underlying truth—an aspect of the character in which the spectator may recognize himself even when his semblance and circumstances contradict that likeness. The duality of the Western is especially marked. It focuses on the image of the cowboy, and that image derives primarily from the rural West, the figure of the hired hand who performed a large part of his chores on horseback.[1] Christian Metz believes that identification in the cinema is not primarily with the image and/or characters onscreen but, rather, with the camera itself: "This is the fantasy of the all-perceiving subject [which] can be recognized in an idealist ontology of film which sees the development of cinema as an increasingly realistic appropriation of the world" (*The Imaginary Signifier: Psychoanalysis and the Cinema,* p. 32).

This view seems to envisage the spectator at an already sophisticated moment of evolution: the first spectators were in such awe of the magical appropriation that they were perforce oriented screenward: it must have taken some time for them to move from identification ("these are *real* people") to probing ("into what unknown worlds will this film move me?"). From the earliest, movies were an urban phenomenon drawing the greatest part of their audiences from cities; and for those audiences, the humble figure of the cowhand would soon acquire an epic grandeur: it is only then that the spectator may have shifted his primary identification from the figure to the camera.

In considering the Western first, we have chosen to move through yet another overlay, that of time. Though most of the actors referred to here played Western roles at one time or another—testimonial to the enduring appeal of the genre—we start with the William S. Hart years, that is to say, roughly the ten years following the beginning of World War I (later we will consider the evolution of the Western in an age of suspicion). We have done so because this was the time when cinematic statements were relatively simple. The genre can be considered to be in its pure form during those years, the truths articulating the character being few in number, constant, and less mediated by complexities of personality or circumstance.

What eventually would be the film industry was born at the end of the nineteenth century. The gold rush, California's struggles for statehood, and its first tenuous link to the East through the transcontinental railroad had occurred in midcentury and were still within the memory of many. The Civil War had ended a scant third of a century back. Oklahoma would not be a state until 1907. From the Barbary Coast to Alaska, Cuba, and Panama, the country was only just settling into its ultimate boundaries. But even within those boundaries, its identity did not yet clearly transcend divisions between East and West, between the urban brokers of power on the Atlantic seaboard and western settlers. These were rifts whose political emblems might be the birth of the Greenback Party and the rise of the Populists but which, at a more intimate level, gave their particular form to an urban dream of escape.

When we speak of the Western, we think of motion pictures. But first came the word. The magma of a culture still seeking solid form was the substance of much of our literature. Fenimore Cooper had found within the wilderness of the frontier the epic figure of Natty Bumppo and the romantic ideal of the noble savage—the great appeal of his stories being reflected in the success of the dime novels that subsequently simplified his moral contrast between the socialized and the untamed. Later, the roistering camps around the Mother Lode attracted the likes of Mark Twain and Bret Harte. And during the period that concerns us here (1914–24), the most consistently best-selling writer was Zane Grey. The year 1920 was that of F. Scott Fitzgerald's *This Side of Paradise:* it sold 35,000 copies. The same year, Zane Grey's *Man of the Forest* was the runaway best-seller, eventually going over three-quarters of a million copies—and at a time before book clubs and best-seller lists could propel a book to popular fame. Of course, by 1920 Zane Grey was widely known: his *Riders of the Purple Sage* (1912) was on its way to passing the million and one-quarter mark.[2]

What Zane Grey brought his readers was first of all a symbolic landscape—the wide open skies under which a man could be purged, in his westward motion, of the infection contracted in a more easterly past. That man, whether redeemer or outlaw, was a loner on horseback with a gun. From the start, *Riders of the Purple Sage*'s Lassiter had been such a figure: a man who had withdrawn from society, a man infused with the darkness of an unrevealed past and, therefore, older. Grey's Lassiters, however, were not free of society: another, more rudimentary society now became the purgatory through which they had to travel, the eye that testified to their contaminated past and the evidence of another contamination they had to eradicate. Even though Lassiter had rejected society, the gun he used with speed and accuracy encapsulated society's ideals of law and morality before its lapse (in his words, "Gun-packing in the West since the Civil War has growed into a kind of moral law").

During this spiritual itinerary, Grey's hero usually encountered a woman who mirrored him. Some mirrored him only superficially and were easy converts: the ones in whom the East remained as an overlay of city mannerisms. Two other types evidenced a deeper resemblance. One was his moral image, flawed through the kind of darkness that leads to saloon or brothel. The other was his physical mirror, the hoyden who was part of the yet-untamed land. As these figures awaited various kinds of redemption within the trajectory of the hero, their function was to show the hero's erotic dimension.

These functional heroines were necessary because the hero's sexual power had to be understood through the litotes of abstinence. The women were the witnesses and the deponents: they either fantasized or fetishized the virility of the hero. They thus testified to the erotic force of the hero but never actually broached the austere mask that signified his purity.

To the extent that one of the few reliable psychological differences in gender is the greater aggressiveness of males (Shibley Hyde, "Gender Differences in Aggression," p. 51), the purity of the hero only allowed him, logically enough, the orgasmic climax of his six-shooter, when he discharged his weapon at last to cleanse the land through which he traveled. Cleansed as he cleansed, Grey's hero redeemed himself along with the space through which he rode, until at last there was nothing left but to populate the clean, vast emptiness and, prudently, to close the book.

One imagines that the bulk of Grey's readers were city dwellers and that his vision of the West, and of the hero who embodied that vision, allowed them to dream an escape into a paradise lost to the constraints and corruptions of urban civilization and now irremediably closing with the end of the frontier—a nostalgia long preserved in popular ballads or in the action of Bill Cody's Wild West Show. While the lost generation wrote for a smaller and smarter set about more exquisite bereavements, Grey's readers could feel within the limited horizons of the city, in its daily oppression, the loss of the bodily and spiritual freedom they might have lived within the openness and purity of those symbolic landscapes.

From 1880 on, the country was in the midst of a huge industrial expansion that fed on cheap labor and swelled the tides of immigration—averaging nearly one million people a year between 1901 and 1910. Fewer of these were coming from the British isles: most were now from southern and eastern Europe.

Mass entertainment at the turn of the century had been provided by popular melodramas and, especially, vaudeville. Because substantial parts of those performances were spoken, access to them was difficult for an increasingly large public with little knowledge of English. One of the many miracles of motion pictures is that they were originally silent: in the first years of the century, they became a hugely successful form of entertainment for those in the lower economic levels: it is estimated that by 1910, twenty-six million spectators attended movies every week. Such a profitable enterprise required larger spaces for its projections: in 1914, the Strand Theater on Broadway opened, its 3,300 seats elbowing the legitimate stages around it. The age of the great movie palaces had begun: the more affluent middle class would now be adding its respectability and its numbers to the masses that had ensured the success of nickelodeons—the rare example of a commercial product rising up from proletarian roots rather than the usual filtering down to them. Exhibitors now clamored for between twenty and thirty new films a week (they were mostly short-length features, five or six of them being required for an hour show). And because all shooting still had to be done out of doors, California, with more hours and days of sunlight, became the cinema's commercial center: Hollywood was born.

When Zane Grey's *Man of the Forest* appeared, Hollywood had hit its stride: in 1921, 734 full-length features were distributed, and of these, one in every seven was a Western (and better than one in five by 1928, the peak year of the Western).[3] Hollywood, ever skilled at identifying the formulas of success, drew many of its Westerns from popular books, and, predictably, Grey was the author most frequently drawn on: over 100 movies were made from his novels. His *Lone Star Ranger* was filmed seven times, a record never surpassed by any other literary work.[4]

As early as 1909, that precursor of surrealists, Guillaume Apollinaire, had said of cinema that it created a surrealist life. One assumes that the surreality of the film lay not in its power to transcend "life" but in its power to capture it—to bring alive within the confines of the magical machine a vastness *out there* into which the spectator could expand. Thus, if Zane Grey was the logical best-seller from whom motion pictures could find grist for their mills, a happy coincidence ordained that motion pictures were also the medium best suited to capture the solemn and grandiose vistas in which the redemptive journey of Grey's heroes was set: here was the possibility to *show* their plenitude, size, and melancholy (Howard Mumford Jones's "significant components" of the western landscape [*O Strange New World,* 1964]). There remained only to give that hero, along with ritualistic gestures, a face: the first and most recognizable one was that of William S. Hart.

Hart never used or appeared in a Grey story. Both shared a more fundamental resemblance: each created, and was created by, the zeitgeist of the times. It was in Hart, every bit as much as in Grey, that "the dominant early twentieth-century version of the western formula came to fruition and achieved its greatest general popularity" (Cawelti, *Adventure, Mystery, and Romance,* p. 232).[5] Though born in upstate New York, Hart was quite literally a child of the old West—at a time when the West was on "the Wisconsin side of the Mississippi" (Hart, *My Life East and West,* p. 14). His father, a miller, moved west in search of mill sites during the eighties. William grew up with ranch hands and Indians (he could speak the language of the Sioux), rode a horse, worked on a cattle drive—and kept graven on his mind the memory of a shootout on the main street of Sioux City.

When his mother's health required him to accompany her back East, Hart returned to New York. To supplement the family budget, he worked at odd jobs, first in New York and later in London and Paris. The Parisian stage awakened his interest in the theater. After returning to New York, for some twenty years between 1890 and 1910, he worked on the boards, becoming in time a reputable actor.

During his time in the theater, he became friendly with Thomas H. Ince and Frank Stammers. Later, Hart recalled,

> I would tell them of a country where there are no spies or newsmongers—only kind-hearted, friendly things; those that would fight to the death in battle, but in peace would shrink from inflicting pain. I would tell them of the land where none are strangled for free speech, where none are stoned for adultery of mind or body, because there is no adultery of mind or body; of the land where all men lie down and rest, and, when they wake, thank the Great Spirit for a better sleep. [p. 16]

In spite of this sentimental view of the West, Hart was offended when he saw his first Western movie: "While playing in Cleveland, I attended a picture show. I saw a Western picture. It was awful! I talked with the manager of the theater and he told me this was one of the best westerns he had ever had. None of the impossibilities or libels on the West meant anything to him—it was drawing the crowds. . . . I did not seek to enlighten him. I was seeking information" (p. 198). Hart had reached an obvious and exciting conclusion: "Here were reproductions of the Old West being seriously presented to the public—in an almost burlesque manner—and they were successful. It made me tremble to think of it. I was an actor and I knew the West" (p. 198). He went West and found that moviemaking was yet another kind of frontier. The set of the New York Motion Picture Company, which Ince now managed, made Westerns in conjunction with the 101 Ranch at Santa Monica: "The very primitiveness of the whole life out there, the cowboys and the Indians, staggered me. I loved it. They had everything to make western pictures. The West was right there!" (p. 200).

Thomas Ince enjoyed an established reputation by now. He had begun by hiring circus riders, cowboys, and Indians as extras for the stampedes of his Western epics: as many as 400 people could be seen hurtling across the vast landscapes of movies that still worked their magic through the huge panoramas they captured and especially through the thundering movement that was their life. Poets like Jean Cocteau (who wrote in 1919 about *Carmen of the Klondyke*) were caught up in Ince's headlong rushes through luminous trails and lyric dust.

Technically, Ince was a superb editor of pictures whose sense of motion and rhythm is preserved in his masterful montages. But in addition to being a cinematic poet, Ince was also a shrewd businessman. The epic size of his movies soon burst its studio banks. After merging the successful Keystone, Kay Bee, and Fine Arts studios, he affiliated himself with D. W. Griffith and Mack Sennett into the huge conglomerate Triangle: what had once been Inceville was no longer large enough, and Culver City was born.

Hart made four pictures for the New York Motion Picture Co. in rapid succession but was told by Ince that directors, not Western actors, were needed in California. It was only after Hart had returned to New York that Ince called him back with the offer of a one-year contract to star in, and direct, his own pictures. Hart's brief but meteoric career in films was launched, as actor *and* director. And Culver City would become one of the vital centers of the motion picture industry as well as the birthplace of the classical Western.

The headlong dash on horseback through the vastness of dusty plains and gaunt tablelands was the stuff of rapturous excitement and dreams of freedom. But as the cinema matured along with its audiences, it began to distinguish within that mass the face and concerns of a single man. Hart's autobiography shows the extent to which he felt the existential reality of the roles he created. And as his fame spread, that conflation of person and persona was confirmed: to the French, William S. Hart was known as Rio Jim, the character he first portrayed in *The Bargain,* one of the movies he made on his first pass through California.[6]

Recollections of Hart focus on his eyes: he was known as the man with light eyes or steely eyes. His detractors said of him what was said of other stars in similar roles (like Gary Cooper)—that his acting amounted mainly to the stare of quiet confrontations. Like Cooper, Hart was in fact a fine actor and one of the few whose transition from stage to moving pictures was achieved through understatement and contained emotion.

Even if we do not look to Freudian fears of castration for its importance, the eye has always been charged with tangible power, as evidenced by the popular evil eye or the Hindu caste system in which the sight of the "unseeable" can cause pollution. Long before *Hamlet* (III.i), it was the abode of the mind: ancient Egypt associated the circular iris with the sun as an emblem of power and intelligence. Whereas activity of the mouth speaks dissipation and shallowness, the eye substituting for a closed mouth denotes strength, acute perception, and solitary individualism. (The Egyptians knew that the only way the mouth could be redeemed was by containing the circular eye, bespeaking the Creative

Word.) There is an atavistic wisdom in idioms that link strong and silent or note that still waters run deep. In Hart's hard, clear eyes, the male spectator could thus project his own unspoken impulses to dominate, to know, to be unafraid: he could be filled with an elation that his everyday existence did not necessarily grant him.

Alongside Hart, in another genre, was the dashing Douglas Fairbanks. Like Hart, Fairbanks was an athletic actor: Hart was a masterful horseman, and Fairbanks a gifted acrobat. But Fairbanks smiled, as do those who disguise the difficult feats they perform. Eventually, Fairbanks's films became essentially the evidence of his energetic activity. A charmer's smile was also the mark of the legendary cowboy of films, Tom Mix, who eventually eclipsed Hart. Though Tom Mix was born on a ranch that allowed him to fully develop his athletic ability, and though he later rode with Roosevelt's Rough Riders, the movies turned him into a matinee idol, the hero in white garb, galloping with guns blazing after indifferent villains. In spite of the fact that many of Tom Mix's movies were based on Zane Grey's stories, they became mostly displays of remarkable acrobatics (for which he seldom had a stand-in) and feats of enthusiastic derring-do. In the cases of both Douglas Fairbanks and Tom Mix, the primacy of the mouth (or of the smile at the time of the silents) over the eyes denoted the overwhelming of character through exuberance—and perhaps also the insinuation of a feminine persona within the male that not all masculine spectators were yet ready to acknowledge.[7]

William S. Hart did not use stand-ins either, but his horse Fritz, unlike Tom Mix's Tony, was not a trampoline for acrobatic tumbling. Fritz was the instrument of a moral purpose. Much has been said about the horses of cowboys as female surrogates and of the moral landscapes through which they galloped. But those symbols could only be informed through the reality of the hero.[8] If the mythical West was a land of redemption, it required a hero to be redeemed. There appears to have been in Hart the nearly religious sense of a fall from grace—a sense that even the redemptive gesture he performed within the illusory Eden of his films referred to a time that had now passed.

In 1923, *The Saturday Evening Post* ran *Tumbleweeds* by Hal G. Everts, a minor writer of Westerns. It was the story of the Cherokee land rush and the cowboys who worked on those Indian lands. The hero, Don Carver, in love with Molly Lassiter (shades of Zane Grey), joins the land rush. Here was the meat of book and film—the stampede through untamed land: it was sufficiently vital for Wesley Ruggles to return to the Cherokee Strip half a dozen years later with *Cimarron,* the only Western ever to win an Oscar. But the Oklahoma land rush that climaxes Hart's picture opens the one based on Edna Ferber's novel: the film had little to say after that.

For Hart, the land rush had to be the final image. In Everts's story, Carver earns the land and the love of his sweetheart after the usual adventures. Hart bought the film rights to the novel and, in his 1925 adaptation, kept its simple plot. But at the end, he gave Everts's story another dimension. Surveying a herd of cattle, Carver (played by Hart) says, as he pushes back his ten-gallon hat, "Boys, it's the last of the West." The herd is penned, and the free cowboy has run out of open horizons and must now turn rancher: the ox and plow shed will henceforth replace the horse. In both book and film, the hero marries Molly, but in the film the sense of a passing, the mournful awareness of a time gone by, clouds the fairy-tale end—an awareness of loss that the urban spectator was more likely to feel than any actual cowboy might have.

At the end of *Tumbleweeds,* Carver marries Molly because that is the way love stories are supposed to end in a society that believes its center to be the family unit. But mocking the traditional ending is the knowledge that marriage also means many kinds of death. The last image of the film shows the tumbleweed caught on the barbed wire of a western fence. That barbed wire may have been historically accurate, but it is not simply another form of palisade: its thorns contribute pain to the end of the cowboy's freedom, for which the tumbleweed stood.[9] The restless horse had carried its restless rider away from social constraints: if the man on horseback was able to purify the society through which he passed, it was only because he was already haloed with the purity of the big sky toward which he rode. To arrest the Western hero in his westward course was to confine his spirit.

Whether Balius and Xanthus, Achilles' immortal steeds, or Roland's Veillantif, the epic records the names of horses as well as the heroes that rode them. The epic quality of the riders passes into their steeds because both grow out of the epic land that designates them as commensurably huge and mobile. They are one with that symbiotic land— raw, young, powerful, and pure. The epic is a myth of youth.

There is always something of the child in the necessarily pure epic hero; it is part of what George Stade terms the American phantasy: freedom from the mother's apron strings. As a result, "all men will remain boys trying to become men," and "real men are those who are free from the control of women even in the form of love" (quoted by Arnold M.

Cooper, "What Men Fear: The Façade of Castration Anxiety," p. 113). The Western will show that dream of freedom to be only a dream. The woman encountered by the hero is only apparently childlike. The one Hart marries at the end of *Tumbleweeds* is Bessie Love. She too had remarkable eyes—but not like Hart's. Rather than reflecting selfhood, knowledge, and strength, they show the fragility of youth, innocence, and need. Molly, incarnated in Bessie Love, makes no personal assertion: she is there so that Carver can illustrate forms of masculine definition as protector, upholder of the law, and dispenser of justice,[10] and, because she allows him those definitions, he is also cleansed in her lustral water.

If her existence is going to affect the hero's, the woman must come to him as a sacred vestal. The woman whose sexual dimension breaks those pristine bounds can only belong to the dark past of the hero, to a time when he was himself steeped in a more primal life. That woman remains invisible, or if she appears in the present life of the hero, her sexual aura infuses the picture of which he is a part but of which he does not partake—she belongs to the world that must be cleansed, the fallen woman in the saloon (frequently played by Louise Glaum in Hart's pictures). She may be a part of the hero's self-cleansing, but she can no longer face him as an equal: at most, she may be saved by him.

Because the vestal cannot detract from the Western hero's epic stature, she mirrors only the pure part that abides in him, the part she will midwife into visible existence as he undergoes his moral molting. Until that moment, like the very ox and plow, she can only be an impediment to the vagrant hero—a source of fertility, a depth of roots that will bind him to the land. Estelle V. Welldon (*Mother, Madonna, Whore*) reminds us that the mother's "uterus has as much power as the [son's] penis, but it is an engulfing, smothering power. Thus nurturing is its only form of dominance: it is the way in which the victim turns predator" (quoted in Rosalind Miles, *The Rites of Man: Love, Sex and Death in the Making of the Male*, p. 25). But, ironically, the female character shifts into that role without any change in her manner or appearance: even as Demeter, she is still a virgin. It is only assumed, as the picture ends, that she has emerged into another dimension—as we assume the hero has.[11]

With all due respect to those who dislike the impinging of "Lévi-Strauss and Company [on] Levi Strauss and Co." (Philip French, *Westerns: Aspects of a Movie Genre*, p. 10), the woman hidden within the hero's maiden may emerge within the hero's horse. If we follow Carl G. Jung's inquiries into the libido, we encounter the mother—original horse of the child

("Kinder Pferd")—in the symbolic horse, and Jung's rider becomes the man returning to the unconscious buried within his earliest life.[12] It is only when he detects a more identifiable mother in the maiden that the Western hero at last abandons his horse. No maker of Westerns ever indulged in such speculations, but the long-lasting appeal of the Western may be evidence that in addition to having common cultural aspirations, both moviemakers and spectators were responding through symbolic surfaces and ritual postures to a common unconscious.

When Joe Franklin attempts to describe Bessie Love, he can think only of exemplary innocence and youth: the candor of Lillian Gish, the child-woman in Mae Marsh, the gamine in Mary Pickford (Franklin, *Classics of the Silent Movies: A Pictorial History,* 1952). But like the Western hero, the virgin conceals dangerous depths. Mythology teaches us the power derived from contact with one's roots: Gaea, the Greek mother earth, bore to Poseidon a giant named Antaeus who recovered strength only in contact with the earth—Hercules killed him by raising him off the ground. Borne out of his past on his steed, the cowboy derives his strength from the horse he bestrides. Though he may well have walked in that eastern past, it is now difficult to visualize him off his mount: on foot, he is desexed. (Even when the hero comes down from his horse at high noon to confront the villain, he does it at the moment of his apotheosis—and at a later date, when it has become important for him to face the enemy shackled: on foot and with his gun in its holster.) We can only surmise, because this is where the story ends, that the woman who pulls him off his horse for good adds to the symbolic plow another ox—a castrated creature now attached to the land.

Separated from his past and awaiting ceremonial emasculation at the hands of a virgin, the hero remains a manly presence during the hiatus of the Western story only through his gun. But his gun is legendary: it fires with the intensity of a machine gun and has a far greater capacity than any six-shooter. Hart, the strong silent man of the movies, spoke so articulately with his revolver that "Quick on the guns as William S. Hart" became an American proverb.[13]

Fire, scourging and fertilizing, is the earliest among the most dangerous of the creative forces. Hermes, the phallic god, invents fire making, allowing it to be drawn forth by rubbing within the female bole the male drill (usually made from an oak, the tree with its deep roots closest to the earth's primal fire). In its symbolic purity and fertility, fire is like semen, which Dante knew to be the purest blood flowing from the heart, too pure in fact to course through the veins (*Purgatorio,* in *La Divina Commedia,* pp. 25, 37 ff.).

Firing his gun, the hero thus returns to archaic myths that attest to his erotic force and his power as the warrior archangel with flaming sword. At the climax of his purifying journey, William S. Hart literally *wipes out* the figures of evil. In *Hell's Hinges* (1916), both aspects of his firing power are combined: Blaze Tracy (Hart, interestingly named) first shoots the evil saloon keeper to death *and then* sets fire to his saloon. But Hell's Hinges is a reincarnation of Gomorrah and like that other City on the Plain can only be cleansed through a celestial conflagration: fire spreads from the saloon to the entire town and burns it down. And, within unconscious depths, the spectator rehearsed a defining memory, for "passing through fear, pain and the shadow of death to attain manhood is as old as human life itself. Rites and ceremonies of initiation reach back to the dawn of time, and the key to their meaning is always to be found in the deliberate ritualized infliction of violence and the sharing of pain" (Miles, p. 74).

Even though William S. Hart knew Indians well and wrote of them with warmth, the Western, of which he was the prime incarnation, spoke to white Christian audiences. We have noted the religious themes of purity and redemption that underlie these fables of the West. In Cawelti's words, "The ultimate result of this confrontation with wild nature and violent men is an affirmation of such traditional American values as monogamous love, the settled family, the basic separation of masculine and feminine roles, and the centrality of religion to life" (*Adventure, Mystery, and Romance,* p. 240). Ironically, the picture never went so far as *to show* these, but the white audience could infer as much from the promissory note (like the one provided by the final caption of *Hell's Hinges,* as both hero and heroine walk away from the blazing inferno, "Whatever the future brings, they will share it together").

In 1916, Hart made what many consider to be his best film, *The Aryan*—a name whose grim resonance reminds us that, four years later, Hitler would be founding the National Socialist Party. In this film, Rio Jim is an outcast consumed with hatred. He has become an outlaw because within the lawful, white world he was dispossessed of his wealth: though white himself, "his heart has turned black," and he now rules over outlaws pitted against white society—but only until the day when Bessie Love appears out of the western wilds: she is part of a caravan that has lost its way and run out of water. She confronts Rio Jim in his evil lair because she must have water in order "to save [those of] her race." True to their beliefs, the outlaws see only an opportunity for revenge and plunder. But Rio Jim heeds a call that transcends mere logic: he turns against his mixed-breed associates to save the whites. And having once again wiped out the corrupt social order around him, he remains alone, too pure in soul even to adapt to the civilizing world he has helped bring into being—even though this time, more clearly than in other films, the moral core of that value system has been made evident.

The land rush that brings about the end of an era for the hero of *Tumbleweeds* had actually occurred only thirty-five years before the motion picture was made. Parts of what is now Oklahoma had been officially designated as Indian territory. But the unspoiled land had become a haven for outlaws because of its remoteness and a lure for cattle drivers because of the richness of its pastures. When the first railroads came through Oklahoma at the start of the seventies, it was no longer possible to keep out the new white settlers. The Indian was thus an adversary among many adversaries—someone fighting for the same land. But there was also a clash of races between those who claimed the land ancestrally and those who claimed it for a new culture.

Western fiction gave this contest a different dimension. For a long time, the Indian remained the most readily discernable adversary, but he also mirrored the fictional cowboy. The latter was not a settler, and a part of his stature was derived from the Indian who, like him, was essentially a nomad, living on horseback, and shaped by the same landscapes. Fictional stylizing raised both cowboys and Indians to an epic level that sublimated all other complexities within a physical confrontation (after all, research confirms that, even in the nineties, "hunting, shooting, killing, as sport, exercise or manhood training have lost none of their allure" [Miles, p. 60]). But, as Fenin and Everson remind us (*The Western*, 1962), it did so with a difference: even when the Indian was seen as a hero, he remained an abstraction, more a symbol than an individual. And French notes that this "faceless symbol became a stereotype: historically a figure to be confronted and defeated in the name of civilization" (*Westerns*, p. 79).

But even as the Indian contributed part of his epic stature to the Western hero, he also contributed the difference of his race to the hero's definition. Created for a white audience, the hero was white and the villains were less than white. The villain's definition might be psychological: "If [he] leered and drooled, he was a *heavy* villain, whose slavering approach to the heroine, or to the material crux of the plot was easily predictable. . . . If he dressed like a parson or gambler, he was a *sneaky* villain to be dealt with after unmasking" (W. H. Hutchinson, "Virgins, Villains and Varmints," p. 35). But more immediately, the alien's race branded him with the mark of Cain: he was the somber and more ominous figure, with swarthy skin, dark hair, and, as likely as not, darker clothing. He contrasted graphically with the luminous purity of the hero and darkened the picture that had to be turned clear in the end.

William S. Hart came along at a time when the mere miracle of the screened stampede was no longer sufficient to captivate audiences: they needed to distinguish a particular person within that relentless motion. Hart introduced the specificity of his face, his manner, and his ethics. But technology never stands still, and in time the size and precision of the screen image begin once again to overwhelm the individual character (Metz's "increasingly realistic appropriation of the world"—a phenomenon we will note in every kind of motion picture we encounter). As a result, it becomes necessary to further magnify the character in order for him to stand out. And the greater the technological advance, the greater the magnification required: by the time we get to huge screens with perfect images, vibrant color, and stereophonic sound, the dimension of the hero must be commensurately complex.

Besides the technological perfection of the modern screen, there may be another reason for the individualization of the modern hero: the alienated spectator, unable to share any longer in a dream of common beliefs or of escapist fervor. A world war, with the entry of women into the marketplace, consciousness raising, and self-consciousness all contributed to a loss of innocence and the effortlessness of simple affirmations. Feminists may still tell men that they live in worlds deformed by a masculine vision, but men are very likely to sense that such a self-definition is delusionary or at least generates less solace than it once might have. And so, the predictable figure of the hero is exploded into a multitude of individual facets, each of which documents an aspect of vulnerability without rising to a symbolic level. In time, the innocent Western is replaced by the adult Western: the hero has an unheroic side, the villains have reasons, a relationship develops between the cowboy and a woman who is no longer a mere embodiment of innocence. When this happens, the very dimensions of the classical Western are altered: the questions raised and cut off by the ending of the old form are now brought into the new one.

The end result of these complications is the very destruction of the Western myth, as in *The Man Who Shot Liberty Valance* (John Ford, 1961; see chapter 10), whose story is the deconstruction of a legend. By 1969, *all* myths had become suspect. That year, Dennis Hopper's *Easy Rider* simply inverted tradition. Riding west, Henry Fonda had been a force for good in *The Ox-Bow Incident* (1943), brought law and order to the town of *Warlock* (1958), and killed the bad man in *Welcome to Hard Times* (1967). Now, Peter Fonda abandoned the West, trading his father's horse for a motorcycle, and headed eastward, into an engulfing corruption he could not redeem and justifying the picture's epitaph, "We blew it." But by now, the individual on which the story focused had become more important than the genre.

NOTES

1. In analyzing the Western, the French, with their amusing fixation on what they interpret as the psychoanalytic content of words rather than on the accuracy of the word's cultural context, have had quite a bit to say about cows (as in "cowboys") and, consequently, "the extent to which the maternal problem continues to obsess" Americans (Raymond De Becker, *De Tom Mix à James Dean,* p. 40). In fact, cows were among the lesser concerns of actual cowboys and among the nonconcerns of the fictional ones. Only in urban-originated mockery, such as Keaton's or Chaplin's, does a cow enter the picture—as a comic accessory, a kind of comic pun on the meaning of the word.

2. See Frank Gruber, *Zane Grey: A Biography* (1970).

3. These are Department of Commerce figures; see also Charles Ford, *Histoire du Western* (1964), and Georges Sadoul, *Histoire générale du cinéma,* vol. 6, p. 37. Much of the secondary literature on the Western is French because the genre very quickly gripped Europeans. For them, the West represented an intensification of what the urban American felt. It was an unknown land, but one aglow with the reality of the spectator's desire—its boundless space, motion, and human rectitude affording him ample vistas into which he could project himself or on which he could comment. In this case, the noble savage was anyway only half a savage—the cowboy, whose brooding and virtues were familiar, even if his horse was not. Until after World War II, little was written in our own country about our most indigenous genre: it was too close for examination.

4. See Jim Hitt, *The American West from Fiction into Film,* pp. 3 and 320–22.

5. In fact, John G. Cawelti links Zane Grey and William S. Hart because "their works have so many points in common" (pp. 232–33).

6. By the time William S. Hart's fame had spread sufficiently far to be of interest even to European intellectuals, they were long persuaded that the initial "S" in his name stood for Shakespeare (it stands for Surrey), so deep was their need to associate this modern catalyst of dreams with more ancient legitimacies. (See, for example, J.-L. Rieupeyrout, *Le Western,* p. 54. As for Raymond De Becker, he calls him "Rio Jim, alias William Shakespeare Hart" [p. 31].)

7. Judith A. Hall and Amy G. Halberstadt write, "A meta-analysis of gender differences in nonverbal behavior indicates that adult females smile and gaze substantially more than adult males do" (p. 136).

8. It is doubtful, as De Becker claims (p. 34), that Tom Mix could be the figure of the reincarnated Centaur because the sexual center was missing.

9. See John H. Lenihan, *Showdown: Confronting Modern America in the Western Film,* p. 14.

10. Betty Yorburg writes, "In small group studies, males typically have taken on the role of leader; females typically have played mediating or tension-breaking roles" (*Sexual Identity: Sex Roles and Social Change,* p. 159). As late as 1988, studies still show that boys "aspire more to peer roles (e.g., being a good friend) and active occupations (e.g., pilot); girls are more interested in family (becoming a good mother) and professional (e.g., doctor) roles" (Daniel A. Hart, *Becoming Men: The Development of Aspirations, Values, and Adaptation Styles,* p. 194).

11. Only if the spectator is directed to follow the hero moving on alone at the end of the picture can one accept Jane Tompkins's thesis that the Western is an attempt to write femininity out of American culture (*West of Everything: The Inner Life of Westerns,* 1992). The usual implication is that the land has been settled, that it has therefore come under the sway of the woman.

12. See "Symbols of the Mother and of Rebirth," "The Battle for Deliverance from the Mother," and "The Sacrifice" in Carl G. Jung, *Symbols of Transformation* (1957–67).

13. See Lewis Jacobs, *The Rise of the American Film* (1939).

2

A Darkness of the Blood: Rudolph Valentino

Baudelaire's poem about "Correspondences" reminds us that perfumes, colors and sounds echo each other. Synesthesia allows us to say that a sound is piercing—that the faculty of hearing can be perceived through the sense of touch. Or we can speak of a *dark* passion, giving emotion a visible quality. Such translation from one sense to another follows psychological or cultural channels deeply embedded within us. We are not likely, for example, to speak of a *light* passion.

On a synesthetic keyboard, the extreme right locates the note with the greatest frequency of vibrations—the one with the least duration and the keenest edge. It is the part of the chromatic scale where a maximum of light, the sun, having fathered all the other colors, blends them into the purity of white. Going leftward down the scale, moving toward black—the absence of color and light—we encounter the visible end of the chromatic and biological order in the darkness of the color red. These somber regions are the ones where the note with the lowest frequency expands; they are the realm of the fertile nether regions belonging to Diana of Ephesus, the dark earth mother—and perhaps, for the male, a reawakening of the boy "who feels in danger of being sucked back by the mother and her desire" (Christiane Olivier, *Jocasta's Children,* quoted by Miles, p. 26).

That depth is perilous: the devil dwells in darkness, assumes the shape of a black cat or hides within Solomon's Black Book where the secrets of demons are consigned. It is also the impure and awesome source of life itself. Here, at the dark red center, is the womb and blood, or, in its symbolic form, wine, denoting intoxication, jeopardy, passion, fertility.[1]

Little wonder then that the Western hero was bathed in light while those he had to eradicate were the spawn of darkness, their lineage showing in their swarthiness, the long black hair that had already given Samson his dangerous strength, their somber clothing and mounts. The synesthetic associations of Western culture showed them to be the antithesis of the present hero and intimations of what the hero once might have been in a more primitive past.

Yet that antithesis was to produce a hero, of an entirely different kind of course, during the very years of Hart's greatest triumphs. As we have noted, the duality of the Western hero as Hollywood first portrayed him was only hinted at: his story chronicled an elevation untainted by the intimations of a former self—his appeal deriving from the virtues that allowed his exaltation. But if the absolute nature of purity attracts, the double-edged radiance of darkness is no less seductive, perhaps harking back to the time when the young boy's dispositions toward masculinity (physiological) and femininity (identification) are still in what Irene Fast terms "undifferentiated array" and which "the narcissistic elaboration of masculinity and femininity within the self [through] object relations" may not transcend as thoroughly as she suggests (*Gender Identity: A Differentiation Model,* p. 53). The origins of the Rudolph Valentino legend are to be found in the perils, riches, and ambiguities of those depths.

At first sight, there was no reason why Rudolph Valentino should have become a legend during his lifetime. Indeed, the first professional steps of this young immigrant seemed to indicate that he would follow the path one might have predicted for a naive young Italian trying to make it in America during the years of World War I—especially a young Italian with olive skin and slightly slanted eyes (Robert Oberfist, *Rudolph Valentino: The Man Behind the Myth,* p. 18). It is necessary to understand why, before noon, on 24 August 1926, the Campbell funeral home in New York City was besieged by at least ten thousand people waiting to see the body of Valentino lying in state—even though they had been told that the doors might not be opened at all: "The first arrivals had been women and girls, but more and more men had now joined the crowd. The average age of the boisterous mob seemed under thirty-five and reporters remarked on the increasing number of men sporting bolero jackets and gaucho hats. Many also wore balloon trousers, spats and the slick hair and long sideburns made popular by Valentino. As mourners they presented a strange assembly" (Shulman, *Valentino*, p. 13).

By two in the afternoon, the rain began to fall, and twenty thousand people clamored to be let in. All around the funeral parlor, north- and southbound traffic through the sixties and crosstown traffic between Columbus and Amsterdam Avenues were at a standstill. The mob finally shattered the glass of the parlor windows and the doors were opened. In the crush that followed, over 100 people were injured. At one time the crowd was said to have numbered over eighty thousand people, mostly shoving and kicking rowdies who nevertheless became sober and respectful once they were inside. Over 100 policemen in the immediate area were reinforced after midnight by an honor guard of Fascist Black Shirts supposedly dispatched by Mussolini himself. Until the funeral, over forty thousand people filed past the glass-covered coffin every day.

Landing in New York just before the outbreak of World War I with neither money nor language, Valentino seems to have had but a single asset—confidence in his powers of seduction. Whether because of prewar jitters or some other reason, America was in the midst of a dance craze: new steps were being created every few days when Valentino first took up residence in a lower Manhattan rooming house. Dance is a channeling of bodily energy into rhythm, the nature of that energy changing the form of the dance. It might involve muscular discipline for the sake of bodily harmony, or it might simply offer release from tensions: a mating dance allows a member of one sex to display strength of bodily control and grace for the sake of an opposite number or in another form might simply involve both partners in a sublimation of sexual attachment. During the heady years just before America entered the war, an emancipative gust was blowing through dance floors, popularizing rhythms from warmer climates that lessened constraint through sensual motion. A prime example of these was the tango.

Rodolpho (as Valentino was called at the time) enjoyed clothes, company, and spending money. He soon became a professional dancer in cabarets that catered to women in search of male partners. More specifically, he became a tango dancer.

Irving Shulman writes, "Such male dancers were referred to as gigolos, even by the women who danced with them, and to the average

American male they were pariahs with effeminate manners" (p. 103).[2] Among these "gigolos" was a distinctive group to which Valentino belonged—the Latin types. These were thought of mostly as continental Europeans, and their charm, for those who found them charming, derived from an intriguing mix: they were both familiar and unfamiliar, more overtly sexual in their body language, their clothing, their response, than the usual American male yet at the same time containing that response within better manners. They were, in a word, exotic, and the allurements of exoticism derive from the same depths that contain sexuality and danger.

Shulman also notes, "Out West, ranchers shot coyotes and other varmints; in New York City, good Americans punched gigolos" (p. 103). This would seem to indicate that someone who had chosen to call himself Rodolpho di Valentina, "with his foreign accent, sensual eyes, good manners and grace on the dance floor" (Shulman, p. 104), had gotten not only to women but to men as well. If he, and others like him, stirred sexual depths in women, depths of discomfort and irritation were stirred in men. Male accusations about gigolo unmanliness echo Strindberg's notion that only effeminate men seek the company of women while the truly masculine remain with males.[3] Even if one disregards the homosexual implications of that preference, it would appear to show a fear of women on the part of certain white American males that translated as vengeful resentment—with which American blacks are familiar. (Janine Chasseguet-Smirgel contends that the boy's "normal contempt" for women—a standard outcome of the Oedipus complex—is a pathological and defensive reaction to the same sense of inescapable maternal omnipotence, rather than a direct outcome of genital differences [*Female Sexuality: New Psychoanalytic Views,* 1970].)

Valentino was not simply the conveyance of a fad: the feelings he aroused were deeper and more intimate; they resonated as they did only because of the peculiarities of a cultural climate. There were two parts to Valentino's darkness, its sinister and seductive sides—the changing nature of the public's response says more about America in the early twenties than about Valentino himself.

By 1916, the then Marquis Rodolpho Guglielmi had gotten himself embroiled in a society divorce scandal, charged with white slavery, and briefly jailed. Once released, he found it best to put distance between himself and New York: the following year, he joined a musical comedy troupe on its way to San Francisco. On the West Coast, he heard that there was money to be made in films and headed south for Los Angeles.

Valentino's first film roles in Hollywood recognized only the sinister part of his darkness. He played heavies whose villainy was manifest because they were foreigners—tainted womanizers, blackmailers, gangsters. When he landed a part that could make use of his choreographic talent, it was as an Apache dancer in *Rogue's Romance*. In her autobiography, *First Person Plural*, Dagmar Godowsky remembers that on first seeing Valentino, Alla Nazimova called him a gigolo and a pimp. Still, for those in the public eye, it is better to be spoken of abusively than not at all. However it happened, Valentino was becoming known. Nazimova, who had come to Hollywood from a successful career on the stage, was a personality in Hollywood, in spite of a succession of ups and downs. Valentino would eventually wed her most famous protégée, Natacha Rambova (Winifred Hudnut) in a second marriage. Nazimova herself would not dwell overlong on superficial appraisals of Valentino; women, more quickly than men, seemed able to see beyond his Mediterranean complexion to the more enticing part of his darkness. Twenty years later Nazimova recalled that even though Valentino appeared fat and far too swarthy, with "grotesque" eyebrows that were black and bushy, she could detect in him the perfect Latin lover and wanted him to play opposite her in *Camille*. But it was another woman, June Mathis, who midwifed Valentino's final emergence as Hollywood's greatest romantic lover.

Mathis was one of Metro's top writers. In 1919 she was at work on a script of Blasco Ibáñez's *Four Horsemen of the Apocalypse*, which Richard Rowland had bought for Metro because it was a best-seller—the melodramatic story of an Argentine family, one branch of which had emigrated to France, the other to Germany. Out of love for a French woman, Julio, the playboy scion of the French branch, mends his ways, enlists, and is sent to the front and killed in combat by one of his German cousins.

When she was through with the script, Mathis suggested Valentino for the role of Julio. She had never met Valentino but had been impressed with his work in a segment of the recent *Eyes of Youth* (again, the eyes).[4] Even though the actor was relatively unknown and Rowland had put forward the name of Metro's successful leading man, Carlyle Blackwell, Mathis prevailed. Later gossip suggested that Mathis did so because she was in love with Valentino. Shulman, Valentino's otherwise reliable biographer, does not believe that "June Mathis, a plain and not too attractive woman, had fallen in love with the man she saw on the screen; there is no evidence to support this romantic confection"

(p. 139). Other than the unlikelihood of people being impervious to sexual attraction because they are plain, there remains the fact that Mathis had been drawn to the face she saw in only a brief film episode. As we have seen, what she saw had something to do with the actor's eyes. Shulman himself says that in Valentino's "role as Julio she wanted him to underplay still more, to show restraint, to feel with his eyes and employ only the slightest movement of his lips" (p. 140). Valentino heeded Mathis's advice, and the rushes showed her to have been right—so right in fact that the script was changed to enlarge Julio's part.[5]

The film was an instant success, in large part because of Rex Ingram's skill as a director: reviews stressed the artistic merits of *The Four Horsemen* as an epic adaptation and, though they praised the actors, had much less to say about them. But the picture stills of Valentino as Argentinean gaucho and as playboy poloist were freely distributed by Metro's publicity department and the glamorous image of a new star started claiming the pages of widely read photomags, such as *Motion Picture* and *Photoplay*.

After making *Camille* and *The Conquering Power,* Valentino moved to Paramount, where his next motion picture was to be propelled once again by a best-seller, *The Sheik*. That book was in fact more than a best-seller: it allowed as no English novel had ever before a descent into powerfully enticing and dangerous depths. For well over one million readers, it offered escape into the forbidden worlds of miscegenation and sexual passion. Its success may have been due to the fact that it appeared to be so clearly a sexual fantasy of its author, Edith Maude Hull. The heroine, self-willed, highbred Diana Mayo, is captured by an Arab sheik who is defined in relation to her as primarily a sexual force and a symbol of nobility. Her breeding contends for a while with her instincts, but the latter finally triumph and she acknowledges her need. Hull, having led her readers through the thrills of improper love and desire too shameful to mention, allowed the end of her tale to reestablish the nobility of the rapist by disclosing that he was in fact a British nobleman. It may have been important that the image of titled ladies not be besmirched in recollection, but the ending was otherwise unimportant: getting there had been more than half the fun.

Once again, Valentino was extremely lucky. As in the case of *The Four Horsemen, The Sheik* was centered on a male character whose allurement was exactly like his. All three were identical in appealing through forbidden paths to an Anglo-Saxon libido—the novel by Blasco Ibáñez, with its Latin hero capturing women through the extension of his phallic whip; the novel by Hull, in which someone of a near-African race was allowed to plumb the sexual depths of a noble British woman; the visibility in Valentino of a dark sensuality that a puritanical culture disguised but which had surfaced in the dancing frenzy of the twenties and on which his representation of masculinity drew heavily (see Studlar, "Valentino, 'Optic Intoxication,' and Dance Madness").

The picture was all Valentino's. He was encouraged to flash eyes and teeth with abandon, to show unbridled gusto in repeatedly kissing and carrying off his prey, while the prey (Agnes Ayres) was reduced to being little more than the passive object of this sexual aggressiveness. And the film, like the book, reached the audience in exactly the desired way:

> Libraries suddenly began to report record withdrawals of books about Arabia and Arabs; police sought hundreds of runaway girls whose destination was reported to be the Sahara; and women neglected their homes and flocked to the picture, even engaged in contests to determine who could see *The Sheik* most often. Women sighed, breathed heavily, gasped as Valentino swooped Agnes Ayres into his arms and kissed her, kissed her, kissed her, while his eyes burned with the pure flame of passion. How he scoffed at convention and disdainfully thrust a woman aside after he had used her! Sighing in their kitchens, parlors and bedrooms, American women longed for burning sands closer to home, demon lovers whose hot kisses seared their lips as strong fingers tore at their pretties. [Shulman, pp. 166–67]

This would suggest that only women were pining away for the sexual symbol the screen allowed them to fantasize about: it ignores the fact that, five years later, men waiting in line to get a last glimpse of Valentino would be wearing bolero jackets, gaucho hats, balloon trousers, and spats—as well as slicked-down hair and long sideburns—none of these being the usual feathers of the American male in his mating dance. Valentino and those who publicized his image had caused both genders to open sexual gates the culture had hitherto concealed.

The advertising for *The Sheik* was frankly prurient: "See the auction of beautiful girls to the lords of Algerian harems," or, "See the barbaric gambling fete in the glittering Casino at Biskra." But once this "barbaric" context had been established, the photograph of the very white Ayres made of the text a rape powerfully informed with the miscegenetic violence required to break a taboo: "See the heroine, disguised, invade the Bedouins' secret slave rites"; "See Sheik Ahmed raid her caravan and carry her off to his tent"; "See the Sheik's vengeance, the storm in the desert, a proud woman's heart surrendered."

The advertising copy, deriving from the novel's words, acquired on-screen the power of visual immediacy: the phantasy suggested by relatively innocuous images was informed by the energy contained within their cultural symbolism. A culture that could not show sexual intercourse onscreen could intensify the audience's more habitual imagination through the sight of a hero in whom dark blood flowed. The act was thus twice forbidden, not only for being suggested at all but because it involved another race, one that was fearsome (as the "foreign" race so frequently is) because of an assumed sexual energy of dangerous strength. Spectators of both sexes thus imagined the act so consistently repressed in the fullest energy of its wildness and primitive power.

The unique confluence that Valentino's screen personality could bring to a particular kind of role was confirmed by the disastrous *Moran of the Lady Letty,* which Paramount released next. In a seafaring role Valentino was out of place and wasted: Paramount hurried back to Blasco Ibáñez with *Blood and Sand.* Nevertheless, because Valentino was such a hot property, casting him sometimes became more important than the roles in which he was cast. Even when the star's exoticism was exploited successfully in foreign roles, like the French *Monsieur Beaucaire* or the Russian *Eagle,* mere exoticism paled in comparison with *The Sheik.* Valentino wearing the powdered wig of Beaucaire became, in the words of critic James R. Quirk, an actor at the expense of a personality: *The New York Times* may have been able to note the "gorgeous" quality of the picture, but the far more numerous spectators who read *Photoplay* felt that the Booth Tarkington story extinguished most of the old Valentino spark. New versions of *The Sheik,* like *The Young Rajah* and, of course, the ultimate *Son of the Sheik,* were what the greater number of spectators wanted.

Until the end of his life, and even after, Valentino remained in the truest sense of the word an idol. But idolatry never swept away those who saw in him the most powerful of socially disruptive forces. Even at the height of his worship Valentino remained under constant attack. And the fear of the threat he represented was so strong that his attackers could only deny the very object of their attack: detractors never portrayed the actor as an open sexual threat but, rather, as a disguised and corrupting force. Even as *The Son of the Sheik* was playing to packed houses, *The Chicago Tribune* fulminated against a face powder machine it had discovered in the men's room of a local dance hall. That machine was for the use of *male* patrons who wanted to emulate the Sheik: the only way to resist a sexual force so intense that it incorporated both sexes was to emasculate it, showing the sexual appeal of *The Sheik* to be effeminate and, therefore, unnatural and, ironically, unmanly.

Rudolph Valentino died in 1926, the same year as the silents that had brought him into the imagination of so many people—1927 was the year of *The Jazz Singer* and a new age. The obituary in *L'Osservatore Romano,* the Vatican's newspaper, recalled Valentino's huge audiences as "evidence of the times' decadence." A dozen years later, *Life* magazine remembered "the romantic dream lover of women the world over" with "his sleek black hair, his mournful eyes, his Roman nose and muscular torso," while in *The Los Angeles Times* Wallace X. Rowles gave the obdurate male version: a "slick-haired, side-burned, bell-bottom-pants Lothario of a hysterical post-war jazz age." Seemingly, there were more than simply the two sides of Valentino's darkness: those "mournful eyes" (contrasting the masculine stare of Hart) seemed indicative of an androgyny to which a large part of the American public had become educated: exotic appeal had become more polymorphously perverse. Many women now responded to a different kind of male, and many men were now aware of a more ambiguous form of masculine seductiveness.[6]

Nevertheless, Rowles may be partially right. It is possible that the tango was a symptom of sufficient magnitude to soon require a symbol: Valentino may simply have come along at the right moment. The virtues of understatement, seriousness, hard work, and physical harshness still provided a cultural ideal for many: they looked to the Wild West and the cowboy for their symbols. But World War I had ended; the temporary euphoria that follows social cataclysms and releases recent constraints is apt to release as well some of the older ones. a growing number of city dwellers were tempted to look away from the virtuous West to older and more appealing corruptions.

And it is likewise possible that *The Four Horsemen* was the ideal vehicle to propel the image of the Latin Valentino at that particular time: like the story's hero, the United States had just fought, in a very real sense, against its own cousins. Ibáñez's novel was the work of a Spaniard. More logically than the American motion picture, it chronicled harshly the misdeeds of those whose blond, white, powerful race it set in deliberate contrast to the darker, smaller, humane Latin. Germanic inhumanity was so strongly emphasized by Ibáñez that some years later it became possible to read into his novel a prophecy of what the Nazi regime turned out to be.

When the Latin Rudolph Valentino was offered up as a sacrifice to that brutality, a victim of the pestilence—war, famine, and death unleashed by Aryans—he showed the failure of what our own culture had regarded as traditional virtues. The dying Julio of *The Four Horsemen* won a significant battle and won it in the very arena of those who had downgraded Latin culture. The Valentino of *The Sheik* would subsequently show the attractiveness and energy of that downgraded culture to those who could now cast aside a part of their traditional overlay.

The role of the sacrificial lamb in *The Four Horsemen* was important for yet another reason. Where the purified and purifying cowboy had either ridden off alone into the sunset or was presumed to have settled down within his cleansed dominion *after* the end of the picture, the heroes of Blasco Ibáñez died. The cowboy could not die in his final Assumption— purity is already an absolute. But the dark blood spilled on French battlefields or in Spanish arenas by the Latin hero was twice proof of his life: lifeblood visibly shed also confirms the sense we have of life in its tenuousness. That visibility of the motion picture added to the seductiveness of a hero whose appeal was the life force of his sexuality.

But that hero was of course not on the screen. Rudolph Valentino lived nearly exclusively in the imaginations of his admirers: women fantasized an ideal lover (the two motion pictures that propelled Valentino into fame, *The Four Horsemen* and *The Sheik,* were for a large part the writing and imagining of women). But one cannot dismiss either the fact that men fantasized themselves as ideal lovers in his image. Valentino was the erotic dream of millions.

But he was only a dream. In real life, the Sheik appears to have been a completely different person. On the first night of his first marriage, Jean Acker locked him out of the bedroom and afterward turned aside Valentino's efforts at a reconciliation. His second wife, Natacha Rambova, was known to be a cold and aloof beauty more interested in her career than in romance: that marriage, too, ended in divorce. The actual Rudolph Valentino may indeed have been the inversion of the traditional Don Juan described by Jung and Marañón. If so, it would be perfectly fitting: the illusory images projected onscreen are not the ultimate reality of motion pictures. That reality is in the image they allow the spectator to nurture within himself. Once in a while, such images may be sufficiently strong to alter the spectator from whom they derive their substance. It may even happen that they are able to affect an entire culture.

NOTES

1. That symbolism has such deep roots in Western culture that, as De Becker points out, even the divine symbol of a dark race becomes fair: as Christ, Jesus is lightened. Interestingly, it is the devil who remains black.

2. Perhaps this is yet another instance of the male fearing the part within him that he senses his role may not have fully overcome.

3. This is not to say that sexuality and homosexuality are as easily compartmentalized as conventional morality might wish. Carl Jung associates Don-Juanism and homosexuality to the extent that both result from the son's mother fixation ("The Mother Complex"); see also the work of Gregorio Marañón, who believes that in becoming an exclusive devotee of women, Don Juan becomes himself the (feminine) center of sexual gravity.

4. The dancer and his eyes become the focal points of Gaylyn Studlar's "Valentino, 'Optic Intoxication,' and Dance Madness" (1993).

5. This creation of Valentino by a woman reminds us of the "woman-made masculinity" that the social vectors of the day encouraged and among which Studlar identifies the "tango teas" ("Valentino, 'Optic Intoxication,' and Dance Madness").

6. Miriam Hansen ("Pleasure, Ambivalence, Identification: Valentino and Female Spectatorship," 1986), Gaylyn Studlar ("Valentino, 'Optic Intoxication,' and Dance Madness," 1993), and Dennis Bingham, whose theory is that "masculinities" contend in the male star with a feminine side (*Acting Male*, 1994), all believe that Valentino's appeal was due to his "bisexuality." We can never know at what unconscious level or exactly how a spectator may be affected by the male star, but it seems reasonably clear that Valentino's male identifier was not going to deliberately take on the actor's female side: he wanted the *consequence* of Valentino's allurement, not the possible convolutions of the lure itself.

3

The Kid, the Kidder, the Kiddush: Charlie Chaplin

Hart and Valentino appealed to two levels of the male psyche. Hart represented to male viewers what they might have consciously dreamed of being, what it was permissible to dream. Valentino allowed the projection of dreams that were more deeply hidden. The cowboy involved the male superego, that self-censoring mechanism born into the original sin of the Oedipus complex. One would be tempted to say that Valentino appealed to the spectator's id—the psyche's primitive needs. In fact, Charlie Chaplin was very likely the one who most nearly echoed those instinctual impulses: alongside him, Valentino appears to represent no more than the male ego, the conscious personality prior to a censoring compromise.

Many spectators were devotees of Valentino, many others of Hart both actors enjoyed a huge cult following. But in a less demonstrative way, practically *no* spectator could help responding to Charlie Chaplin—and for more compelling reasons than laughter. It is a relatively safe guess that Valentino's audience was composed principally of women and that Hart's was predominantly masculine. If our assumptions are correct, Chaplin's world was more likely to be a man's as well. Hart and Valentino engaged the spectator on the level of a conscious discourse, but a more immediate subtext ran through Chaplin pictures that returned the spectator to a preconscious awareness. Today, most of Chaplin's films are still seen, whereas those of Hart and

Valentino have disappeared: the id is less sensitive to fashions than the ego or superego.

In *Jokes and Their Relation to the Unconscious,* Freud appears to distinguish two levels of laughter. The child's laughter expresses sheer pleasure. Even when that pleasure is evidence of superiority, the child does not demonstrate Freud's sense of the comic—does not measure against something *else* the accomplishment that occasions laughter. The adult, on the other hand, *judges* the child at whom he or she laughs, whether it is the child's excess expenditure of movement or deficient expenditure of intellectual effort. That judgment evidences the adult's sense of the comic—laughter informed by a comparison. Here Freud echoes Hobbes, who had seen laughter as sudden glory arising from an as sudden sense of our own eminence by comparison with the infirmity of others "or with our own formerly" ("Human Nature," 1651). Hobbes's *previousness* and Freud's distinctions suggest that adult laughter results from the recognition of a now-transcended part of the self, from knowledge that the laugher is in fact better than what one contrives to be or triumphs over what one remembers being.

Possibly, part of what can be said of Chaplin can be said of all comics: their success is proportional to their skill in re-creating postures of childhood whose excesses and lacks were once the spectator's very own but from which he can now separate himself through his laughter. But Charlie Chaplin's genius takes him a step further: it allows him to slip so perfectly into the somatic and mental world of the child that the spectator also enjoys the "sheer pleasure" of *being* a child once again, *before* he realizes that he has now transcended that stage, before his sense of the comic moves him to a second, more conscious level of laughter.

The immediacy of the spectator's first reaction is perhaps the reason for the staying power of Chaplin's movies: the spectator is not laughing at the punch line of a gag (a gag cannot preserve its punch through repetition) but, rather, is experiencing a *renewable* satisfaction, one that remains alive within him. Both reactions taken together may account for a remark made by André Bazin: referring to a scene in *The Adventurer,* he notes, "I have 'listened' to that gag twenty times in different places; when the public, or a part of it at least, was made of intellectuals (students, for example), a second wave of laughter of a different nature would sweep across the spectators" (Bazin and Rohmer, *Charlie Chaplin,* p. 14).

To find the screen suggestion that flowed most directly into the spectator, bathing him once again within his infantile world, we must look to the very earliest Chaplin—the mainly one- and two-reelers made for Keystone, Essanay, and Mutual. In 1917, Chaplin signed with First National, for which he would do eight films, ranging from the two-reel *Shoulder Arms* to the six-reel *The Kid*. Here, a change is apparent: length, especially in a picture like *The Kid*, introduces other concerns resulting in a more mediated picture. After starting his own United Artists (with Douglas Fairbanks, D. W. Griffith, and Mary Pickford), Chaplin would make only full-length features from 1923 on. Although the watermark of the old Chaplin remains in all of his pictures, those that follow *City Lights* (1931) are caught up in the sophistications and complexities of the post-silents world: from *Modern Times* (1936) through his final *Countess from Hong-Kong* (1967), it is no longer possible to talk of the predominance of subliminal effects that were so powerful in his earlier work.

In 1916, Chaplin made *The Vagabond,* not quite two and a half years after his very first picture. It was a two-reeler, his third film for Mutual, and his fifty-third feature. By now, his cinematic identity was fully established. He was able to affix his logo to the opening scene, the swinging doors of a saloon disclosing at the bottom only the famous oversized shoes and at the top the equally familiar bowler. The title echoed the previous *Tramp* (1915) and prefigured *The Immigrant* (1917), chronicles of the outcast and wanderer, here shaded as the Wandering Jew through the Semitic fiddle seen in Charlie's hands once the saloon doors swing open.

The Wandering Jew is a complex figure of guilt, fear, atonement, and freedom. Condemned to remain marginal until Judgment Day, he can only pass through the structures society has erected for its own comfort and protection. He does not benefit from them and, therefore, does not respect them. Perhaps mindful of his own childhood in London's Kennington slum, Chaplin's earliest pictures show him with few exceptions to be a social outcast. His very first appearance was as a swindler in *Making a Living* (making a living, the necessity of keeping body and soul together, would remain an important theme: the Wandering Jew was also condemned to never have more than a few small coins in his pocket). Later, when Chaplin found a more permanent identity, his clothes denoted the loss of affluence—with only his tie, cane, and bowler emerging from, and emphasizing, sartorial misery.

The one who is forced to live on the other side of boundaries feels, and is made to feel, suspect: to be out of bounds is to be very nearly out of law—both the outlaw and the transient are excluded from legal protection and rights. The outcast cannot free himself from the fear of authority. The shadow of the law reaches into nearly every part of Charlie's universe. The policeman, the boss, and the upholders of moral custom loom over him as constant and punitive judges. Those fears merge his world with the child's.

To start with, these nemeses dominate Charlie physically. According to Uno Asplund, Eric Campbell "was well over six feet tall" (*Chaplin's Films*, p. 176): he was the terror who bent lampposts in *Easy Street* (1917), Charlie's boss in *The Fireman* (1916) or *The Floorwalker* (1916), a rival in *The Rink* (1916) or *The Adventurer* (1917), the malevolent waiter in *The Immigrant* (1917). Mack Swain, another giant of a man, played threatening fathers (as in *The Idle Class,* 1921), foremen (*Pay Day,* 1922), and Big Jim McKay, who, in a hunger-induced hallucination, saw Charlie as a chicken in *The Gold Rush* (1925). Alongside these Goliaths, Charlie was an especially frail David.

And he was frail in other ways as well: starting with his nickname, he was diminutive.[1] In "What People Laugh At," Chaplin notes the deliberate contrast of his small frame with the hugeness of his opponents meant to elicit the audience's sympathy for the underdog. By contrast, his adversaries were so inhumanly large that the audience could sense them as the full weight of social repression. But size was not the only aspect of that repressive force. For the outcast, the policeman need not be a giant: he is invested with persecutive power, and sooner or later a policeman crosses nearly every one of Charlie's paths.

Some of the women (played early on by actresses like Phyllis Allen and Alice Davenport) were oversized too—Oedipal giants and punitive mothers with whom Charlie kept colliding (*The Immigrant* or *The Circus,* 1928), in whom he attempted to hide (as often in the first pictures with Mabel Normand), or by whom he was turned into a collapsing infant (*Tillie's Punctured Romance,* 1914). While the punitive men reduce Charlie physically, the punitive women shrink him into a child. Already, like other infants, he has difficulty with his clothes—he is in a *pre-vestiary* stage of development. His clothes are too large for his small size; they do not fit well.[2] The ill-fitting shoes are a further problem. Without necessarily going as far as Parker Tyler, who believes they are weighted with the very body of death (*Chaplin, Last of the Clowns,* 1972), the fact is that they fetter Charlie's walk as they would a child's. In a famous scene from *Easy Street* (1917), Charlie, for once a cop, turns to confront the imaginary bully behind him only to discover that it is he, Charlie, who has tripped himself. The child steps into his parents' shoes to assume the trappings of adulthood but is hobbled as he does so. In fact, all of Charlie's clothing expresses a quest for adulthood—if not for its power, then at least for its dignity. It is an exaggerated quest, one that hampers him because it does not fit.

The child who has not yet mastered the intricacies of clothing is very likely to be defeated by objects adults handle every day. In *A Night Out* (1915) Charlie tries to pour water from the telephone; the tiger rug and the wall bed decoy him in *One A.M.* (1916); his Model-T Ford stalls every time he climbs into it (*A Day's Pleasure,* 1919). These objects of the adult world become impediments just when Charlie most needs to be quick, as he is so frequently pursued. And if not actually chased by the enforcers of social ordering, he finds himself caught in another part of the child's nightmare—he is late. He must move ever faster to catch up with his world, but he is on a psychological treadmill: like Jack the Bear, he runs like hell but he gets nowhere. The revolving door in *The Cure* (1917) becomes an accelerating trap, as does the assembly line in *Modern Times.* His totem is the up escalator he tries to go down in *The Floorwalker.*

Still, that flight is also the child's dream of freedom, and if Charlie is forever pursued—pursued by others, pursued by time, pursued by objects—he is also forever escaping. He escapes into dreams, as in *His Prehistoric Past* (1914), at least until the inevitable Keystone cop wakes him up. He fantasizes heroic deeds in *The Bank* (1919), until he wakes up caressing a floor mop instead of the girl of his dreams. He imagines the ultimate escape through his ascent to heaven in *The Kid,* until a celestial policeman brings himself, and Charlie, down to earth. At the end of so many films, he escapes down the empty road that leads to extinction—but even that return to the womb is illusory: it lasts only until the next film that starts the chase all over again.

Chased and beaten, the child dreams his escape. Defeated by objects he cannot handle, the child turns them into a personal metaphor. He domesticates the recalcitrant object by changing its original function to one of his imagining; moving from fear to vengeance, he destroys the adult object—it no longer serves as it was meant to. Charlie becomes a doctor to the alarm clock of *The Pawnshop* (1916) through stethoscope and reflex hammer. He uses the street's gas lamps to anesthetize the bully in *Easy Street.* Pursued in *The Adventurer,* he dons the lamp shade at the foot of the stairs and turns into an innocuous floor lamp. And any number of times, his cane becomes the prehensile appendage, endowed with a virile power he lacks, that extends his arm for purposes of dalliance, theft, or revenge. Having brought the adult object under his own control, the child is twice avenged within a world intended for the use of his elders only.

Charlie becomes offensive in his revenge. He steals money from a (false) beggar in *His New Profession* (1914) and a hot dog from a child in *The Circus* (1928). He wedges the bandaged leg of Eric Campbell in the revolving door of *The Cure*. It is not enough to simply escape the tyranny of laws and objects: it is as important not to know that this escape is fraught with consequences or in conflict with moral imperatives. A pre-ethical child is in evidence from the start. In his first two-reeler, *Mabel at the Wheel* (1914), Charlie not only turns a car racetrack lethal by making it slippery but also "froths and rejoices in his vindictiveness with a dyonisical joy that verges on sadism" (Jean Mitry, *Charlot,* p. 30). In the Keystone days, such exuberance in destruction was warranted by the dynamics of Mack Sennett's fast-paced comedy. But when the figure of the tramp suggests intimations of a soul, an undertone of cruelty deepens the character. Theodore Huff sees Chaplin's first Keystone characters as those of "a sharper, a heel, an annoying blunderer, a thief, an obnoxious drunk, who is cruel, sometimes to the point of sadism," but adds that this was before "the real 'Charlie'" (*Charlie Chaplin,* p. 35). While it is true that the *real* Charlie may have become less obnoxious and annoying (as the pacing of his comedy was refined), Charlie's subsequent cruelty and sadism persist and are no longer simply mechanical aspects of comedy.

Until after *City Lights* (1931), Charlie is not a specific character. He is a generic morality figure, the outsider, as are those around him, nonparticularized figures of impediment, of repression, of love. In Mitry's words, Charlie was merely a way of being before the world. But because this way of being was the social underdog's, the ensnared spectator could likewise kick his boss, bring down the plant in which he worked, flee to freedom along a trail of destruction, become smitten with the female incarnation of that freedom. His satisfaction in so doing accounted for his deepest laughter.

On second thought, that satisfaction manifested itself in social laughter—a more conscious comment on the spectator's position in society. If William S. Hart preserved for city dwellers pent up by the system a dream of freedom and open spaces, Chaplin allowed them a dream of reclamation inasmuch as the hostile adult symbolized by bosses, policemen, and the idle rich were also actual bosses, policemen (their infantry), and the idle rich. They located Chaplin and the spectator within a specific class that the spectator could momentarily destroy thanks to

Charlie, who subverted the class structure by refusing to accept it. The child who appropriated for his own use the objects and ways of adults was also the one downtrodden who, however much society tried to repress him, reemerged as he had always been—the insistent mime appropriating for himself the symbols and ways of the oppressor. In *The Gold Rush,* he refuses to chew on his leather boot with the desperation of one who is starving: instead, he turns the desperate moment into elegant, high-class dining, filleting with gourmet delicacy what can no longer be viewed as a shoe.

Free and/or avenged, Charlie dances his triumph. His dance is proportional to his dream: no earthbound adult can dance like that, and the dance is therefore already an escape. In *The Floorwalker,* he evades the clutches of the long-suffering Eric Campbell by rhythming a mad gig around him. In *Modern Times* (1936), Charlie's dance is his first emancipation from the factory.[3] The gesture is so subversive that he is sent off to a mental ward. Later, released from the ward and subsequent imprisonment, he dances on roller skates his joy at being free in a child's equivalent of heaven: the toy section of a department store.

Drink is supposed to be the escape of lesser men; in Chaplin movies, the dance of freedom often assumes the mask of drunkenness. He becomes drunk sooner or later in nearly every picture, but his is a particular kind of drunkenness, one that affects his body but not his face. It is yet another form of dance. In Jean-Louis Barrault's words, Charlie shows intoxication "like a whirling planet"; "and," adds the French mime, "he never overdoes it!" (quoted in Mitry, p. 19). Charlie's drunkenness is casual; he does not seek escape in drink, but the accident of his drinking releases the child, the anarchist, the dreamer within his dream, who is no longer subject to any law, whether social or physical.

The drunk, like the dancer, subverts the social order. There is a good reason why the enforcers of law and order are after Charlie: when he is not running away from them, he is very likely destroying what they mean to preserve. In addition to all the forms of sobriety and seriousness that Charlie subverts, social integration requires gainful employment. Most of the time, Charlie is unemployed. Miming the world of adults, he plays at doing things—at being a boxer, a fireman, a scene shifter in a movie studio, a soldier, a windowpane fitter. He works, sometimes very hard, but practically never holds down a job for any length of time. He can envisage the routine of work only as a child might, with a short attention span. He is distracted, loses concentration. Finally, the actual effort defeats him.

We have already drawn attention to the fact that Chaplin begins his work in pictures as a con man in *Making a Living*. Still the con, he attempts legitimacy as a reporter by stealing another reporter's story: the picture ends with a scuffle between both men. Now neither appears to be respectable: the con's anarchy has corrupted legitimate work. Granting that this was Chaplin's first try and that reporting was not a likely job for Charlie, it should be noted that even as a professional clown he would not succeed. In *The Circus,* he becomes the star attraction for a while, but only by accident, trying to escape from an ill-tempered donkey. It is not a job he can hang onto for long. He then tries a balancing act on the high wire but is unsuccessful. At last, the circus leaves town without him.

Unemployed, and very likely unemployable, the political Charlie refuses to accept that he is less human for being expelled from the exchanges of market capital: sooner or later, he subverts the job he attempted and rushes back to his hounded freedom, a free-floating signifier recklessly redefining accepted signifieds. Charlie's jobs are brief—like his victories. In fact, the most optimistic aspect of his world is its episodic and improvised nature: the defeat, like the victory, is but a disjoined interval.

Together with a steady job, the family is another underpinning of society, and the child attempts to mime that representation as well. Scenes of married life in the earliest pictures, with Mabel Normand and more shrewish incarnations, are simply pretexts for conjugal accidents. But when Charlie tries to be a credible father, he can assume the role only for another child, another waif, as in *The Vagabond,* when he washes and delouses Edna Purviance. But this fathering merely frees the (female) waif who then escapes. Five years later, Chaplin wrote himself a fathering role with a happy ending in his first full-length motion picture, *The Kid* (1921). Critics felt the upbeat finale contrasted too strongly with Chaplin's vision and made the rest of the film appear maudlin. Chaplin did not repeat that mistake.[4]

It is of course in the nature of men and women to meet and pair off. That encounter will likewise be mimed by the child, even though social and erotic distinctions are not yet clear to him. The waif may be a girl but is primarily a waif. Like Charlie himself, the female waif is mistreated by the powerful who always dominate the weak, and he must save her. But her liberation is a form of his own liberation; it does not intend, nor does it turn into, sexual possession. This is a world in which pecking replaces kissing.

The appealing women who played opposite Chaplin were both young and young looking. Edna Purviance, who would appear thirty-five times with him, had turned twenty the year before she was first seen in *A Night Out* (1915). In his autobiography, Chaplin recalls his first meeting, when he was nineteen, with Hetty Kelly, a fifteen-year-old dancer in a chorus line: "One looked off and caught my eye. . . . I was suddenly held by two large brown eyes sparkling mischievously, belonging to a slim gazelle with a shapely oval face, a bewitching full mouth and beautiful teeth—the effect was electric. When she came off, she asked me to hold a small mirror while she arranged her hair. This gave me a chance to scrutinize her. That was the beginning" (*My Autobiography,* p. 104). And Chaplin adds that at the end, although "I had met her but five times, and scarcely any of our meetings had lasted longer than twenty minutes, that brief encounter affected me for a long time." Later, he concluded, "the episode was [to me] the beginning of a spiritual development, a reaching out for beauty" (quoted in Maland, *Chaplin and American Culture,* p. 42).

Chaplin's first wife, Mildred Harris, was sixteen when he married her. At the age of fifty-four, he married his last one, Oona O'Neill, then eighteen.[5] This led to a sometimes malevolent conflation by critics (and the American Congress) of Chaplin and his fictional persona.[6] It is not uncommon to see his private and artistic lives bound up as "the search for Hetty Kelly."[7] Still, there can be little doubt that in his pictures the child woman is the only possible companion for the child hero who is merely aping the social forms of courtship. That child hero is so frail that even a frail woman would overwhelm him; he must be matched with that "slim gazelle," a woman whose frailty is exaggerated by childhood—or, in this symbolic world, by brutal guardians, physical affliction, or poverty.

Sensuality is absent in these relationships. (The sensual Charlie is not the one who makes love but, rather, the one who performs with a passion, like the frenetic dancer previously referred to, or the one who eats with such obvious enjoyment in *The Gold Rush.*) Under these circumstances, the woman's gender is not sufficient to keep her within Charlie's focus. Nysenholc recalls that even Edna Purviance is turned into an object when she disappears from the seat on which she was sitting with Charlie and he looks for her under the cushions (p. 96). At that moment, the comic mechanism requires that even innocent Edna be no more a person than were the dangerously large and shrewish women desexed through their size or nastiness in Chaplin's early Keystone comedies. The woman as object is one more of the things the subversive underdog is entitled to: Charlie, no less than those who weigh down on him, feels entitled to their trappings, and these include a woman (or at least the childlike imitation of a woman).

When the libido is so unclearly focused, Charlie himself may turn out to be the woman. There are of course the early Chaplin characters in drag, as in *A Busy Day* (1914), *The Masquerader* (1914), or *A Woman* (1915). Those roles have a certain crudeness to them: in a sense, they emphasize for comic purposes the very masculinity of the disguised male. But there is a different kind of femininity that seeps through many of Chaplin's characterizations, a far more subtle one that Marcel Martin refers to as *troublant* (either sexually "arousing" or "disturbing").

That sexual seepage occurs frequently. In many of his pictures, Chaplin becomes at some point a mincing character; he feminizes himself, usually in order to escape from or to placate a threatening presence. Critics like Mitry and Huff believe this tactic results from the childlike nature of the character. Mitry feels Charlie relies on "a sexual ambiguity," finding his "safety in a certain femininity. A strictly psychological femininity which is like the avowal of his weakness, his need of protection. [He plays at being] the one who needs to be consoled. He seeks maternal attention" (p. 50). That regression is the moment when the child makes himself even more childlike by taking on the sex whose traditional role stresses frailty while allowing at the same time engagement of the adversary through flirtation rather than confrontation. It is the moment when the male waif, out of self-protection, turns into the female waif, when the child becomes the innocent flower child.[8] When that regression is not modulated through comedy, it introduces the sentimental Chaplin, the one who is close to tears and self-pity—the one who needs to justify a return, if not to the womb, then at least to the maternal breast.

But the child is not all innocence. In fact, it is questionable whether Charlie is ever innocent, for innocence is so often no more than the disguise that helps circumvent actual jeopardy. As such, it is part of the here and now. But the child also lives a dream life in which he overcomes adversity by escaping from it or defeating it. Central to that dream is the idea of freedom. But however gloriously Charlie is able to implement that dream, it remains tinted with fear: judges and chastisers lie forever in wait. This has led critics like Hannah Arendt (and especially the French, who have contributed the lion's share of the literature devoted to Chaplin) to stress the Jew in the Wandering Jew.

Chaplin denied at one time that he was Jewish. It is very doubtful that he ever spoke, or even heard in his home, the kiddush—the traditional prayer recited on the eve of the Jewish Sabbath. In his autobiography, he goes to some pains to emphasize his mother's later attendance at "Christ Church in the Westminster Bridge Road" even though (or perhaps because) the "skeleton in our family cupboard" was that her mother "was half gypsy" (*My Autobiography*, pp. 18–19, 22). Still, most biographers feel that "gypsy" is a euphemism, and Huff notes that the "name Charles Chaplin does not appear in the records of Somerset House where all English births are recorded, suggesting that Chaplin might not be his real name" (*Charlie Chaplin*, p. 10).[9] Huff goes on to assert that Chaplin's father "came of an Anglicized French Jewish family."

The reason why most critics ignore Chaplin's denial and take his Jewish ancestry for granted is because they sense the pariah's pain in the comic gesture (see Arendt, "The Jew as Pariah"). Jean-Louis Barrault felt the density of persecution settle on the back of Charlie as he watches his home go up in smoke: "In *The Great Dictator* [1940], Charlie looks at his house burning down; we see him from behind: he is absolutely immobile; but that back contains every tragic element of the longest dirge" (quoted in Mitry, p. 19). The pain becomes evident if one compares Charlie Chaplin to the other great comic actor of the twenties, Buster Keaton. Starting with the toughness of his nickname, Buster Keaton appears to be a far more *solid* presence than Charlie. He too faces a hostile world, but it is a world of material obstacles that must be overcome or circumvented. Keaton's problems are mechanical, private, and limited in their consequences. They do not result in human entanglement. Keaton's malevolent objects finally turn him into a kind of intelligent object: he has no fear.

Whereas Chaplin is usually escaping, Keaton heads directly toward the obstacle, deadpan, concentrated, purposeful. Keaton is propelled by the confidence of the athlete: he moves ahead in a straight line; Charlie is anxious, and his paths are devious. Keaton's relentless motion forward is finally the very motion of his film: Mast notes that in *The General* (1926) "every gag, every piece of business, is subordinated to the film's driving narrative" (p. 156). Keaton knows things will work out: he can turn the threatening lobster claw into a cigar cutter (*Three Ages*, 1923; Nysenholc points out that if Charlie is given real pliers with which to work [*Laughing Gas*, 1914], he will pull out the wrong tooth).

Keaton's spectator anticipates the triumph that will result from the collision. Charlie, in trying to avoid his, fears and finally encounters human disasters along the way: the spectator is aware of his own tenuousness in Charlie's latent jeopardy.

If the schlemiel is the waiter who spills the soup and the schlimazel is the one who gets it in his lap, Charlie is both. But he has other Jewish inherences as well. Marcel Martin reminds us that he is also the schnorrer—the unregenerate beggar who takes advantage of others' generosity (p. 15). Charlie may be a beggar, but he is also a survivor, and surviving has made him hard, with little time for gratitude or social graces, even though he might mime them from time to time. (Whatever his better intentions, he always forgets to remove his hat—a further reminiscence of the Jewish figure.) He can be unjust and, as we have noted, even cruel. In *The Champion* (1915) he picks up a good-luck horseshoe just before entering a training camp where he hopes to make some money as a sparring partner; when he sees the other sparring partners being carried away from the ring one after another, he makes sure the charm will work by stuffing it into his boxing glove: fairness in an unfair world comes after self-preservation.

Surviving, he remembers the threat with a kick or a punch. Speaking for more than just the Jewish spectator, Elie Faure says that in getting his own back, Charlie "avenges all of us, those that were, those that will be. [What's even better, his vengeance] forces the others to bear a part of his humiliations" (*Fonction du cinéma,* p. 56).

Most of our examples have been drawn so far from the earlier Chaplin movies, the ones that are still most frequently shown today because of the immediacy of their appeal to the spectator's preconsciousness. Just as the spectator does, they and Chaplin himself rely on their collective infancy (infancy, from the Latin *infans*—the one who cannot yet speak)—that moment before the comic and his camera are concerned with ideas.

Throughout the thirty-five pictures made for Keystone, the fifteen for Essanay, the twelve for Mutual, the nine for First National, and the first four at United Artists, the films are silent. And within them, Chaplin is wholly silent: his mouth does not shape the words that cannot be heard. He has other ways of speaking. The scene from *The Adventurer* for which Bazin heard different kinds of laughter is the one in which Charlie, having escaped from Sing-Sing (no less!), reaching behind him for a stone, feels with his hand the shoe of the dreaded guard who has caught up with him. There is a momentary hesitation while Charlie, through his hand, takes in this calamitous turn of events. He then attempts facing up to it (but without turning to face it): with the same hand, he tries to make the threatening shoe disappear by covering it with some sand. More powerfully and more immediately than any spoken word, that pathetic gesture conveys the magnitude of human jeopardy and the futility of assertion. Little wonder that, in looking back at pictures like *Shoulder Arms, The Kid,* or *The Gold Rush,* Chaplin felt that "sound would have added nothing to any of them. Quite the contrary" (quoted in Pierre Leprohon, *Charles Chaplin,* p. 138).

These early pictures are primary in a number of other ways as well. Grey tends to fall out because of the contrasting image—the essential statement is put down in black and white. That essential quality is to be found in the film's rhythm as well. The faster projection rate of post-silent pictures makes them seem much jerkier than they were intended to be. But even in their normal projection, Chaplin sought an accelerated and more purposeful rhythm, one in which threat and wish fulfillment are more immediate. The early pictures show us the essentials of an action rather than its analysis. As Leprohon points out, the jerkiness imposed by the twenty-four-frame-per-second projection does not falsify our perception: the action was stylized and spare to begin with; the modern projector merely emphasizes the intent (p. 122).

The film that elicits the spectator's immediate response avoids certain kinds of analysis. Minute scrutiny of a human quandary probes its object and so magnifies it. But analysis turns comic when it attends to a surface, as when it breaks down and mocks the fluidity of human action. One way of countering that fluidity is to speed up the camera, which alters human motion into something mechanical in the truest sense of Bergson's definition ("of a mechanical imposition on what is alive," *Laughter,* ch. 1, V.ii): that camera reduces the actor. The stylization of the early Chaplin movies, achieved through the reduction of a human gesture to its symbolic equivalent as pantomime, is thus the idiom of comedy. Chaplin himself stressed the fact: "I am a comedian and I know that pantomime is more important in comedy than it is in pure drama" ("Pantomime and Comedy").

Chaplin was conscious of the necessity of a direct and simple statement: the spectator was to *be* the child, instantly, before he could think of what else he was. In various interviews at the end of the twenties and the start of the thirties, Chaplin said he loathed talkies not only because they ruined "the great beauty of silence" but especially because he believed they defeated the *meaning* of the screen. He objected

mainly to talk; he soon acknowledged that "sound effects and syn-
chronized music are certainly useful" because they might facilitate the
conveyance of that meaning (quoted in Leprohon, p. 139). He was set
against the trappings of an art that would weigh it down and require
for its understanding more than could be instantaneously perceived.

Such was the ideal of the earliest Chaplin—the physically nimble
creature constantly on the move through a young medium yet unen-
cumbered by the concerns of more complex mediations. But by the
end of the twenties, both Chaplin and the medium were aging, *slow-
ing down,* moving from visceral immediacy to reflection. We have already mentioned that critics found *The Kid* to be overly sentimental in
contrast to its happy ending: what was being contrasted was a reflection on childhood misery. City streets and tenements, which in previous films had been merely the neutral space within which a threat developed or an escape began, were analyzed as a slum in *The Kid,* the
place of a specifically engendered misery. And there were other indications that the Kid was growing older. In 1923, Chaplin scripted and
directed (but did not appear in) *A Woman of Paris* (1923), a straight
drama of unhappy love and moral redemption.

If *A Woman of Paris* was the indication of changes to come, it was
also something of an exception. Two years later, Chaplin made *The
Gold Rush* and three years after that *The Circus.* But the thirties were
on their way, and moving pictures had definitely come of age; grey was
also starting to show through the tousled hair of the tramp. Chaplin
made one last picture still strongly steeped in the old idiom, the 1931
City Lights, a largely silent picture at a time when the screen was expected to have a voice and one that showed him in his symbolic raiment when surfaces had become scrupulously recognizable and denoted specific circumstances.

At the start of *City Lights,* Charlie is still the tramp, the unspecified
figure of the free outcast. His clothes are a little less ragged and fit better than they usually do, but only temporarily, in order to contrast his
later destitution. He is discovered sleeping within the bosom of a female statue as it is unveiled, from which he is routed. The temporary
breast is hard, unyielding stone (it is missing altogether in the child
woman). Charlie's first image thus establishes the waif's dereliction
within the city. It also establishes his disrespect. It is not enough that
he has ruined the official unveiling, which was already mocked (together with movie sound) by turning the city fathers' speeches into in-
comprehensible and muffled words. He now extends the mockery: as

he clambers down along another figure of the sculptured group, his profile comes in contact with its splayed hand, allowing him to thumb his nose while the national anthem is being played—one of Chaplin's more blatant images of contempt for the system which un-American committees would later remember. True to his usual persona, Charlie is hounded, compliant, and subversively hostile.

The image of the victim and the anarchist is continued in the next scene. Jeered by street urchins, he moves into traffic only to find the dangerous figure of a cop coming his way. In order to escape, he reaches the curb by going through a parked luxury car. The child is threatened by those who enforce discipline but escapes from them by appropriating a part of their property and converting it to his own use.

When Charlie slams the car door closed, he attracts the attention of a blind flower girl. She is standing near what appear to be the metal railings of a park. The vignette may contain more than one reminiscence of Hetty Kelly, who, long ago, had promised to meet Chaplin on their first date "at Kennington Gate at four o'clock on Sunday afternoon" (*My Autobiography*, p. 105). The girl, thinking a wealthy customer is in her vicinity, holds out a flower to him. The reduction of her bouquet to a single flower stresses its symbolic meaning: it is at once the emblem of love, of pathetic frailty, and the contrasting image of bucolic purity within the city. (Later on, when a momentarily affluent Charlie buys her flowers by the bunch, they turn into mere comic objects.) The flower girl is not only obviously poor (in the tradition of flower girls) but blind as well: at this stage, she is the only kind of woman Charlie can encounter, one enfeebled through her sex and circumstances to an even greater degree than he—the child woman.[10] Chaplin buys her flower with what few cents he has left and sits near the railing, enthralled. But this tender scene is not allowed to develop: the blind girl empties her water pail on him.

In contrast to Chaplin's previous cityscapes, this one is realistic, with bright shops, broad sidewalks, and bustling traffic. Before, the streets had been Chaplin's own reminiscences of the Oakley Street basement in which he lived, the Lambeth workhouse, the garret at Pownall Terrace—decaying walls, miserable stores, and eateries glimpsed only long enough to convey an abstract tone of urban wretchedness. Once Chaplin specifies the city, Charlie must contend with it for our attention, as when he disguises the voyeur in him so as to admire a nude statuette in a gallery window, stepping back as the connoisseur, but unfortunately into a street elevator.[11] Chaplin had always analyzed parts of previous streets in order to provide Charlie with a specific dilemma; the difference in *City Lights* is the persistence of the realistic set alongside the part analyzed—the gag loses some of its spontaneity because of the logic of its integration.

At evening, the tramp and the flower girl go their separate ways. She enters what is intended to be a genteel slum but has the cardboard look of second-rate Hispano-Californian scenery. The awkward stylistic change returns the set to a symbolic function: the female waif, like Charlie himself, is outcast, denied residence within the shining metropolis. Similarly, Charlie finds his way under an emblematic bridge near a river where he encounters an amiable drunk trying to commit suicide. In the process of saving him, objects turn once again against Charlie: first it is the stone intended to weigh the drunk down that falls on Charlie's foot before nearly drowning him altogether. Later, when the no-longer-depressed drunk invites him to dine, Charlie swallows paper streamers that have become entangled with his spaghetti. Finally, quite drunk, Charlie dances his way through the restaurant into complete mayhem—a vengeful moment provoked by the outsider who was never allowed into such an establishment.

Night dissipates Charlie's drunkenness but not his aggressiveness. With the help of his newfound friend's car and money, Charlie buys the flower girl's entire stock and drives her home. Money has made him her master: when Charlie asks to see her again, she answers, "Whenever you wish, sir." She is the imitation woman to whom this imitation patriarch, along with his derby, cane, and impudent mimicry, is entitled. Emerging temporarily from slave to wealthy master (someone who can afford to buy out the girl vendor), Charlie loses with the flower's symbolism his own sense of humanity: in his luxurious car, he follows a man with a cigar; when the man discards the half-smoked stogie, Charlie jumps out of the car and kicks an old tramp out of his way in order to get it. The cruel instinct of the survivor is not mitigated by the awareness that he is driving a Rolls Royce. The cigar is, after all, very important: it is the capitalist emblem par excellence.

Charlie will be returned to the straight and narrow by the news that the flower girl, already twice frail, is now ill and requires medical treatment she cannot afford. She has reached the point of destitution that not only reduces her far below Charlie's level but leaves him as the only one who can help her. A man in the society whose ways Charlie appropriates may be homeless, moneyless, and wretched, but he has the right nevertheless to be better and stronger than one symbolic woman. The economically jeopardized spectator of Depression days would recognize that fact with some degree of solace.

By this time, Charlie's rich friend is sober and has deserted him. Charlie makes the usual abortive attempts at holding onto a job. First, he becomes a street cleaner. We see him with the emblems of his trade, the brush and scoop, but he does little actual work. Next, we see him persecuted by a parade of animals including an elephant. (The child's scatological humor contrasts the virginal quality of his encounters with the child woman.) He then loses the job altogether because he has once again subverted it, spending more than the time of his noon break with the girl. In another recognizable move, he tries to make some quick money as a boxer: when he sees the size of his prospective opponent, he reverts to the female in him in order to disarm the enemy. He does this with such success that the brute hides behind a curtain in order to change into his shorts. It will not, however, prevent him from knocking Charlie out once they enter the ring.

The adventure having ended disastrously, Charlie is back on the city streets where he encounters his rich friend, happily drunk once more and once again generous. Charlie will now be able to give the girl sufficient money to leave for Vienna (the city whence all medical salvation comes) in order to have her sight restored. Unfortunately, the drunk sobers up before Charlie has time to leave with the money, and once again his nimble and nasty alter ego must come to the rescue. He snatches the bills that are no longer his and rushes off to give them to the blind girl. A vestige of nasty Charlie first thinks of keeping one of the large bills for himself, but ultimately he relents. Nemesis follows: he is dragged off to jail for theft.

Several months later, it is fall—the time of decline. Charlie is released from prison, considerably worse for wear. He is bereft of even the jaunty cane with which he once worked the doorbell of his rich friend. The girl, who has regained her sight, now owns a flower shop. When a young man whose wealth is evident in his top hat enters the store, she smiles in happy anticipation, believing for a moment that he might be her benefactor.

The street urchins are once again pestering Charlie, and the girl watches them, amused, through the shop window. Charlie catches sight of her and is rendered motionless. Seeing him staring at her, she laughs and says, "I've made a conquest." She repeats her earlier gesture, offering Charlie a flower. This time, however, it is with a coin: the symbolism and her world have changed. As she presses the money into Charlie's hand, she recognizes his touch and her smile fades. He points to his own eyes and asks, "You can see now?" Indeed, she can now see: what she sees is the final image of Charlie's face, with a painful smile that, though it might express happiness, is certainly charged with apprehension. That fear is justified after what we have seen of the girl in her new life: her expectation that her savior is handsome and wealthy, her laughter at him through the store window, the loss of her smile when she recognizes him. Most important, she is no longer the waif, the child woman—Charlie's only possible companion and his only possible claim to patriarchal status.

City Lights was studded with familiar images. It was Chaplin's last incarnation of the tramp adrift within the city. Even though he would keep his tramp's outfit for parts of *Modern Times* and *The Great Dictator*, he would no longer be a simple figure of freedom and deprivation; both pictures placed him within a specific part of the urban world—he became a character rather than a suggestion. Conceivably, some of that freedom had already been lost in *City Lights*. Although he precipitates the manic dance of destruction in the restaurant, Charlie dances his insouciance for only a very brief moment. It happens, ironically, as he is going to be locked up: he flips his cigarette over his shoulder and, as it is about to hit the ground, catches it with a back kick. This will be his last gratuitous gesture.

Much of *City Lights* is about seeing: the flower girl's loss of physical blindness, followed by her blindness when she actually sees Charlie; the blindness of the rich man, whose humanity is awakened only when, as Eisenstein puts it, he is blind drunk; Charlie's own perception that his happiness is dependent on the girl's blindness (when he tells her about the miraculous cures of the Viennese doctor and she exclaims, "Wonderful! Then I'll be able to see you!" he realizes his imminent jeopardy before putting it out of his mind; and the film's last scene focuses through a close-up on the agonized question in his eyes). But *City Lights* is also about a camera learning to see. We have already alluded to the city streets that were always an important but neutral space in Chaplin's pictures and which here acquire a competing role thanks to the camera's sharper sight. The modern camera would continue to see more and more keenly, to hear with ever greater acuity, to imitate every surface with absolute precision.

Chaplin had subtitled *City Lights* "A Romantic Comedy in Pantomime," but by 1931, he must have known that his very medium was dooming the essentiality of pantomime. Chaplin may have been dragged into the modern times of motion pictures kicking and screaming, but he was dragged in nevertheless. His own camera became larger and crisper, his sound expanded: eventually, even the hateful *word* had to be accepted. It was no longer possible for Chaplin to limit himself to the kind of simple statement his spectator absorbed without unnecessary mediations. In fact, motion pictures were conditioning that very spectator out of such responses.

When Chaplin was forced by his camera to pay attention to the physical world around Charlie, Charlie became secondary to the meditation on that world that had already accounted for the second level of laughter in earlier films. But in *Modern Times, The Great Dictator,* and *Monsieur Verdoux* (1947)—in all the pictures that follow *City Lights*—that thought displaces the image's immediacy. There are still wonderfully comic moments, but they are the interruptions of other concerns, from which the spectator as well is drawn away when he laughs. *Modern Times* is of course a satire of the industrial age; *The Great Dictator* is, as Bazin puts it, Chaplin's response to Hitler for having stolen his mustache;[12] *Monsieur Verdoux* contrasts the paltry numbers of a mass murderer like Landru with the devastation of the atomic bomb. And in *Limelight* (1952), the spectator is allowed a shocking glimpse of the naked, doleful face beneath the clown's mask, forcing him to sense his own pain across the distance that separates him from a specific character. Chaplin further enlarged that distance by elevating Calvero (in which name critics have read *calvary*) to a Christlike level of suffering. This avowal of undisguised pain draws the picture toward Chaplin himself and reduces the universality of the figure to which generations of spectators had so spontaneously responded. Calvero's character calls for a spectator who *understands* his pain, instead of the child who once reexperienced pain.

The modern camera was to alter more than only Chaplin's pictures. By the time *City Lights* was shown, both comedy and serious analyses had to acknowledge the motion picture's realism. Whether intending fun or sorrow, the character would henceforth be determined to a large extent by the assertiveness of a photographic instrument that had become too complex for the limitations of a simple statement readily recalled but not necessarily articulated by the spectator's conscious mind. When Charlie Chaplin first walked down the sidewalk of a specific street lined with particularized shops and individual passersby, their aggregate statement asserted itself alongside his. That aggregate statement resulted from a medium that now included sound, a crisp and precise lens, an increasingly nimble camera, and was soon to discover color and size. The archetypal figure could not long survive within such explicitness: it was only a question of time before the universal and symbolic hero was displaced by the singularities of a particular individual.

NOTES

1. Sergei Eisenstein contrasts the diminutive Charlie and the great Chaplin in his essay "Charlie the Kid": *"The Kid.* The name of this most popular of Chaplin's films is worthy to stand beside his own name; it helps to reveal his character just as 'The Conqueror' [designates] the spirit of William who conquered Great Britain" (*Film Essays,* 1968, p. 108). Other than in *The Kid,* there are not many children in Chaplin's movies: *he* is the child, adrift in a world of adults.

2. Nysenholc has noted the diaper-like safety pin that holds up his baggy pants (*L'Age d'or du comique,* p. 34).

3. His bondage within its assembly line had been a dance of an entirely different kind—the manic rhythm of dehumanizing repetition.

4. When at the end of *Modern Times* he and the waif are allowed to go off into the sunrise—when exceptionally Charlie is not left alone—it is after they have escaped once again from their pursuers and their incarcerators. As dawn comes up, they are at a crossroads. They leave together. But as the two dark figures holding hands across the highway's dividing line shrink from sight, trailing their shadows behind them, the spectator is left wondering about the precariousness of their choice.

5. He married his second wife, Lita Grey, when she too was sixteen. (Interestingly, most critics give her real name as Lolita McMurray, although there is some evidence that it was really Lillita.) Chaplin does not mention her in his autobiography.

6. De Becker writes that Chaplin had a nymphette fixation (p. 99). Columnist Westbrook Pegler accused him of moral turpitude, and Representative John E. Rankin said he was "detrimental to the moral fiber of America."

7. See Wes D. Gehring, *Charlie Chaplin,* p. 29.

8. Gehring writes, "[Chaplin's] tramp, so often associated with Pan, the figure from Greek mythology who was the god of fields and forests, might also have been called a flower child, both because of his inherently rural view of the city (as something negative and ugly) and his persistent use of a flower motif in the films, forever a sign of the purity and innocence of nature" (p. 134).

9. Martin feels the name may have been Kaplan (p. 10).

10. The actress who played her role, Virginia Cherrill, though still fairly "gazelle-like," was a little old for the part. In fact, she "was a party girl given to

staying out most of the night. Many mornings she would appear on the set somewhat the worse for wear" (Huff, p. 222). Chaplin was not happy with her work and, at one point, even thought of replacing her with a sixteen-year-old—one Marilyn Morgan, who later on became the more famous Marian Marsh.

11. This is an instance of the woman's reduction to an object that the child may safely appropriate. Enjoyment of the female body is possible (but only furtively) when it has been miniaturized and turned to inert matter.

12. Talk and thought somewhat mar the ending: Chaplin's final speech sounds weaker today than the film's images.

Part 2

The Star in Transition (the Thirties)

4

The Taming of the Great Lover: Charles Boyer, Clark Gable

Valentino was more than a bombshell—he was a drug injected directly into the bloodstream. He was the first major star to flaunt a sexuality that had been permissible only in women—perhaps because a largely masculine industry projected its fantasies and desires onto women while concealing the male libido through an impassive surface equated with manhood. Theda Bara, who had come to motion pictures playing the "Vampire" in *A Fool There Was* (1915), was one of several women (Pola Negri, Nita Naldi, Gloria Swanson) whose image was in fact an erotic promise. (It is interesting to note how many of these names, especially when they were contrived, flourished a final, latinate vowel—in contrast with which William Surrey Hart and even the somewhat equivocal Charles Spencer Chaplin have an honest down-home ring.) Although Theodosia Goodman came from Cincinnati, as Theda Bara she was meant to evidence the sexual power supposedly possible, permissible, and visible only beyond our borders—in her case, Egypt. She and her sisters turned the movie into a peephole—a not quite licit opening through which a glance could be *stolen* at exotic sexual worlds. Bara was successful enough to coin the word *vamp*, a diminutive of the persona that encapsulated the male's sexual desire and fear, combining Eros and Thanatos—which publicists were prompt to point out in the anagrams of her name, death and Arab.

In reality, Theda Bara was little more than packaging—an *image* of lasciviousness with no echo. She evolved as a container of sexual intensity through film action that remained unaffected by it. In Valentino, the Eros-Thanatos (Arab-Death) image was more powerful if for no other reason than that it was unusual—and perhaps also because the actor was really Rudolph Valentino.

The figure of any revolutionary pales within the context of his successful revolution and because of it: Valentino made things possible that had not been possible before him, and he was ultimately dwarfed by the horizons he helped open. In retrospect, one realizes that the relatively innocent images of *The Sheik* could not sustain much longer the shudder at miscegenation once Valentino had brought one of our periods of innocence to a close. Miscegenation would now have to await the arrival of stronger images derived from the reality of a more open culture rather than simply the mind of the spectator. Meanwhile, Valentino established the appeal of the Latin lover. Imitators, like Antonio Moreno and Ricardo Cortez, were found south of the border. The most successful was Ramon Novarro, whom Rex Ingram had cast with Valentino in *The Four Horsemen*. Ingram developed Novarro into a full-fledged star who took over from Valentino during the second half of the twenties.

The thirties were a different time for motion pictures: by the end of the decade, 65 percent of all Americans would take in a movie a week. Spectators habituated to films were more demanding and more critical, at least with regard to the medium's technical realization. Sound was a staple, color soon would be. Society was changing as well, and the silver screen reflected those changes. The days of a unidimensional Theda Bara had passed, and if sex appeal was still an important female characteristic, it needed to be incorporated within a person that exhibited other dimensions as well. The evolution of the vamp into a different kind of woman is more evident than the evolution of that new woman throughout the thirties, but it continued nevertheless. When Fanny Hurst's *Back Street* was first filmed in 1932, it featured Irene Dunne as a small-town belle who goes to New York, where she becomes a figure defined by her love for a married man rather than by any occupation of her own. The picture's second incarnation in 1941 removed the dolorous female and replaced her with Margaret Sullavan as a wisecracking woman who helped run the family business. (In the postwar version, exactly thirty years after Irene Dunne's, Susan Hayward was no longer confined to even the family business and later becomes a successful dress designer in her own right: she was by a now a full-fledged executive flying around the world.)[1]

The masculine image was undergoing changes as well and along with it that of the Latin lover. The idea that sex was more powerful and more interesting in proportion to its distance from our shores remained, but in modified form: gone with the smoldering of a Theda Bara was the smoldering Sheik whose look alone could ignite a full house of spectators. The eye was the nearly single attribute of the silent idol. Now, that figure had a voice as well and was caught up in the specificities of a story determined by the acuity of the camera's eye. The new Latin lover was evolving from an undefined darkness into a character with cultural particularities. The country whose sexual myths were most widely established in the popular mind was France.

In contrasting French culture with others, Sanche de Gramont identified it as a lightness:

> It is like passing through a decompression chamber and entering a lighter atmosphere. Lightness means tipped foils instead of sabers, a sauce without flour, a dress that is elegant because it is without superfluities, the ability of an employer to rebuke a subordinate without offending him, politeness without obsequiousness, irony disguised as flattery, indifference disguised as attentiveness, gestures that are understood before they are completed, the importance of nuance, like the difference between sports and athletics or between strength and power, and knowing the right tone to adopt, the precise gradation between familiarity and deference when bantering with a lady. [*The French* (1969), pp. 461–62]

Americans may have been sensitive to some of those distinctions. But for the more generalized sense of what the French man represented to the American, one must go to lesser-known and older definitions:

> So long as a man faithfully observes his marriage vows, the lenient opinion of America will not so carefully scrutinize his conduct to his parents and his children, his brothers and his sisters. Above all, it will hardly trouble itself to inquire whether he behaves agreeably at home, or permits himself, within doors, the luxury of complete freedom from uncomfortable self-control. In France, on the other hand, where the family is so deeply rooted in national affection, no man can neglect his homely domestic duties without braving public opinion. For this severity there is a touch of compensation. So long as he does his faithful best in his domestic relations, his conjugal vagaries may perhaps be held secondary—much as domestic vagaries might be held among ourselves. [Barrett Wendell, *The France of Today* (1907), p. 141]

Or, again, "[The Frenchman is] anxious to show himself "a bit of a dog," because this is a passport to popularity amongst certain of his compatriots. He boasts of his conquests, real or imaginary, with the gusto of a sportsman recounting his bag or the fisherman his tally of fish. . . . The most quiet Frenchman will, under certain circumstances, avow himself a perfect demon for pleasure of a questionable sort" (Charles Dawbarn, *France and the French* [1911], p. 33).

To the popular American mind of the thirties, the French man was thus something of a sexual gourmet, admired for his suave manners and understood with a sly wink. These traits were embodied throughout that period in the person of Charles Boyer and magnetized by what contemporaries referred to as the dark velvet of his eyes and the dark velvet of his voice—a rich bass timber authenticated by a charming but discrete French accent.

Charles Boyer substituted for traditional Mediterranean courtesy the boulevardier's urbanity. Where the Sheik might once have been brutal while paying due regard to forms (carrying his victim but never pushing ahead of her into the sacrificial tent), no hint of brutality could even be thought of in connection with French savoir-faire. It was important at a time when American women were starting to enter hitherto restricted preserves of men[2] and, with newly disclosed minds and tongues, that they not confront a man who was supposed to bowl them over simply by looking at them: there was a real and present danger that he might no longer be able to do so with such a paucity of means. It is not that women ceased to succumb but simply that they required more reasons than before.

Just as Rudolph Valentino was really Rudolph Valentino, Charles Boyer was in fact Charles Boyer. Although he later became a naturalized citizen, Boyer was born in France where he received an intellectual's education, first in philosophy at the Sorbonne and then at the Paris Conservatoire. He began his professional life on the *boulevard* stage—an exercise in the kind of lightness Sanche de Gramont refers to, which led later to the understatement and elegant intelligence he brought to his motion picture roles. Because American films of the thirties required that lands of sexual awareness be more remote than accurate, Boyer was first cast in roles that justified an accent, though not necessarily his. In 1935, Walter Wanger cast him as a Frenchman opposite Claudette Colbert in *Private Worlds* and as a half Chinese–half Russian opposite Loretta Young in *Shanghai*.

But Wanger was aware of more than simply Boyer's accent. Beneath the actor's charm that generated immediate sex appeal, Wanger saw and exploited a darker mood likely to cause deeper turmoil. In *Shanghai,* European urbanity hid Dmitry Koslov's secret: the spectator, like Loretta Young herself, was deceived—Koslov-Boyer was not a successful Shanghai businessman-cum-boulevardier but a half caste, a Eurasian who had made his way to the top. When Boyer disclosed his dark past to Young, a conflict was set up between the sexual magnetism of the star and the socially conscious intent of the picture.

At first, the revelation causes those around Koslov, including Loretta Young, to recoil from him in horror. But the script allows that if the half caste is sufficiently attractive, race becomes much less of an impediment, and a young Charles Boyer with practically no Oriental makeup was more than equal to the task. Young finally understands that one doesn't leave a Charles Boyer that easily and comes back to him, setting the scene for the picture's final thrust: the lovers cannot remain together because the reality of the world will not allow it. (One is of course left wondering whether that socially conscious and unhappy ending was not due in part to the strong taboo against racial intermingling that still existed at the time.)

The following year, *The Garden of Allah* discovered some of the same depths beneath the same Gallicized Russian accent. This time, following the outline of the 1904 novel by Robert Hichens, Boyer was a Russian monk who had fled his Trappist monastery in Algiers. The picture had all the earmarks of commercial appeal—a technicolor vehicle set in North Africa, pairing two actors considered to be among the sultriest: Charles Boyer and Marlene Dietrich. But once again the director (Richard Boleslawski) was able to descend to a second level in Boyer with the revelation of his past and to move from surface charm to inner conflict.

On the train where the two meet, the more somber Boyer is first disclosed: instead of being the suave Parisian, he is rude. Boyer and Dietrich will become lovers later on, ostensibly because he saves her from knife-wielding Arabs in the city's ill-famed quarters. But, in fact, Dietrich has already discovered on the train the sorrow that provokes unsociable behavior: Boyer's deep voice, dark eyes, finely chiseled nose and cheekbones have once again given the Frenchman away. And, as in *Shanghai,* the brooding is stronger than its urbane mask: in the end, Boyer-Androvsky must make things right with his God, and the two lovers are parted.

The bittersweet ending that brought so many of Boyer's films to a close (including *Back Street*) resulted from substance contradicting the promise of surface—a surface so powerfully attractive as to greatly intensify the sense of loss. But there was also time for escapism. A film like *Tovarich* (1937) found Boyer cast once again as a Russian, but this time as an émigré prince in an urbane fable (originally, a French boulevard play) where surface was all. As a stylish butler to crude, nouveau-riche employers, Boyer could display all his charm, with literally no mental reservations, for the benefit of a different and presumably smaller audience—one interested in the pleasure of badinage rather than in dreams of romantic redemption.

But alongside the comedies, the serious Boyer remained as well throughout his long career, sometimes reaching into evil, as in *Gaslight* (1945), sometimes not quite, as in *Hold Back the Dawn* (1941) and *The Thirteenth Letter* (1950). This hidden persona within the sexually appealing male tells us something about Boyer's talent as an actor, and it tells us a lot more about the evolving expectations of those (women especially) who were going to movies in the thirties.

The perspective of the woman in the picture house was not so very different from that of Marlene Dietrich when she meets Charles Boyer in *The Garden of Allah*'s opening train scene. She was first presented with an unusually appealing male surface—a surface that, in Valentino, had promised little more than carnal knowledge. But at a time when women were acknowledging other possibilities in themselves, being able to move through a sexual surface to yet another human level was important. Where Valentino projected the immediacy of a simple truth, Boyer's message was more complicated. It appealed to the mother in the woman but also to the one who was now helping run the family business and would soon be jet-setting around the globe—at least in films. Reality may have been somewhat different for the average spectatrix, but within the picture house such facts were relatively unimportant: what a part of the film recognized was the changing nature of her fantasies.

The fantasy was of course ahead of the social reality. In *Together Again* (1944), Irene Dunne told the father of her dead husband that he belonged to "a dying race" for thinking that public service was a poor alternative to a woman's more traditional role, assuring him that women could live perfectly well without men and that it was only the man's fear of losing his emotional power over women that made him think they could not. The wartime emancipation of women may have accounted for this remarkably avant-garde speech. Unfortunately, the shadow of Charles Boyer was lurking in the background, still powerfully enough for Irene Dunne to surrender, in the words of Molly Haskell, "to precisely that emotional power . . .

when, in the end, she forsakes her mayoralty to go off with Boyer" (*From Reverence to Rape*, p. 129).

Valentino and Boyer were evidence of the extent to which the screen could impose a visceral truth. The compelling force of their sexual image transcended deficiencies of movie thought and inadequate words—or even the well-articulated point of a feminist position. Comparing the 1932 and 1941 versions of *Back Street*, Haskell remarks that "the idea of a woman 'giving up all' for Charles Boyer is a lot easier on the pride than the idea of 'giving up all' for John Boles" (p. 173).

But fashions change, or rather, expectations are altered as social and economic evolutions affect the spectator. Charles Boyer made sixty-six films during his lifetime and was a reliable box office draw, yet today they are shown little more than are those of Rudolph Valentino. The world has shrunk, boundaries are no longer distant, and what was once exoticism is now within reach. The screen lover who brought with him the mystery of an enticing part of the world had been dispelled through many kinds of familiarity, and women had learned for some time that Latins could be lousy lovers. Boyer understood that mystery might no longer be a function of exoticism, that geographical distance might now afford less mystery than the distance between an outward appearance and what it hid. Unfortunately, even such depths as the movies of the thirties plumbed were not always sufficient to propel their characters very far into the more problematic years of the postwar. Throughout the thirties, no single film of Boyer's is as incendiary as *The Sheik*. He remained pretty much from film to film the same veiled sexual promise—but one that could not sufficiently excite the now more sophisticated female audience or reach their male escorts.[3]

As exemplified by Boyer, the appeal of exoticism in the thirties is one that evolved from sexual enticement pure and simple to the enticement of more diversified mysteries. The dialectical nature of Charles Boyer's appeal may have been in part cultural; it certainly derived from a country that privileges dialectics over pragmatism. Perhaps we are saying that Boyer was essentially an actor. Whatever the case, he remained mainly a woman's actor; for men, he was too removed culturally to be either a threat or a model. It is also conceivable that the hard times following the Great Depression were not contributory to the kind of foreign craze that had allowed Valentino to draw even men.

But men were not necessarily the only ones for whom exoticism could become distance stretched to the point of disinterest. A more immediately accessible figure like Valentino, but homebred, no longer receding into the shimmer of heat rising from a now unconvincing desert, was provided by Clark Gable. Gable was evidence of the here and now, proof that raw sexual energy, as potent as any import, could be produced in the good old United States. In the words of Charles Champlin, Gable "soon built up a reputation as the most total male who brawled his way across the screen" (quoted in Gabe Essoe, *The Films of Clark Gable* [1970], p. 16).

Including brawling within the "totality" of the man, Champlin identifies an equation of male self-identification and sexuality with aggression (one that had already been suggested, perhaps intentionally by American filmmakers, in *The Sheik*).[4] The difference between the sexualities of Boyer and Gable can be seen in their respective smiles. Boyer's was an entrapment, the disclosure of another person within the smiler; his smile drew its object toward him. Gable's smile was athletic, open, aggressive: it moved toward its object; it was in fact a first embrace.

What might thus be properly termed Gable's engaging smile assumed instant victory in an encounter with a woman. But women were not its only target: Gable, smiling, "established immediate camaraderie with all men" (Champlin, p. 16). Gable made only a few more pictures than Boyer: his greater and more enduring popularity may be due to the fact that he was also a man's actor.[5] For the male spectator, he was just as much a sexual ideal—the more so for having a screen persona that was believed to be an extension of the man he actually was,[6] an encapsulation of all the easily understood virtues the culture equated with virility. He was an outdoorsman and an athlete (at fourteen, when he left school, he was already six feet tall), he "drove fast cars. He ate like a tiger and drank prodigiously" (Champlin, p. 16).

The definitive Gable projected the male spectator's sexual fantasy of possessing a woman with ease, few encumbrances, and no consequences. Champlin describes "Gable [as] a roguish, down-to-earth, adventurous man's man; a sort of vagabond whose roots were only in himself" (p. 16). The American "man's man" was the one who believed he could take a woman and leave her, no matter how exalted her station or her sense of herself: "Jean Harlow, Joan Crawford, Norma Shearer, Claudette Colbert, Greta Garbo, Myrna Loy, the most desirable, witty, elegantly emancipated women in America bantered with him and fell in love with him on the screen. As often as not, he could resist them, walk out on them and go back to his work" (Champlin, p. 15).[7]

Though the new fashion in criticism has tended to emasculate Gable,[8] how much passivity and weakness actually informed such a male character can be seen, perhaps only in retrospect, in a picture like *Wife versus Secretary* (1936). Gable, playing the role of a publishing tycoon, is drawn into seemingly innocent situations with his secretary which appear sufficiently compromising to provoke his wife's jealousy. (Whatever the picture may have said explicitly, the stars' myths were meant to make the spectator feel even more than the wife, Myrna Loy, that such suspicions were grounded: the secretary was played by Gable's frequent partner, the original *Bombshell,* Jean Harlow.) Though tough as nails in his business dealings, Gable swings without any appearance of will between the two women. It is Loy who leaves Gable; his love-'em-and-leave-'em manhood is demonstrated only through his willingness to find an adequate replacement in Harlow. But when Harlow (the truly active principal in this film) finally confronts Loy, brings her back, and throws her into the arms of her husband, he accepts this, the movie's last embrace, with equal passivity. But the spectators were evidently meant to interpret Gable's irresponsibility as proof of his masculinity, while "Loy is made to seem a nag, and the audience is asked to resent *her* rather than a state of affairs weighted heavily in man's favor" (Haskell, p. 115).

Gable's particular screen personality evolved from his early work as a heavy.[9] His first major role while still in silents was that of a convict on death row in *The Last Mile* (1930). Elza Schallert, of the *Los Angeles Times,* recalled "the fierce, bloodthirsty, vindictive and blasphemous way he tore the part open." In his first talking role (*The Painted Desert,* 1931), *Film Daily* recognized his "brutish mannerisms." That same year, Gable played a gang chieftain in *Dance, Fools, Dance,* and the next a gangland leader in *The Finger Points*—but this time *Film Daily* detected his "fine voice and magnetic personality."

That was also the year Gable had a supporting role in *The Secret Six;* another in the supporting cast was the woman with whom he would frequently co-star—Jean Harlow. Their first major pairing was in *Red Dust* (1932), in which Gable played a rubber plantation boss in Indochina and Harlow a prostitute. The *London Film Weekly* allowed that in this film Gable was "perhaps more gruffly virile than ever before" and added that he "and Harlow make an excellent team." Their reputation was established by 1933; the same *London Film Weekly* said of the two in *Hold Your Man,* "Being themselves is the job at which Harlow and Gable have made good. [The film] is hardboiled, cheekily smart stuff, just right for these two."

What Gable hadn't achieved as successfully was attempting roles in which he wasn't "himself"—roles from which even intimations of the heavy had been expurgated. In *Laughing Sinners* (1931), Gable was the Salvation Army worker who befriends down-on-her-luck singer Joan Crawford. *The New York Times* commented, "Leading man Clark Gable is rather unconvincing as the saviour of fallen Joan Crawford." Opposite Greta Garbo, he fared little better in *Susan Lennox* (1931) as an engineer who shields Garbo from her brutal father. Even though there was by this time what *Variety* termed "Gable's vogue," Richard Griffith felt that Gable "occasionally lapses into moments of amateur play-acting." The difficulty of Gable's transition, and an indication of the tincture that would be necessary for the successful image of the star, was summarized by *Variety*. Referring to *Possessed,* released a month after *Susan Lennox,* the article notes, "Gable again is the stiff, cold-blooded manly leading man. Since graduating from gangster parts he has failed to register any strong emotion. Happy or sad, it's always the same Gable. Only when the script calls for a snarl or for him to slap Miss Crawford in the face, to call her a 'little tramp' and to tell her to scram, did anything register on the Gable horizon."[10]

Perhaps because of the brutalizing climate of the depression, sentimentality (so essential to the American spectator) needed a disguise more in keeping with the times. Norma Shearer, who had also been pushed around by Clark Gable (*A Free Soul,* 1931), remarked that "Gable made villains popular. Instead of the audience's wanting the good man to get the girl, they began wanting the bad man to get her" (quoted by Chester Williams, *Gable* [1968], p. 39). That the disguise was not meant to displace the sentimentality is evidenced by the fact that, in *Broadway Melody* (1938), a teenager like Judy Garland could sing, "You made me love you," to a photograph of Clark Gable: brutal though he appeared to be, the King could be recognized by even a young girl as basically safe.

It is possible that the girlish Garland of *Broadway Melody* and the streetwise Harlow of *Wife versus Secretary* both had the same intuition: that this character could be taken in hand by a woman. Taking in hand means taming, bringing inside (within the kind of area the cowboy once made safe on his westward passage). The woman who can achieve this corralling must be of a specific kind: she must be self-confident and must herself be *inside* (what the French quite properly term "une femme d'intérieur"), as opposed to those who remain outside (the kind that are called in all languages women of the street). The outside man may tempt the woman for two reasons: he is magnified, like Gable's Rhett Butler, by the epic quality of the dangerous world in which he dwells, and he therefore represents an interesting force to bring "inside," within her spell (which his stature magnifies in turn).

For the man, the desire of the woman to domesticate him is flattering and sets in motion the politics of rescue (already evident in Charlie Chaplin's relations to very young women): his own desire to possess interposes him as a protector against other potential possessors and makes him see the woman as more vulnerable than she is (a role that she may herself assume, as, for example, the cliché southern belle was supposed to). Until the man realizes the full consequences of this game, he is ready to accept as his own the adventurer's mantle that makes him so appealing. Men were thus most likely the ones who projected Gable, through their own fantasies, to mythical proportions: when *It Happened One Night* required Clark Gable to strip down to his bare chest, he wore only a shirt so as not to break unduly the rhythm of the scene; male spectators by the tens of thousands assumed, however, that manliness was no longer compatible with undershirts, and, Kathleen Gable recalls, "after seeing this movie, males from Azusa to Zanzibar just refused to wear undershirts" (*Clark Gable: A Personal Portrait* [1961], p. 29).[11]

Eventually, Clark Gable ended up as a force that was fed by his fiction but transcended that fiction. Few spectators could accept that Gable was no more than an actor playing a part in a movie. Even though the depression had made the paying job a most desirable commodity, Gable's pictures seldom showed him holding down a job: his mythical persona was too large for anything but the outdoors and was unlikely to be held down by even a disastrous economy. He was the outdoorsman (the man from "outside"); his was a physical world, to be confronted physically: in the fiction of films, Gable finally became the oil rigger his father wanted him to be (*Boom Town,* 1940)—or its equivalent as flyer, trapper, plantation overseer, rancher.

On the few occasions when a desk job threatened to rope him in, he escaped outside—as a reporter or a globe-trotting executive. He remained indoors only when danger subverted the indoors—as a gambler or gangster. In the end, he grew so huge that even sacred Hollywood codes could not always contain him: in 1939, he gave *Gone with the Wind* the first swear word uttered by the talkies (the codes that finally did keep Gable bound were more subtle).

Everything that had gone into the making of Clark Gable reached its acme in *It Happened One Night,* a picture no one really wanted to make. At the request of Frank Capra, Columbia Pictures, a struggling company in the early thirties, had bought a magazine story by Samuel Hopkins Adams called "Night Bus," which was shelved and about which Capra himself had forgotten. When he decided to start working on the property, casting became a problem. Constance Bennett, Miriam Hopkins, Myrna Loy, and Margaret Sullavan turned down the part of the spoiled heiress who runs away from her Florida home and encounters a bohemian painter on the New York bus. Rebuffed by the female leads and hoping that a big masculine name would reverse the women's negative response, Capra rewrote the script to make the male lead more attractive as a reporter—moving the man from the "inside" studio to the outdoors of the investigative reporter, with all the intimations of savvy and tough assertiveness implied by the job. Robert Montgomery was finally contracted for the part, but at the last moment, Louis Mayer withdrew Montgomery and sent Clark Gable to the minor league studio in order to punish him for the problems he had caused MGM's management (a drunken Clark Gable is said to have growled when he first visited the Columbia lot that the place was a smelly Siberia [Tornabene, *Long Live the King,* p. 173]). Gable grumbled but had no option but to sign, and Capra was able at last to get a female lead—Claudette Colbert, who had to be bribed out of a Sun Valley vacation in order to take it.

It Happened One Night was released in February 1934 to middling reviews and enjoyed first-run status for only one week. But once it was in the local theaters, it took off. Even though they jar present sensitivities, the jobless reporter Peter Warne and the heiress Ellie Andrews struck a sympathetic chord of surprising magnitude and accuracy in depression-era audiences. Gable and Colbert created a pairing that allowed men (and to some extent, women) to dream their fondest dreams and sublimate their most vexing frustrations while at the same time they enjoyed the solace and security of a moral code—and all through the same improbable cocktail.

That heady and amusing cocktail was provided by its two principals for nearly the totality of the film. After Gable's (and Colbert's) hostility had subsided, Capra gave Gable his lead: "He was playing himself, and maybe for the only time in his career. That clowning, boyish, roguish he-man *was* Gable. . . . Whatever came natural to him, I let him do" (quoted in Tornabene, *Long Live the King,* p. 174). By this time, the Gable image was established: he was the actor whose (male?) fans were identified by *Variety* as those who expected him to call his leading lady a little tramp, tell her to scram, and push her around to ensure her compliance; and he was also the male through whose gruff virility women could see a domesticable man. Claudette Colbert as the spoiled brat and dominated heiress allowed Clark Gable to exercise that persona while the circumstances of the plot gave a social dimension to his gruffness.

In the first part of the picture, Gable and Colbert are seen as equals. In fact, Ellie is insufferably rude to Peter, unable to react in any way but brusquely to a show of warmth—as when she discovers that Peter made her night's sleep on the bus comfortable or when he provides her with shelter from the rain in the motor park. Her prickliness is not unjustified: she is a babe in dangerous woods (her first neighbor on the bus tries to take advantage of her—driving her, with sure instinct, to Gable, whom she dislikes but does not fear). Also being a lamb among assorted wolves, she will allow Gable to enact the role of the rescuer. Meanwhile, her brusqueness is matched by Gable and topped in the second part, when his manliness requires that his response to Ellie's love be masked by an increasing raspy tone.

Ellie's reason for running away stems from the fact that she has upset a Lévi-Straussian system of exchange in a tribe where the circulation of women and goods is carefully prescribed: she met in New York and secretly married an English pilot.[12] This is simply unacceptable to her father, and dissolving her marriage is as unacceptable to Ellie. Her refusal gives her a curiously split personality: she is as rebelliously stubborn as her stubborn father but is nevertheless an object her father has always bent to his will and intends to continue bending.

Because he knows his daughter well, Alexander Andrews first tries to keep her aboard his yacht by tempting her with food: he has two elegant trays brought to the cabin and urges Ellie, if she will not eat, to simply inhale a perfectly done piece of steak. Still a creature of plenty, Ellie bats the food away and dives overboard toward what she believes to be her freedom. As she dives out and away, she adds to her appeal: though still at heart the vestal of the hearth, her moving out gives her the appearance of the woman who is emancipated—who no longer dwells within the manse—thus combining in an unstable but pleasing mix the immediate allurements of sexual attractiveness and the eventual virtues of domesticity, preserved for such a time as she will inevitably return to her various fathers.

The world into which she escapes resembles the one from which she flees to the extent that, for someone like her, it too is ruled by the power men feel it is their right to exercise over women. Ellie is able to handle the small-time mashers whom she arouses but will have more difficulty evading Peter's equally selfish reasons for using her, even though they are not sexual: having lost his newspaper job because of his insubordination, Peter is hoping to get it back through an exclusive reporting of the heiress's elopement. It will be up to her to detect his Oedipal weakness—the ankle around which a fetter can be snapped.

To say (as Peter in fact does) that he is interested only in his hot scoop is to indulge an extravagant litotes: Gable's persona exudes sexuality to such an extent that he does not need to give it verbal confirmation. His assertions are as thin as the "walls of Jericho"—the blanket that Peter hangs between their twin beds in the motor camp room and which the spectator knows will come tumbling down long before the final trumpet blast is heard. Still, hanging up that symbolic blanket emphasizes another part of the Gable persona. He is not only the male who can demonstrate his sexuality by resisting it, he is also the take-charge tinkerer who knows how to propel himself effectively through the world. It is to be expected that his mere presence dissipates other sexual threats in Ellie's vicinity, but he is also the first one to assist the woman whom hunger has caused to faint on the bus, the one who (when he is not converting one bedroom into two) can turn two haystacks into as many bedrooms, the one who finds food when their money has finally run out. He fares better than does Ellie because it is his world—the world of the proletarian bus (rather than the affluent train) and of the motel rather than the hotel (a fact not likely to be lost on depression-era spectators).

Ellie's quite natural irresponsibility with money accentuates another one of Peter's traits—his frugal management: he knows the value of a dollar, which she obviously does not (another wink at the Great Depression spectator). On an impulse, he pulls out a bill to give the son of the starving woman and is still considering the consequences this action might have when Ellie snatches the money out of his hand and forces it on the kid. All the while, the spectator expects that in the end she will be drawn into Peter's wage-earning world and able only to intend, not to satisfy, the squandering impulse that defines her as a kind person. But then the fairy tale muddies the tracks beyond recognition: the spectator expects just as confidently that Peter will be drawn into her world, and never more in need of riding the bus, and that it is he who in the midst of affluence will preserve the instinct not to squander money.

Peter's purposeful motion counterstates and stresses Ellie's ineffectuality: she is terrified of being alone in spite of her sassy mouth; she cannot eat the carrots Peter has unearthed for them—true to another one of her anthropological definitions that classify her as belonging to the advanced state of civilization that requires cooked food. And cooked food is what Peter will fix her the morning of their first night alone (he is as skilled at scrambling eggs as he is at other workaday chores); what sex was unable to do (as Peter's self-definition is based on manly abstinence) food will achieve: the spoiled, willful brat melts into a loving woman. She is now ready to submit to the surrogate father who will replace the one from which she has run away.

The eroticized relation of that father and child is shown in a curious scene whose otherwise gratuitous inclusion appears to stress its symbolic meaning. On their way to the road that will allow them to hitchhike the remaining distance to New York, they are unaccountably required to ford a large but shallow stream. Gable rolls up his trousers to his knees and then throws Colbert over his left shoulder, with her rump conveniently in front of his face. She giggles that she has not ridden piggyback since she was a child. Although her position suggests she is a bundle slung over Gable's shoulder rather than someone riding piggyback, it emphasizes a regression in her and leads to a disquisition by Gable on piggybacking, his theory being that the rich know nothing about it and that it is a luxury enjoyed only by those with roots among the common people, like Lincoln.

Even though the scene is tinged faintly with hagiographic reminiscences (St. Christopher the Child-bearer fording the stream, or Bunyan's Christian on his pilgrimage to the Celestial City), Peter tossing Ellie over his shoulder is an act of custody but one executed in such a casual and effortless way that it looks like an assumption of chattel— Ellie being now one of his articles of movable property and his slave. But as such, Ellie assumes a complete femininity that had only been intermittently apparent in the sassy brat. Her nether and posterior sexuality having been kept well within Gable's sight, the erotic charge of the spanking he must necessarily give her is emphasized.

The character created by Gable is an improbable mix of ingredients dosed to ensure success even though they appeal to contradictory sentiments within the spectator. Gable maintains the raspy toughness of previous roles, but, because this one debates the problem of wealth, he does so with more justification. The man who draws himself up to his usual paternalistic height in order to castigate the "little" brat or tell her to scram has valid reasons: he (not she) shares the audience's knowledge of how necessary money is and how difficult life can be without it. Illogically, but forcefully, the fundamental importance of money will be demonstrated by the world in which Ellie and her kind live: starting with the opening shot of her father's yacht, the audience will be allowed entry into the wonderful world of wealth; it will be given glimpses of elegantly curved steel, restrained sumptuousness, and soft lights that contrast markedly with the grim truth of the depression beyond the picture house.

Finally, in a last twist that favors gratification over logic, Christian Peter will be rewarded with possessions both material and sexual for upholding Puritan principles. Having regarded luxury as sinful and dominated pleasure through continence, having presented Ellie's father with an itemized bill for minimal expenses instead of claiming the $10,000 reward for finding her, Peter will be granted all. He will be vouchsafed that stroke of uncanny good luck that befalls the virtuous Horatio Alger lad because of his fundamental honesty and his steadfast, cheerful diligence: he will be free to marry the boss's daughter.

The depression spectator had it all as well: he luxuriated in upper-class wealth, deprecated it, possessed an attractive woman through the sexual power of a smile, and was never possessed by her—the picture ending before further questions could be asked. Women were not immune to the Gable smile either, but they may have read beyond the picture's surface, as Jean Harlow had already done when she foisted regularized matrimony on him in *Wife versus Secretary* and as teenager Judy Garland would do, singing to a sex symbol recognized as ultimately safe—knowing that this rugged he-man would not hurt a woman but was in fact a protector. The rough-and-tumble Gable was really a tease—only implying the possibility that he might not be quite honorable, even though Harlow, Garland, and Colbert know all along that he really is. They (and the audience) had many clues, starting with the hagiography provided by previous films. Nor were they blind to the convention of male response to personal distress through drink (when Peter loses his job and later when he loses Ellie), which shows a dependency the story had claimed to be Ellie's alone. This difficulty in dealing with emotional crises subverted the image of the take-charge male more deeply than did Ellie's resort to sex in order to demonstrate Peter's ineffectualness as a hitchhiker (or as a piggyback philosopher).

In any event, a good time was had by all. When official judgments confirmed the box office verdict, Hollywood crowned *It Happened One Night* best picture of the year, with Academy Awards in every other major category as well: best actor, best actress, best director—

and, to round out the list, best adaptation. Meanwhile, the picture had given Gable superstar status. When, in early 1934, he went on a personal appearance tour, "women of all ages blocked traffic while he was playing at the [New York] Capitol Theatre. They fought to get in. On the street outside the stage door was another mob of fur-coated teenagers. The police requested him not to leave between shows, which meant staying backstage from noon to midnight, and eating his meals there" (Charles Samuels, *The King*, p. 182).

It Happened One Night soon fanned Gable's fame far beyond Manhattan. He created the same havoc in the hinterland: upon his arrival in Kansas City, more than 2,000 women rushed into the station trying to get his autograph. By summer, the scene was repeated in South America: "At Santiago, Chile, women chased him into the suite of his friend Henry Moscowitz. They broke down the door, roughed up both of them, stole Moscowitz's pajamas, combs, hairbrushes, toothbrushes, shorts, thinking they were Gable's possessions" (Samuels, p. 183).

When Clark Gable died in 1960, more people felt a sense of personal loss than had any for an actor since the death of Rudolph Valentino. His career had lasted three times as long as Valentino's.

NOTES

1. The classic text that documents these changes is, of course, Molly Haskell's *From Reverence to Rape* (1974).

2. Perhaps this was more in their fantasies than in reality. Still, daring to entertain the fantasy is the first step toward any future change. That fantasy may have been entertained because the women of the thirties had taken a few steps beyond their sisters in the twenties, and women in the labor force had even reached something of an economic apex: by "1939 the average year-round, full-time female worker earned just 61 percent of what the equivalent male made. By 1977 she made just 57 percent as much" (Lester C. Turow, *The Zero-Sum Society* [1980], p. 19).

3. When there was the slightest danger that he might loom as a threat, men found security in pointing out that he wore a toupee. As a masculine model, he occasioned mainly ironic imitations of a heavy mock-French accent.

4. London psychotherapist Adam Jukes writes, "Masculinity is predicated on violence" (*Men Who Hate Women*, quoted in Miles, p. 8).

5. He was able to reprise in *Mogambo* (1954) the romantic lead he had played twenty years before in *Red Dust*.

6. We will attempt to show in the next chapter why this kind of spectator perception may not have been inaccurate.

7. For a more negative note on the same subject, see Jane Ellen Wayne, *Gable's Women* (1987).

8. On- and offscreen, Joe Fisher feels the brutality and speed of his love-making (whether fictional or actual) were protection against loss of manhood (premature ejaculation) ("Clark Gable's Balls: Real Men Never Lose Their Teeth," 1993).

9. This is an ironic reversal of the earlier real-life person: Clark's father, an oil driller, "took his son with him to the Oklahoma oil fields, determined to make an oilman out of him. Clark hated the violent, dirty world of his father" (Champlin, p. 19). Nor did William H. Gable give up: even when Clark had become a successful film actor, his father said to him, "Kid, why don't you get out of this silly business and do a man's work?" (Lyn Tornabene, *Long Live the King*, p. 165).

10. Even at the height of his success, Gable still felt the need to assert himself as a serious actor. In 1937, he made *Parnell* for Metro-Goldwyn-Mayer. If one considers that the Irish nationalist was a frail, nervous, and sensitive man, it is easy to see why the task might have been beyond Gable's talent even if his range had been broader. It is said that whenever Gable hinted he might try again, Carole Lombard forestalled future disasters by hiring a plane and dropping leaflets on the Culver City studio saying, "If you think Gable is the world's greatest actor, see him in *Parnell*, you'll never forget it."

11. This led to protests from underwear manufacturers who felt that "Gable's bare chest bankrupted a small but stunned portion of the garment industry" (Tornabene, p. 175).

12. The glamour implicit in this competitor's avocation is dispelled when we meet him, first as a crook willing to be bought off (the exact antithesis of Peter Warne) and later alighting from his flying machine in a ridiculous top hat.

5

The Adventurer (I):
Edward G. Robinson,
James Cagney

The great comic actor sees the human quandary with a shrewd eye: his art requires reduction to a symbolic level of the essential postures that define people and their actions. There is most likely no great comic actor who is not first of all a great actor. The noncomic actor in whom the actor prevails is the one who conforms to the author's vision of a character (and is therefore called a character actor), who steps out of himself to become consciously a particular presence. But films turned out another kind of serious actor as well, the one whose talent (and it was no small talent) was in being himself—the personality actor, of whom Clark Gable is a most conspicuous example. Here and abroad (among the French, one thinks of the Jean Gabins, the Michel Simons, the Raimus, the Arlettys, etc.), the screen was well served by generations of those whose offscreen personas became the substance of their roles, those of whom Sklar says, speaking of Cagney, "You could tell [they were] the real thing the minute you saw any other actor try to take on, as a role, what [they *were*] almost by birthright" (*City Boys: Cagney, Bogart, Garfield*, p. 13). They often came from lower- or working-class roots that contributed the tough truth of city streets to their portrayals.

We will have little to say about the first kind of actor, for we are looking for reflections of the American male, whether as fantasy projection or accurate portrait—portrayals of men like those watching the movie. Even when the conscious actor attempts such a character (rather than one with specific traits that limit recognition), it will be a more mediated creation than that of the personality actor who already *is,* to a greater or lesser extent, that man in the audience *before* he becomes his screen image as well. When one considers the Hollywood image of the American man as adventurer, Edward G. Robinson is the example of the conscious actor who was sufficiently gifted to first establish the gangster genre as a national awareness but who created a type without reflecting an ethos.

Edward G. Robinson was shaped by sixteen formative years on the New York stage. Before finally coming to Hollywood, he had done more than thirty plays on Broadway, eleven of which were with the Theatre Guild and, in his own words, "about ten with Arthur Hopkins, who was perhaps the most literate producer we had on Broadway" (quoted in James R. Parish and Alvin H. Marill, *The Cinema of Edward G. Robinson* [1972], p. 16). Robinson remained conscious of the difference between acting and personality: "Now, everyone has dramatic instincts, but I began to realize the scope of it. To be entrusted with a character was always a big responsibility to me" (quoted in Parish and Marill, p. 16). Able to shape himself to innumerable parts, he nevertheless did not look enough like what an American masculine self-projection might require: "If I were just a bit taller and I was a little more handsome or something like that, I could have played all the roles that I have played, and played many more. There *is* such a thing as a handicap, but you've got to be that much better as an actor" (Parish and Marill, p. 16).

It was because of Robinson's fame as a stage actor that Hollywood sought him out—and it was perhaps because of his particular look that he was first cast in hoodlum roles. He played secondary gangster parts in *The Hole in the Wall* and *Night Ride* (both 1929) before getting the gangland lead in *Outside the Law* (1930). But it was not until the following year that he would turn a Hollywood staple—the gangster movie—into a major genre with *Little Caesar.*

The first of the major gangster movies was in fact not Robinson's: it was *Scarface,* also made in 1930 though release was delayed until 1932. That picture is worth recalling for a few reasons, in particular for a reflection articulated by the chief of police when he thinks of the difference between the bad men of Westerns and gangster thugs: the first ones showed a measure of honor; they at least faced you openly. The thugs are simply that—unredeemed cutthroats. His words are meant to underline the picture's socially conscious thesis—that the government should be doing something about the growing evil of gangs. This appeal to the government is spoken explicitly in the film by a newspaper editor to a group of social do-gooders who feel the press is playing up gangsters too sensationalistically and turning them into heroes. The editor's defense of the press's freedom and responsibility does not really answer their charges—charges that could just as easily be brought against the very picture that claims to be an exposé: Paul Muni's portrayal of Scarface (Al Capone's nickname) is not necessarily unsympathetic, and he is certainly redeemed at least to an extent by his love for his kid sister and the loss he feels when she dies and leaves him bereft of affection.

But there were more than simply front-page headlines behind the allure of the gangster, just as there was more than simply a sympathetic Paul Muni allowing spectator identification with the fictionalized Al Capone. Robert Warshow sees the gangster genre as "an experience of art universal to all Americans"; it is certain that having created the part, a far less sympathetic Edward G. Robinson would be recognized for years as Rico, the protagonist of *Little Caesar* ("The Gangster as Tragic Hero," in *The Immediate Experience*, 1962).

Warshow offers us a number of clues to the spectator's empathy. To begin with, the gangster is denied escape into the plenitude of the American dream. He is a prisoner of the city, Warshow writes, "not the real city, but that dangerous and sad city of the imagination which is so much more important, which is the modern world" (p. 131):

> The gangster's whole life is an effort to assert himself as an individual, to draw himself out of the crowd, and he always dies *because* he is an individual; the final bullet thrusts him back, makes him, after all, a failure. "Mother of God," says the dying Little Caesar, "is this the end of Rico?"— speaking of himself thus in the third person because what has been brought low is not the undifferentiated *man,* but the individual with a name, the gangster, the success; even to himself he is a creature of the imagination. [p. 133]

The successful gangster movie is, thus, tragedy translated into the idiom (language and gestures) of the times: the depression-era spectator who felt himself to be a victim of the city (and very likely the *real* city) could rehearse the exhilaration of Rico's rise up the economic ladder and feel in his own defeats the bullet that brings Rico down at the end.[1]

Rico dying thus created Edward G. Robinson, the star, but also branded him. If parts of the spectator resonated in the circumstances of Cesare Bandello, he was not a figure in whose body and gestures the spectator found a comfortable fit or into which he wished to fit. Robinson's character was, because of Robinson, too much Warshow's "individual with a name," a specific person, someone else whose fictional circumstances might well have condensed the psychological landscape of the times, but whose stubby, five-foot-five frame stood apart from it. Robinson understood this and put his considerable talent acquired on the stage to use in a variety of other roles. Another kind of hood was needed who was more important and more intimately recognizable than his filmed trajectory. Throughout most of the thirties, that figure would be James Cagney.

Fiction allows its characters one of two dimensions. They are either subordinate to the story and become the means by which it moves forward, or they are more important than the story, in which case they tend to internalize the action of the story. Cinema was so conditioned by the miracle of motion that for a very long time films favored the first type of character—one whose trajectory was more important than he was. The early films of James Cagney belong to this group: they are action movies with largely stock characters. Within this kind of vehicle, the personality actor becomes specially forceful because his own dynamism will fill the character's relative vacancy: it is a safe bet that early film fiction characters were relatively close to the actors' offstage individuality. *The New York Times* certainly thought so of James Cagney, analyzing his performance as that of someone who "was and continues to be so brilliantly right in his interpretation of a particular type of American male, a type that has been spawned in large numbers out of the slum districts of New York and Chicago [like Cagney himself, so] that it is a natural thing to suspect that he is not acting at all" (quoted in Patrick McGilligan, *Cagney: The Actor as Auteur,* p. 184).[2]

In titling his book on Cagney *The Actor as Auteur,* McGilligan is making exactly that point. He believes that Cagney belonged to that small group of actors who were able to impose their personas on a film in the making: "Whether he rewrote his dialogue (as he frequently did), sat in on story conferences, advised casting, contributed ideas for scene design . . . , his impact on the average production was enormous" (p. 200). And what Cagney was contributing to the "Cagney vehicle" was "the always-evident implication that he represented the 'little guy,' from the strong belief generated among critical circles and fans that the Cagney persona was intended to typify the average American. This implication came partly from Warner Brothers but mostly from Cagney himself, who always described his persona in a strictly American context. He usually played a New Yorker, for example, occasionally a specifically small neighborhood Brooklynite" (McGilligan, p. 184).

Reminiscing about his childhood in a working-class neighborhood on East Ninety-Sixth Street, Cagney sounds like a character out of one of his own pictures—street-smart, street-tough, smart-talking, and sentimental:

> We didn't *know* we were poor. We realized we didn't get three squares on the table every day, and there was no such thing as a good second suit, but we had no objective knowledge that we were poor. We just went from day to day. . . . We simply didn't have time to realize we were poor, although we did realize the desperation of life around us. I recall the Fitzpatrick family on Ninety-sixth Street who were put out on the sidewalk because they couldn't pay the rent, and this not long after they had seen their little child run over by a refuse wagon. The Cagneys never had that kind of experience, thank God, and it never occurred to us, despite the poverty, to hang our heads or feel sorry for ourselves. We just did the best we could. [*Cagney by Cagney*, p. 6]

It may well be that what McGilligan saw as the "intention" of Cagney's portrayals to remain within the mainstream—the image of the scrapper risen from New York streets—was less character creation than simple transfer.

After the end of World War I, the United States enjoyed a decade of relative prosperity until the stock market crash in October 1929, an economic disaster of such magnitude that it was not overcome until World War II. By 1932, a quarter of the labor force in this nation was idle, and industrial production had shrunk by approximately one-half.

During the good times of the twenties, the country presented a sometimes religiously moral front behind which the social fabric raveled: after World War I, the Eighteenth Amendment to the Constitution made Prohibition national, while flappers and their escorts drank bootlegged alcohol. The constitutional change meant to uphold morality brought huge wealth to major crime figures who had been confined previously to gambling and prostitution. Among these, the one who rose to mythological dimensions was Al Capone.

The man who would one day be the most famous of all U.S. gangsters was born six years after his parents had emigrated from Naples to the slums of New York. The saga of the Capone family reveals perverse facets of the American Dream. It failed the Neapolitan emigrants who found themselves trapped within the lower depths of the city but allowed their son to rise from those lower depths by dint of industry and grit. (It is estimated that at the time of his conviction in 1931, Al Capone was worth over one hundred million pre–World War II dollars; though he was associated with several killings, and in particular the Saint Valentine's Day Massacre, it was his failure to pay taxes on this huge wealth that put him behind bars. Furthermore, he was not killed by the forces of law and order as in the motion pictures spawned by his legend: he was given an eleven-year sentence that was cut short in 1939.)

That mythic figure fascinated millions, among them writers like Ben Hecht and William Burnett. And Hollywood was drawn to books like *Underworld* and *Little Caesar* in the expert knowledge that where there are millions there is money. At the end of the twenties, having a voice was a condition of success in the new world of the talkies; at the beginning of the thirties, being able to step into a gangster part was a ticket to stardom. Edward G. Robinson burst onto the scene in January 1931; four months later, it was James Cagney's turn.

Early in 1930, Cagney was starring on Broadway as, to quote him, "a sniveling murderer" (*Cagney by Cagney,* p. 37) in the short-lived *Penny Arcade.* The play appealed to Al Jolson, who bought it and then sold it to Warner Brothers, stipulating that Cagney and the female lead, Joan Blondell, should also be the picture's principal actors. It was made that year as *Sinner's Holiday* and led to another part for Cagney as second lead in the gangster movie *Doorway to Hell,* which turned out to be a box office success. *Doorway to Hell* pulled Cagney out of the bit parts he had in the subsequent *Other Men's Women* and *The Millionaire,* both made in 1931. John Bright and Kubec Glasmon were turning their "Beer and Blood" into a film script for Warner Brothers; they remembered Cagney in *Doorway to Hell* and got him the lead. That picture, *The Public Enemy,* made Cagney into a major star overnight.

The picture was a rags-to-riches chronicle, the rags part of which took place in the Chicago slums before World War I. The slum emphasis contrasts perhaps too symbolically with the bourgeois gentility and moral values of the Powers family: the mother is a compendium of lower-middle-class Irish virtues, while the father is a cop who takes the strap to young Tom for general sassiness and suspecting that he has stolen a pair of skates. Half a century later, Cagney thought those values informed young Tom as well: "In *Little Caesar* the main characters were hard-bitten criminals from the start, but this was not true in Bright and Glasmon's script. The story begins with Tom Powers and Matt Doyle as a pair of high-spirited boys and follows them through the ranks until they achieve full-fledged criminal status" (Doug Warren with James Cagney, *Cagney: The Authorized Biography,* p. 74).[3] In fact, the boys are more than simply high-spirited: they are shown right from the start to be thieves who even work for a fence.

Nevertheless, there was a good reason for Cagney to assume that bourgeois morality was an important ingredient of the picture. Once he has grown beyond teenage larceny, Tom is shown performing a string of ugly deeds, many of which seem motivated more by sadism than story logic: after shooting a policeman during a robbery, he shoots the fence in a deliberately cruel way, shoots the horse that threw and killed his boss, and, in one of the most frequently anthologized of all film excerpts, crushes his breakfast grapefruit into the face of the woman of whom he has tired. Yet for all of this portrayal, Cagney is not meant to be unsympathetic—a fact that worried Warner Brothers enough to frame the picture within disclaimers stating their intention not to glorify the gangster.[4]

The first reason for not disliking Tom Powers is of course Cagney himself. Cagney had begun his stage career in the drag chorus line of *Every Sailor*—a revue Cagney himself termed "a knockabout act, purely burlesque" (quoted by McGilligan, p. 18). For more than ten years before coming to Hollywood, Broadway called on Cagney for song and dance, comedy, and straight drama; later, that underlay showed through the Hollywood gangster and eventually obliterated it. Throughout his film career, Cagney returned to his professional roots ("A song-and-dance man, which is what I am basically, becomes one over many years of unrelenting work" [*Cagney by Cagney,* p. 71]),[5] and throughout he kept what his fellow actor Pat O'Brien called "that crooked Mick grin." Though callous and evil as Tom Powers, he was also, in Kenneth Tynan's words, "equipped with charm, courage and a sense of fun" (quoted by McGilligan, p. 32). His small frame was a powerfully coiled spring that exuded driving energy. He was a survivor with grace, never down for very long, bouncing back with the hint of a dance step remembered from his early days as a hoofer, giving as good as (and better than) he got, and all the while with his mouth half open, on the edge of a smile or a wisecrack.

But the character of Tom Powers held deeper appeal as well. From their start as Brewery gang enforcers, Matt and Tom rise to become important members of a bootlegging group. Eventually Matt is killed by rival mobsters, and Tom confronts the killers: in the shoot-out that follows, he is seriously wounded, and as he stumbles along the rain-swept curb he realizes, "I'm not so tough." This prepares the hospital scene in which his mother (whose favorite he has always been) reconciles him with Mike, his war hero brother. The happy ending that might have been anticipated is aborted: rival gangsters abduct and kill Tom; when Mike answers the family's apartment doorbell, Tom's bandaged body falls forward like a horribly grotesque mummy—or, as Sklar speculates, like the swaddled mother's baby he has always been, an aspect of the Cagney portrayal to which we will return. That final scene should have been sufficient to obviate the picture's second disclaimer and satisfy the moral imperatives of the Production Code. But it was not: something kept Tom near to the heart of Ma Powers and the 1931 audience.

Ma Powers keeps affirming that her son is a good boy in spite of repeated assertions to the contrary by the far more trustworthy Mike. Not only do Mike's words (along with factual evidence) fail to convince his mother, his war medals fail to displace Tom in the public's affection: during the confrontation in the family dining room, the young hood dims the war veteran's luster by telling him contemptuously that a good life can be had only for the taking. He then strides out the door to his life of beer, women, and crime and confirms his assertion by soon being shown in evening dress and on the arms of elegant women—allowing the spectator to glimpse a more affluent life from which he was cut off.

But for the fictional gangster, the dream of possession is a dream of gratification, not of change. However high he rises, he remains within a social idiom the spectator can understand—that of the lower-class underdog. Tom's rise through the underworld is accomplished by hard work—whether driving a beer truck, stealing, or acting as an enforcer, he is always doing a job or looking for a job to do.[6] In the words of Heidi Dawidoff, this is a criminal "whose alienation from society commands respect and whose courage to stand up and make some mark on the world commands a following" (*Between the Frames: Thinking about Movies* [1981], p. 71). His costly suits, fast cars, and fancy women are the kind of instant wish fulfillment the impoverished might readily dream, entailing neither special gifts nor special consequences.

Women are merely emblems of those dreams: no more than any other form of luxury are they a responsibility to be assumed. They would lose their value, as they did for Clark Gable, if the ever-poor boy at the center of the wealth that now possessed them was in danger of being possessed by them. The difference is in the layers of toughness that dressed the Gable and Cagney types. The toughness of Gable's characters allowed their fundamental decency to remain visible: a few scrapes turned their gruff rasp into the awkward disguise of modesty. It took considerably more, usually a fatal bullet, to reveal the inner person in the Cagney gangster, and because the change was greater, the moral butterfly that emerged from the rough chrysalis seemed purer by contrast.

Women play a curiously recessive role in *The Public Enemy,* the emblem for which is the hospital scene: the bandaged face of Tom is on the right end of the bed, his brother Mike sits at the left end. Between the two is the mediating mother. Behind the mother, visible but silent throughout the whole episode, is Tom's sister, whose only function is to be a presence dismissed. In the same way, Kitty will be a woman whom Tom can first subdue and then drop when conjugality palls. For a spectator trapped by economic circumstances from which there seemed to be no escape, and who also knew that sex had to be paid for through a lifetime of responsibility, the fantasy of Tom's double evasion was especially compelling: the grapefruit shoved into Kitty's face was a vengeful gesture likely to have been repeated inwardly by many men in the audience—as Sklar reminds us, reviewers of the 1930s never mentioned that scene.

Tom can thus measure how high he has come up the corporate ladder of crime through the price of his women—the price he pays for them as evidence of his wealth, which also turns them into disposable objects. At its highest point, he meets Gwen Allen, played by Jean Harlow. She is different mainly in the satins she wears and the careful waves of her platinum hair. Her vernacular self-assurance is also evidence that she will be willing to jettison the moral principles that bind Tom's family. But once Gwen speaks, she repeats a familiar submissiveness to the male who glories in his predatory instinct. She tells Tom about the men she has known who were nice, polished, and considerate: "Most women like that, Tommy, I guess they're afraid of the other kind. I thought I was too. But you're so strong. You don't give, you take. Oh Tommy, I could love you to death." The man's character is defined by the submissive woman's, which it helps define in turn: Gwen is tough and gutsy because that is what it takes to approach someone like Tom.

Gwen says she *could* love Tom; but in fact, she doesn't. Their relationship is perverse: he can brutalize but not possess; she has no trouble keeping him out of her bed. Gwen's brief appearance contributes another degree of perversion: her words combined with her rejection of Tom make her sexual enjoyment appear to be mainly masochistic. But that masochism affords Tom the only sort of female companionship he can sustain. Proof is given when Tom does end up in bed with a woman: in that scene, the woman initiates the process. For her to do so, Tom must be drunk (his retrospective excuse the morning after). But while he is drunk, she turns him into a child, sitting him on her lap (just as Gwen cradles his head in her arms) and putting him to bed. When Tom can reassume his brutal superego in the sobering light of day, he throws out the woman who penetrated him.

The mothering woman who recurrently dominates Tom is an unsatisfactory surrogate for the genuine mother seen in many of Cagney's pictures,[7] to whom the son can return only through her female substitutes. The producer of *The Public Enemy,* Darryl F. Zanuck, defined Tom as "a no-good bastard but he loved his mother, and somehow or other you felt a certain affection and rooting interest for him even though he was despicable" (quoted by McGilligan, p. 168). That despicability was actually washed away by the presence of the loving mother from the very first *Sinner's Holiday,* in which the small-time hood ended up begging for his mother's forgiveness. Perhaps because of Cagney's small frame and youthful face, the image of the child came naturally to Zanuck:[8] he had envisaged for that picture Cagney crying on his "mother's breast" and saying, "I'm your baby, ain't I?"—a line Cagney refused to speak (Warren with Cagney, p. 63).

But from the early gangster parts through *Yankee Doodle Dandy* (1942), Cagney was frequently some mother's baby, whether in the 1939 *Each Dawn I Die* (1939) or ten years later as a dependent Cody Jarrett on the lap of Ma Jarrett, dwarfed by her formidable presence. One of Cagney's first comedies, *The Irish in Us* (1935), gave him lines to his screen mother that indicated more clearly than those he had refused to utter the character's relation to women: "I'm not the marrying kind. What do I need with a wife? I've got you, haven't I? You're my sweetheart." That mother—the one the athlete never forgets to salute at the end of his most trying feats—is the character through whom the audience reenters the world of conventional morality: she forgives and grants atonement, allowing the uncritical sentimentality of the spectator who may endow the brutal acts of the hero with a redemptive sheen. The other women begin as wonderful wages of sin and end up as irritating satiation: they are only the barometers of the hero's success and limitations. Once the spectator and the fictional hero have had their fill of the gangster's simplistic pleasures, both are ready for the Schadenfreude awaiting them within the mother's bosom.

The mother's acceptance of her gangster son taints her. Ma Powers uses as a centerpiece for the festive table celebrating the return of

Tom's brother, the war hero, a keg of Tom's bootlegged beer; later, Ma Jarrett will become the head of the gang when Cody is locked up. But these unhealthy intimacies spelled family nevertheless—and perhaps even of the most recognizable kind. McGilligan believes "the appearance of [Cagney's] 'mother' in his films represented roots: the past, a tradition and the hope of future" (p. 168)—a curious comment, considering the nature of some of those figures, but one confirmed and reconfirmed by the box office.

People in the breadlines of the early thirties felt that the government had failed them: unable to avert economic collapse, Hoover would be turned out in 1932. At some point, the hostility of the spectator coincided with that of the fictional gangster and may have accounted for the mythologizing of Al Capone—an identifiable individual set against the social order by which the spectator felt victimized. When the screen spread and amplified that myth, the spectator's empathy was reshaped by other, and sometimes contradictory, feelings. The hero risen from the city's dregs was not only Horatio Alger's boy who made it big; he was the one who, in making it big, could throw off the constraints of a moral code and achieve brutish dreams of sex and power—satisfying what Cawelti has termed "a fascination with untrammeled and amoral aggressiveness" (p. 77). But in decreeing the hero's ultimate downfall, the Production Code appealed to more than morality—it granted the spectator additional satisfaction by updating the plight of Icarus, who plunged into the sea for having flown too close to the sun: knowing full well that he would never contrive wings on which to soar, the spectator avenged his inadequacy through the gangster's single but terminal failure.[9] The son of Daedalus fell into the Icarian sea, Cagney's gangster died within his mother's bosom: his version of the myth gave the spectator better cause to feel self-righteous.

Not all gangsters were created alike. Edward G. Robinson's gangster benefited from the same desires and frustrations in the spectator and could elicit the same empathy, admiration, or envy. But lacking Cagney's charm, he remained, even as a specific character, a figure that was primarily allegorical: he did not seduce the spectator into accepting his incarnation. When he died at last, the morality play ended, but he was not mourned. Cagney, on the other hand, made sure the final separation would be bittersweet. He brought to his roles the full glamour of stardom: before his screen role gave him a particular definition, he was already, in Otis Ferguson's words, "everything everybody would like to be." His smile and the tough quality of even his tenderness (expressed more frequently through a mock punch than a caress) added to the blandishments of the gangster epic the personal dimension of his own attractiveness.

That attractiveness, which turned women into pushovers, also contributed to the hero's isolation: women too easily seduced became too quickly cloying; the female conquest ended as an emptiness. She was also an object of mistrust because her value was proportional to her cost: the gangster bought her after having seduced her and resented her transformation into a creature of money. The fantasy of male gratification achieved instantly, and turned to disillusion nearly as fast, required the compensation of sustaining danger and physical pain (perhaps another reason why the gangster's success could never propel him into a different world). It also romanticized friendship. But because women could become friends only when they did not serve to demonstrate male virility defined as unconstrained sexual aggressiveness, this usually left the Cagney mobster his mom and other men. In *The Public Enemy,* Tom loses Kitty and Gwen (to mention only the main ones), but Matt, who came before them, also outlasts them: when Matt dies, there is nothing left for Tom but to return to the womb.

Male bonding remained a feature of Cagney films even after the gangster period. One thinks of the ever present Frank McHugh or Pat O'Brien, who provided the subtext of so many films (*The Irish in Us, Torrid Zone, Ceiling Zero, Here Comes the Navy)* in which women were a flimsy fabric drawn over what McGilligan sees as "stories about love between men" (p. 177). And the male spectator was allowed to dream the purity of that "profound and honest evidence of male friendship" even after the Hayes Office ceased to be satisfied with disclaimers and forced Warner Brothers to give Cagney a symbolic badge so as not to have to alter his persona in *G-Men* (1935) or *Angels with Dirty Faces* (1938).

That surface shift in Cagney roles was one of many. His accomplishments as a song-and-dance man and his attractiveness allowed him to shed the gangster's trappings without giving up too much of his former self.[10] By actual count, he was a gangster in only one-quarter of his more than sixty major films, but the toughness he brought to other roles preserved in the public mind his original image as a particularly appealing hood.

Still, with the sloughing of the gangster skin (if not the hood's residual toughness), a different story could be told, allowing another kind of woman to step into the picture. She was the one who could keep up with the rough-hewn hero, his smart-talking, fast-moving, tough-and-tender counterpart—a type frequently portrayed in the early thirties by Joan Blondell. Molly Haskell saw her in *Blonde Crazy* (1931) as "a synthesis of snappy-smart and gentle," allowing a partnership with Cagney "in which she occasionally gets the best of him without humiliating or emasculating him and without appearing overbearing" (p. 130). Such an ideal of feminism suggests a blandness in which give and take are equally matched and the battle of the sexes ends in a tie. But Blondell was not keeping count of points scored: in *Blonde Crazy* (Blondell's fourth appearance in a Cagney movie), she enjoyed free rein as Cagney's thieving sidekick. Cagney was still on the other side of the law but now for comic effect. This turned the male challenge into a primarily verbal thrust, which Blondell parried verbally—something she was exceptionally good at.

The chemistry between these two through seven pictures made them one of the more popular screen couples during the early thirties. Theirs was a relationship that raised movies to the only erotic level allowed by the Hays Office—the snappy intercourse of quick-paced patter. In McGilligan's words, theirs was a sexual encounter "symbolically represented by the back-and-forth, artful, witty, pseudo-antagonistic and suggestive debate. Cagney and Blondell were the first twosome to refine and popularize the exercise of romantic rivalry and double-edged repartee" (p. 162). In Joan Blondell, the spectator had someone better than the girl next door: she was a knowing and willing sexual presence but not the carnivore who ate men whole or the dominating force that would turn proprietary through passion. She represented a masculine ideal of sex that was both safe and lasting because it existed as friendship within what Dawidoff sees as the tough evenness of their relationship (p. 19). Because, in other words, it was not so different from friendship with men.[11]

Blondell and Cagney made movie history: they were the first of the famous teams that embodied intimate friendship between the sexes through crisp, funny patter and zany situations, as Myrna Loy and William Powell or Cary Grant and Katharine Hepburn would later do in a somewhat different and more elegant moment—that of the white telephones. But meanwhile, and thereafter, Cagney continued to be seen by the whole country as he had been by his old friend Pat O'Brien: "With Babe Ruth, Jack Dempsey, F. Scott Fitzgerald, the early Stutz Bearcat car, the last of the beaded, speakeasy hostesses, he was the image in the American scheme of things; of the Roaring Twenties and the Tepid Thirties, of the dust bowls and the bread lines and gang wars . . . the saga maker of the hard kid who couldn't be pushed too far." The spectator who was granted entry into Cagney's world (especially his hoodlum world) for an hour and a half was the one who might have been more easily pushed around—by the breadlines, the dust bowls, or by lesser vexations of the thirties, a time that could be called tepid only to the extent that listlessness and depression can be thought of as lukewarm.

NOTES

1. Robinson himself felt that Rico was an epic figure: "Finally I was given a version [of the William R. Burnett story] that made some difference, reading more or less like a Greek tragedy . . . or one by Shakespeare. . . . I think it has sustained itself throughout these years because it was constructed as a Greek tragedy."

2. In the line of new critics who look for the culpability of the male actor in his offscreen reality, Lucy Fischer also conflates Cagney's roles with "the issue of maternity," which she locates in the actor's personal life ("Mama's Boy: Filial Hysteria in *White Heat*").

3. Miles writes, "The boy child is . . . allowed to explore more freely than a girl, play more adventurously, make messes and get dirty" (*The Rites of Man*, p. 21).

4. The Production Code, which had been adopted the previous year, would not be enforced until 1933. Sklar assumes that the sympathy was due to recognition of a familiar type: "The Times Square movie crowd responded . . . to the intrinsic doubleness of a figure familiar in the neighborhood[:] the roughneck sissy—a type that could evoke feelings of joy and fear and pity, and rise from a sociological case to a tragic hero" (p. 32).

5. The last words of his autobiography are "thanks for giving a song-and-dance man across the years all those heart-warming encores."

6. In another reminiscence, Cagney himself says, "I almost can't remember a time when I wasn't working" (*Cagney by Cagney*, p. 20).

7. One is struck here too by how prevalent this aspect of the national ethos was and how much Cagney himself had always fit into it: "A question people have asked me through the years is why the Cagney boys didn't get involved with guns and crime the way my old Sing Sing pals did. The answer is simple: there wasn't a chance. We had a mother to answer to. . . . In Sidney Kingsley's play *Dead End*, one of the kids says to his mother, 'Look, Ma, I'm dancin',' . . . a vital, sobering line because it reminded me that in our mother we always had somebody we could show off for" (*Cagney by Cagney*, p. 25).

8. This was a sore point with Cagney: "For reasons unknown to me, people are always interested in my exact height. The literal truth is, I don't know what

it is. I haven't measured for years, and I'm really not interested enough to do so" (*Cagney by Cagney,* p. 56).

9. Cawelti believes that this satisfaction preserves an American archetype, "the traditional moralistic pattern of the destruction of the criminal over-reacher" (p. 60).

10. His attractiveness seems to have affected women less strongly: *Variety* estimated that 90 percent of those who lined up to see his pictures in the thirties were men.

11. McGilligan notes that after she stopped acting as Cagney's screen partner, Joan Blondell was replaced by Pat O'Brien.

6

The Time of the
White Telephones: Cary Grant

When Joan Blondell met James Cagney as an equal in a world of words, it was clear that two fundamental changes had occurred: the male character left the arena of physical action that had been a large part of his previous definition, and his woman was now raised from object to foil. That change was possible because of the huge audiences motion pictures now commanded. Most products of industrial capitalism are at first limited in their availability to the more prosperous; typically, they then filter down the economic ladder toward mass consumption. Motion pictures reversed this scheme: they had first been an industry meant for popular consumption, and only slowly, as their acceptance grew among those who were better off and/or better educated, did they start acquiring a truly diversified public.

By the end of the thirties, when three-quarters of all the people in the country were going to the neighborhood picture house at least once a week, there was an audience for motion pictures that were not derived primarily from motion, the magic that had been the cause of the medium's nearly instant popularity at its birth. The success of Blondell and Cagney had demonstrated audience interest in a battle of the sexes that was not physical and whose outcome was not predetermined.[1]

In displacing that battle to a verbal level, its very terms were altered as well. To start with, the battle became more important than its consequences: the fun was in the thrust and parry rather than in their result. And the fun was actually fun; where James Cagney's famous grapefruit scene had literally been a one-shot occurrence fraught with hostility, the idea was to make his verbal exchanges with Blondell last: physical action anticipates a resolution, but verbal action of this kind is pleasurable in its extension and exists, therefore, largely for its own sake. The logic of this fact led eventually to a motion picture that existed primarily as a vehicle for crisp, funny dialogue. The vogue set in around the middle of the decade, and, although it never quite died out, it faded with the forties.

That being said, studies differ in their labeling and understanding of the genre, which is sometimes termed "screwball comedy,"[2] while other authors designate many of the same films as "romantic comedy."[3] Regardless of labels, the majority of these films evidenced similarities born of a same inner logic, and in time those similarities became defining. Once the premise of a smart, funny verbal film was accepted, a number of other necessary factors had to be called into play—all of them devolving from the kind of fun that was intended.

Gehring suggests that the new kind of comedy "was tied to a period of transition in American humor" (*Screwball Comedy,* p. 1), away from the verbal comedy of what he terms the "cracker-barrel type"—exemplified by Will Rogers, who judged and mocked the world's foibles from a vantage point of native common sense and self-confidence. Gehring feels that the change from the cracker-barrel wisdom of the "able" character to the humor of screwball comedy's "incompetent" (whom he calls an "anti-hero") came about because of the magnitude of crises that now overwhelmed the ability of folksy wisdom to contain them. "Incompetent" does not seem to designate accurately the William Powell of *The Thin Man* series any more than it does the Cary Grant of *The Awful Truth* (1937) or *Holiday* (1938).[4] To term the films' protagonists "anti-heroes" seems a little out of place as well; but these movies that seem oblivious to both the Great Depression and the coming world war are obviously not part of the mainstream: they are sparkling shards of a world enduring beyond its time presumably because that world never quite existed. And they are further removed from the mainstream in that their veneer of upper-class urbanity sometimes distills a European waft (traces of which subsist in the aforementioned Grant and Powell). Yet these comedies are linked by common threads, as are many others made during those years.

Whether or not this new kind of comedy was tied to a period of transition in American humor, it was certainly tied to a period of social transition with psychological implications. As is frequently pointed out (see, for example, Reinisch, Rosenblum, and Sanders's *Masculinity/Femininity: Basic Perspectives*), a girl growing up was already more likely to be allowed to cross over into masculine-defining roles (e.g. tomboy) than a boy seeking the reverse. Concepts of masculinity and femininity were becoming just a little harder to define, and to the difficulty of making clear-cut statements within the psychoanalytic realm had to be added the difficulties of societal pressures that were now beginning to change as well (see Patricia Elliot, *From Mastery to Analysis*). Indeed, the shift was tenuous—a character like those portrayed by Joan Blondell was not the result of the androgynous revolution social psychologists like Sandra Bem would one day predict: rather, she represented the assimilation of women into hitherto masculine roles (and, as we shall see, even *that* assimilation was precarious).[5]

When the man-woman relation between Cagney and Blondell develops as a verbal exchange, it is the exchange of workers (even if their work is less than fully legal): their words are a break—for them as well as for a picture bogged down in a sluggish moment. But talk is not their ultimate object: they do not have the leisure for it, nor is it (perhaps for that very reason) a particularly prized pastime of the social group to which they belong. For talk to become important—more important than, say, a job—the talkers must first have free time to indulge it (to the extent that *Holiday* is about anything, it is about Cary Grant's refusal to accept any job, no matter how attractive) and a greater belief in words than in action. Verbal comedy is thus more likely to be the comedy of leisure classes in the characters it contrives and perhaps also in the audience for which it has the greatest appeal.

The high-society protagonists of these films belong to a world which the Italians labeled that of *i telefoni bianchi*, the white telephones. Although there are studio shots showing Cary Grant handing Elissa Landi a white telephone in *Enter Madam* (1935) or Irene Dunne listening to one in *My Favorite Wife* (1940), the object and its color are only emblematic of a world that seems white because of its remoteness from the more sordid and soiling aspects of everyday life (Little Caesar may have used a phone, but it could never be a white one). It is the world represented by Jean Harlow's pale satins and careful grooming in *The Public Enemy* but now displayed by those who have legitimate claim to them. And the dangerous suggestion to post–Great Depression spectators that not having a job might be enviable may well have been counterbalanced by the spectator's pleasure in being admitted for a while to the pristine luxury of that world. That audience may have had less interest than the fictional characters in the circumstances of their momentary dilemmas, but there can be little doubt that they enjoyed their glamorous surroundings and that the stars' attraction suffused the elegance of the fictional worlds in which they moved.

What Gehring identifies as cracker-barrel humor implied the superiority of rural common sense. It was a form of the pastoral inasmuch as it opposed, at least by implication, the virtues of clear-sighted simplicity to the folly and deception of big-city complications. By contrast, high-society comedy was solipsistic: it ignored (or was genuinely ignorant of) other worlds, being comfortably insulated within an urban setting—more particularly Manhattan—except when it transferred its urban glamour for an occasional weekend to a countryside seldom more distant from New York than Connecticut. In Manhattan, it never moved too far from apartments atop high-rises—worlds whose dominant tone one remembers as white (or at least light),[6] with a view of other high-rises similarly distant from streets that the Cagneys and Robinsons of different fictions might still have trodden.

James Harvey describes as "high life and smart talk" the "classy" comedies produced between 1929 and 1933, but the terms seem particularly applicable to the films that concern us here—those made during the second half of the thirties that displayed a particular kind of verbal and visual dazzle. What occasions the smart talk has to do as often as not with what Jacques Lacan might have termed the purloined marriage (which, as he says of Poe's letter, occurs as it should have all along but only after an extended detour). Many of these comedies may have been termed "screwball" because their participants belonged to an economic class that does not have to live by the books. This privilege, which the spectator might have resented, is turned into mild eccentricity and becomes in American lore a way of excusing what could have been otherwise the misuse of surplus wealth: rich people, already alluring and witty, are at worst just the tiniest bit off their rockers—it adds to the fun of their words.

When Joan Blondell matched James Cagney barb for barb, it marked her rise up the ranks in the battle of the sexes. The high-society woman was emancipated at birth: her looks, her wit, and her wealth *were* her difference and made other distinctions less important[7]—though her privileged life could result in a personality flaw that gave the picture its only serious look at the characters. Determining by what means that flaw would be corrected, those movies ended up modernizing in a variety of ways *The Taming of the Shrew.*

The more eccentric character was usually the male whom wealth affected in odd but superficial ways. He might drop out of his usual life momentarily and unaccountably, as does Harvard man William Powell (the never inebriated alcoholic of the *Thin Man* pictures), who becomes temporarily a very suave bum in *My Man Godfrey* (1936)—just as millionaire Ray Milland would turn into a clumsy busboy in *Easy Living* the following year. The character's peculiarity was often a childlike whim—the kind of spontaneous and unpredictable behavior one associates with those who have not yet learned to live by adult rules (as in so much of Chaplin's comedy). In the case of the affluent, it was a matter of not having to, and if a director like Frank Capra wished, that resistance to adult patterns could be raised to the level of a political statement, as in *Mr. Deeds Goes to Town* (1936) or *Mr. Smith Goes to Washington* (1939). Otherwise, the child in Cary Grant could either be a klutz (as in *The Awful Truth* [1937] and *Bringing up Baby*) or a compulsive acrobat (*Holiday,* 1938), while Gary Cooper could not remain free of a spouse in *Bluebeard's Eighth Wife* (1938) any more than he could of his tuba in *Mr. Deeds.*

These childlike traits humanized the affluent suburbanite, as did a dog opportunely brought into the picture when the man needed to demonstrate his loving nature.[8] By contrast, the woman's character, if already flawed, appeared the more so. What saved the childlike man from emasculation was his gift for snappy repartee (at his most bumbling he could remain a match for her, just as once Joan Blondell could remain a match for him), and this prepared the final scene in which he was redeemed through marriage to either the right woman or a woman he had helped make right.

This final marriage, or at least the righting through conventional solutions of the interpersonal quandaries that had been the picture's justification, showed that, however wild the fairy tale, it was still contained within accepted myths. The picture's conclusion allowed the spectator to assume that the characters, however madcap, however much their wealth had made them temporarily (though amusingly and inoffensively) insane, would now be drawn back into a recognizable fold. The high-society comedy was an excursion, a brief journey undertaken for pleasure with the intention of returning to a point of departure firmly established at least in the spectator's mind. The fun was that of any excursion—a brief transit through the kind of desirable world it is nice to visit but in which one cannot live, in this case the glamorous preserves of elegant and witty people seldom concerned with either money or jobs. But no more than the poor kid who made good in gangster pictures did the spectator intend to be changed by what he possessed for the duration of his excursion: dissipating the threat these characters might have posed had they been sufficiently real to persist beyond the end of the screening, the spectator's conventions were allowed to reappropriate them just before the lights went on.

Screwball comedy mutated after the war in pictures by directors like Howard Hawks (*I Was a Male War Bride*, 1949; *Man's Favorite Sport*, 1964) or Preston Sturges (*The Miracle of Morgan's Creek*, 1944; *Unfaithfully Yours*, 1948) and several others. But the genre we are concerned with, high-society comedy, started losing its appeal during World War II. The end of the Great Depression and the impact of television advertising turned many Americans into more conspicuous consumers (while the television set began keeping them at home), making the world of high society less exotic. It was most likely replaced by the splash and glitter of musicals—a more total and less dialectical fantasy. Movies were becoming ever more slick, with a commensurate loss of bite. Harvey believes the war and the attendant loss of foreign pictures intensified the control of moral censors over Hollywood "until at times the industry seemed almost like a branch of the Legion of Decency" (p. 405).[9] One needs but compare *The Philadelphia Story* (1940)[10] with its musical remake *High Society* (1956) to note the direction and evolution of the postwar years.

The Philadelphia Story is generally considered to be the crest of the genre, and because of Katharine Hepburn's formidable presence, it is impossible to locate Cary Grant except in relation to her character. In 1939, Hepburn was appearing on Broadway with Joseph Cotten and Van Heflin in Philip Barry's very successful play. Barry had already made his mark in the 1928 *Holiday* (ten years before the motion picture) as a satirist and redeemer of the leisure classes. His *Philadelphia Story* had been written with Hepburn in mind (it is even said that she collaborated with him in the writing of her part). This suggests an interesting dimension of the personality actor's power to shape a role— for Katharine Hepburn was certainly known as a personality among personality actresses in Hollywood. The power of her personality eventually extended beyond her roles, affecting the very image of the males opposite whom she appeared.

Her father (like Humphrey Bogart's) was an eminent medical man— a surgeon and urologist. Her mother was a blueblood in her own right, one of the genuine Boston Houghtons, a cousin of Alenson Bigelow Houghton, who at one time was Ambassador to the Court of St. James. But this woman, with her B.A. from Bryn Mawr and M.A. from Radcliffe, was a particular kind of blueblood—a suffragette who picketed the White House, long before the activity was common, to help Woodrow Wilson make up his mind on women's suffrage, and who crusaded among other causes for birth control. Even if her parents had not had liberal ideas about the education of children, it is very likely that young Katharine would not have grown up like those of the common mold.

From her father, a partisan of "a healthy mind in a healthy body," she acquired her athletic ability, and from her mother, her socially progressive ideas. After having private tutors and attending the Oxford School for Girls in Hartford, Katharine was sent to her mother's alma mater, where a precocious theatrical interest nearly caused her to flunk out during her freshman year, and an illicit cigarette came close to getting her expelled a little while later. Upon graduating from Bryn Mawr, she acted her way to Broadway and in 1932, on the strength of her New York reputation, was brought to Hollywood. Hollywood was not prepared for this "strong-minded, extremely promising, and much too frank Katharine Hepburn, a rebellious lady *par excellence*," who, with her angular looks and upper-class Connecticut speech, did not fit the customary pattern and who, to make things worse, showed a "general unwillingness to adhere to the rules of the game" (Homer Dickens, *The Films of Katharine Hepburn* [1971], p. 1).

Oblivious to conventions, she "hired a Rolls Royce to take her about the film capital, dressed casually in slacks and sandals, wore little or no make-up, refused to coo in the established starlet fashion" (Dickens, pp. 1–2). This and the fact that she had been chosen over several established actresses to play the lead in *A Bill of Divorcement* (she was never to appear in a supporting role) were calculated to make her poison in Tinseltown. Her steady decline at the box office delighted detractors, and she eventually returned to Broadway and the Philip Barry play.

Thus, if Tracy Lord in *The Philadelphia Story* is modeled on Katharine Hepburn, we can readily see the traits that defined the character. Interestingly, those traits were by common acceptance negative ones. Here was a woman who came to Hollywood during a time of economic depression with money and flaunted it: her hired Rolls Royce spoke louder than the habitual glitz and glitter of other Hollywood aspirants; it showed a disregard of conventions that was more likely to irritate than to entice. She also displayed discernible elements of education in a culture that tends to equate it with wastefulness when it goes beyond the practical and which at worst demonstrates traits that run counter to the prized virtues of directness and simplicity, which define for us fundamental human honesty.

Her angular and athletic body was a further affront in that it clashed with the accepted notion of the starlet, the young woman analyzed (or fetishized) as face, breasts, and legs. Not only did she show no desire to feminize herself (refusal to wear makeup), but she actually usurped masculine prerogatives. Having allowed slacks and sandals to rob men of her legs and the high heels that should have extended them, she also assumed the male privilege of wearing what was simply most comfortable. If one then considers that she was brought to Hollywood in order to star in her first picture, and that she would never derogate from that position in the future, it is easy to see how there could be no forgiving the slacks, the independence, the Connecticut accent, the Bryn Mawr degree, and all the rest. Long after those considerations had become irrelevant, they still composed her aura and, by extension, that of the screen characters she played.

Philip Barry's Tracy Lord has a number of those attributes: though the story transfers Connecticut's old money to the Philadelphia Main Line, we are in the same social register world. Its people are beautiful, moneyed, and/or just a little crazy—and they all have the impudent wit their social position allows, their culture enjoys, and their closed world understands. That world is invaded by interlopers Macauley Connor and Elizabeth Imbrie, two journalists assigned to cover the society wedding of Tracy and George Kittredge. This has happened as the result of a deal worked out by Tracy's former husband, Dexter Haven, who still feels a strong sense of allegiance and affection for his in-laws: if *Spy* magazine is allowed to cover the wedding, it will not investigate the indiscretions of Tracy's father and a Russian dancer. Dexter Haven comes along with the reporters whom he passes off as family friends in order to make possible their entry into the closed sanctum of the Lords.

In the center of that sanctum is Tracy, a woman not unlike the Katharine Hepburn imagined by her detractors, exuding the cold beauty of a metallic radiance that extends into steely, though amusing, comments uttered in upper-class tones. Her immediately apparent sin is that she does not suffer fools gladly and is quick to spot them. Her kind and slightly eccentric mother, who would not say a bad word about anyone, is as negative as her gentle nature allows in explaining that "Tracy sets exceptionally high standards for herself"—meaning, presumably, that Tracy is unkind to the point of holding others to standards that are unacceptably rigid.

If Tracy's standards are too high, the men who are measured against them do not provide much of a yardstick. Her father has admittedly deserted his wife for a more exotic and younger creature. Her fiancé is a parvenu for whom access to the world of the Lords represents the culmination of his rise up the economic ladder. As for Macauley, the reporter, James Stewart plays him in his most rustic manner, even though he is supposed to be a writer with the soul and style of a poet. This leaves Tracy's ex, Dexter Haven, played by Cary Grant.

Like those of Katharine Hepburn, Cary Grant's real and fictional lives were indistinct in the public's eye. Charles Champlin remembers him with the woman to whom he was married at the time, Dyan Cannon, watching couples on a dance floor:

> "I don't know," says Grant, grinning. "When I dance with a girl, I like to hold her. I mean, that's the pleasure of it." He gazes at the floor space between the dancers and lifts his eyebrows in the look of startled, innocent disbelief which generations of light comic actors have tried hard to duplicate.
>
> "Uhn-uhn. Don't like it." Grant was saying. "And another thing. Bucket seats. Bucket seats are an abomination." His hands measure the vast, incommunicable gulf between bucket seats. "I don't know what the world is coming to." He grins again, wraps his arm around Miss Cannon and they move off to say good night to their hostess.
>
> It is a Philip Barry moment—an urbane, amusing, romantic encounter in the world of the rich and beautiful. [quoted in Donald Deschner, *The Films of Cary Grant* [1973], p. 2]

Such a tautological definition shows the extent to which the personality actor is assumed to be the incarnation of his role. In Cary Grant, to quote Champlin again, the role was one that satisfied a particular desire in a particular spectator—his dream of social grace: "To be the man who knows what to say and do and be in any social situation, and most particularly to be able to move with assurance through the world of the successful, is enviable beyond price and the charm of a figure who can do it is immense" (p. 3).

In all fairness, the tautology that links Grant and his roles is such that he seldom had to move out of the worlds that he defined—in most of his pictures, certainly in those that concern us here, he gave its special cachet to "the world of the successful." But the assurance that made the spectator think he might indeed be able to move through any other world as well was always one of the personality actor's defining traits—Cagney and Bogart had it too. The difference is that whatever else enabled a Cagney or a Bogart to move through those other worlds was backed up by muscle. In Cary Grant, that ability was mostly contained within the charm of a smile and the aptness of a turn of phrase— even though he was also a big man whose masculinity could not be diminished by wearing either glasses or a frilly negligee (as in *Bringing up Baby*). And although he was the male replica of screwball queen Carole Lombard, "a clown really, [his] name became and remains the synonym for masculine glamour" (Harvey, p. 301).

This is the man pitted against Katharine Hepburn in *The Philadelphia Story*. Yet debonair Dexter Haven is not really better than the other men arrayed around Tracy. The first image we have of him is that of the brutal male in the lineage of other such charmers: as he comes out the front door of the Lords' estate, he applies his hand to the face of Tracy and pushes her with such force that she falls down. Later, we learn that Dexter was also a drunk and this was the reason Tracy divorced him. But urbanity and charm dispel a multitude of sins and will give Dexter, along with the other males, the right to judge Tracy.

And judged she is. Her mother's analysis is confirmed by the men. Each in turn calls her a goddess, and they inform the term with considerable negativity: it first denotes their inability to possess her. It also alludes to the fact that they feel betrayed by her beauty: she is irresistibly attractive, but that attractiveness conceals her less desirable traits; her intelligence is perceived as impatience, her freedom as self-centeredness, her wit as arrogance. And confirming their mortal status alongside the goddess, each man blames her for his own frailty. Her fiancé blames her for his inability to match her stride: he sees her freedom as a sign of moral failure and feels that self-made men are clearly designated to be the judges of such lapses. Her father blames her for his philandering: a man is supposed to prolong his youth through a young woman; if his daughter will not play the role, he is entitled to look elsewhere for a substitute. As for Dexter, he claims that if she had not sat in judgment over him, he might have been less of a drunk and perhaps even a more accomplished lover.

Tired of the shaming pedestal on which they all want to put her, Tracy turns her attention to her harshest critic, Macauley, who has been engaged in verbal class warfare ever since he entered the Lords' precincts. Presumably because her unconscious is already starting to tire of her businessman fiancé, she is taken by the poetic quality of Macauley's book the moment she discovers it in the local library. He is likewise captivated by her the moment she focuses her magnetism on him. Although she cautions him not to treat her as a goddess, and though he promises not to, Macauley falls as hard as only the converted can: "There's a magnificence in you, Tracy. A magnificence that comes out of your eyes, in your voice, in the way you stand there, in the way you walk. You're lit from within, Tracy!"

At the height of his rapture, Macauley adds this revealing exclamation: "You've got fires banked down in you, hearth fires and holocausts!" It appears that along the Philadelphia Main Line, goddesses, unlike gods, are not composed of fire: their most obvious characteristic is that they are cold and unapproachable. But, poet that he is, Macauley knows about the fire in Tracy: it is simply that her fire has been banked down. Should it be rekindled (by a man), that fire will be the hearth fire, the warmth of home and family life. But if it is not kept within rightful bounds, it can reach the power of a holocaust, a term that in 1940 only meant total destruction by fire. So, through the bypass of his poetic fervor, Macauley reaches essentially the same conclusion as the others: Tracy must be tamed, made to be a woman within the definition of men, lest she should become once again a destructive force.

Hepburn, conferring her parafictional life on Tracy, splits the cast of characters: she alone defines Main Line aristocracy; Cary Grant as Dexter Haven abdicates that privilege in order to become a spokesman for the audience's traditional morality and to punish her. That Dexter speaks for those beyond the Lords' compound is amply vouched for, starting with his belief in drink, which he shares with the writers of the script. We have already noted the different ways drink defines the strong man: it demonstrates his virility when he can prevent it from affecting him; it demonstrates the manliness of his sorrow when he is driven to it for consolation (Dexter's excuse for his alcoholism). But in a motion picture that is awash with various images of drinking, Tracy has been defined as someone who can lose her control only when she is drunk (we are told that there have been only two such occurrences previously). Drinking, which is proof of virility through male dominance of the drink, becomes evidence of female sexuality through the woman's surrender to drink.

It is this necessary surrender that the males around Tracy are so eager to effect for her own good: as long as she remains superior, she is in fact inferior to an ideal definition of womanhood. To start with, a woman acquires her unwonted superiority at the expense of her sexuality. And Tracy's sexuality has certainly been impugned, first by her father (he tells her, even though she has been married and is about to be married again, that she is a "perennial spinster") and then by Dexter, who lumps her with other "married maidens" and for whom she represents an especially frigid divinity, the "chaste and virginal" moon goddess. Because this is a fairy tale with a happy ending according to the audience's understanding, Tracy must receive her final comeuppance: she will get gloriously drunk, along with Macauley, who is after all more of a poet than a he-man.[11] And although her two previous drinking episodes had no lasting effect, it is assumed that because this one comes at the conclusion of the men's indictments, the results will now be permanent: she will finally acquire the "understanding heart" her father and Dexter had found lacking in her. And because the exceptional individual is essentially maladjusted, she will feel so much better for it, admitting to her father the morning after that she now feels "like a human being."

As previously suggested, the Main Line was a nice place for the spectator to visit but not one to live in. *The Philadelphia Story* does a patient job of surgery in separating the glamour from the moral tone. The world of the beautiful people endures: Dexter, the ex-drunk who never touches anything stronger than orange juice throughout the picture, emerges at the end as Cary Grant, the reality that defined Philip Barry characters, still in possession of all the attributes that make him desirable. The born-again Tracy, now able to appreciate those glamorous attributes, remarries him once her station has been lowered: she allows him, as he dictates the terms of the ceremony, to maintain the whip hand that will keep her happy in her womanhood.

Again like the poor boy within the big-time gangster, the rebellious character will remain as a conventional person within the swanky world of the upper crust—a world that retains all of its appeal and its arrogance in spite of its allegiance to the conventions that regulated in 1940 the relations between men and women. George Kittredge, the self-made man, is shown many times how unfounded are his claims to that world: he cannot ride a horse properly or wear appropriate clothes naturally; he knows nothing about sailing; he does not understand Tracy's emancipation (nor do the others, of course, but because he is beyond the pale, he cannot understand her *by definition*). Far from being Ted Sennett's "mocking [of] the idle rich" (*Lunatics and Lovers* [1973], p. 15), this comedy suggests that their world is a vision of Eden once that other apple—the golden apple of discord—has been removed.

Even Cary Grant is said to have wanted to be Cary Grant, so one can readily accept at least a part of Pauline Kael's assessment: "Cary Grant is the male love object. Men want to be as lucky and enviable as he is— they want to be like him. And women imagine landing him" (quoted by Harvey, *Romantic Comedy in Hollywood* [1987], p. 297). Perhaps not all men wanted to be like him, and Hollywood knew this—there was the Bogart man and there was the Gable man, just as there had been and would be others still: the makers of demigods knew the limitations of demigods and therefore believed in diversification. And though it is very likely that all men wanted to be as lucky and as enviable as Cary Grant, it is questionable whether they wanted to be like him. They were most likely too realistic for that.

The first level of appeal is skin-deep: the screen lover is handsome. But where, beyond that surface, a Clark Gable promised physical love and a Charles Boyer promised subtler entrapments, Cary Grant remained on the surface: what you saw of him was what you got— charm, fun, wit. Norman Mailer had described the ideal demigod of motion pictures as the one who fought well, with brawn or gun, was resourceful, and was sufficiently dashing to love well—and love many. That definition, penned in 1960, seems to indicate that Mailer had the Gable model in mind, even though Grant had been proving for one-third of a century that there were those who believed in other kinds of seduction—those who were delighted to discover beyond the surface a mental rather than a physical dimension.

The Cary Grant of the white telephones was not distinguishable from his surroundings. He and his domain were one: it was as difficult to imagine him in a tenement slum as it was to imagine him making passionate love in even one of the art deco bedrooms through which he moved—either scene would have subverted the world he invested with verbal and physical grace. One assumes that the average male spectator found his sexual projection most readily in Gable and that women were more tempted by Boyer's promise than men were to imitate it. Likewise, there was no imitating Cary Grant; but Cary Grant was only a part of a larger symbiosis, and that symbiosis was enormously appealing—even to male spectators. And the fact that he could finally reduce even a female figure as powerful as Tracy to conventional moral dimensions contributed in no small measure to that appeal.

NOTES

1. It is noteworthy that, in the forties, those over fifty tended to go to pictures less than half as often as those in the youngest group (those under twenty-four): people for whom motion pictures had not been acceptable entertainment as they were growing up tended to be less assiduous and very likely more critical spectators than their children, for whom this kind of entertainment had always been commonplace. One would imagine that it was to this more reticent group that the new kind of verbal motion pictures appealed most.

2. The genre is so termed in Wes D. Gehring's monograph by that name (1983).

3. James Harvey surveys Hollywood from Lubitsch to Sturges in his *Romantic Comedy* (1987). And, in a lengthy attempt at a redefinition, Brian Henderson concludes that the term offers no agreement, neither from critic to critic nor within the work of a single critic ("Romantic Comedy Today: Semi-Tough or Impossible?" 1978).

4. Nor for that matter does it designate the Clark Gable of *It Happened One Night,* which Gehring lists as a screwball comedy.

5. See, for example, Alison Thomas's "The Significance of Gender Politics in Men's Accounts of Their 'Gender Identity.'"

6. For example, the kind of "enchantments" James Harvey remembers in *The Palm Beach Story* (1942) include "the penthouse and the yacht and the dance floor surrounded by palm trees and the art deco mansion with its vaulting white rooms and staircases" (p. 601).

7. Even though Katharine Hepburn did enjoy the company of a leopard in *Bringing up Baby* (1938), Irene Dunne performed Dixiebelle's stripper song in *The Awful Truth* (1937), and Carole Lombard was crowned queen of screwball for at least half a dozen madcap roles.

8. This was often the same wire-haired terrier, Asta, who, with Nick and Nora Charles, was part of the central trio in the *Thin Man* pictures.

9. Compare James Agee's sense of a growing genteelness in the American movies of the forties (*Agee on Film,* 1958).

10. *The Philadelphia Story* went into actual commercial release on 17 January 1941.

11. *The Philadelphia Story* received five Academy Award nominations: for best picture, best actress, best director, best screenplay, and best supporting actor. Only the screenplay and the supporting actor, James Stewart, made it, and the long intoxication scene is generally credited with having earned him the award.

Part 3

The Fall from Grace (World War II and After)

7

From White Telephone to White Collar: Gary Cooper, Spencer Tracy

Familiarity may not breed contempt, but it does preclude a sense of awesomeness or even the exceptional. By the time of World War II, motion pictures had certainly become familiar. Stars still cast enough of a spell to warrant klieg lights and crowds around Grauman's Chinese on premiere nights, but it was a spell that the keen eye of the camera was starting to limit. As movies became a habit rather than an event, spectators required an immediacy of recognition in place of the films' dissipating magic. As we have already noted, technology propelled by spectator demand made of representation an ever more accurate approximation of the real world's surfaces: the camera was becoming too scrupulous to maintain much longer a screen image at the distance required for the star's semidivinity.

More often than not, the star had been a projection of a part of the spectator's fantasy, the possessor of some radiant power—sexuality, beauty, brute force, wealth; his solitude gave him an aura of absolute purity, and his gregariousness gave the luster of ineffable social grace. But as the sharper lens of the camera pierced distancing veils, the spectator entered a world whose familiarity was as unlikely to mythologize anyone else as it was to mythologize him. Even the comic actors of the past were now magnificently remote: they had conjured worlds both more perverse and less actual than the spectator's through a special charm of movement that was theirs alone. Within the familiar world of the screen, the spectator needed someone more like him to match his stumbling.

In their quest for the visible layers of everyday life, movies would become colorful and larger; they would track sound more accurately; for a while they would even attempt to duplicate stereoscopic depth and olfactory stimulation. Meanwhile, within a world that was so much like his own, the spectator was starting to look for someone very much like himself—not the self he hoped or imagined he might be, but the self he knew as instantly as he knew the surfaces around it. Because capitalism requires a recognizable commodity to market successfully, the personality actor keeps being resurrected in box office blockbusters like Harrison Ford, Arnold Schwarzenegger, or Sylvester Stallone (none of whom appears in the index of Kristin Thompson and David Bordwell's *Film History* [1994]), but they are isolated stars in a pallid sky. The firmament resplendent with personality actors started fading as, one by one, each took on the coloring of surroundings that were ever less distinct from the spectator's. This is not to say that gangster movies, cowboy epics, and romantic, musical, and even screwball comedy died out—it means only that there was now a sufficiently large demand for that oxymoron, the everyday hero, to require his creation.

A few months after MGM released *The Philadelphia Story,* Warner Brothers came out with *Meet John Doe.* It starred Gary Cooper, an actor who already had fifty-four movies to his credit (and who would go on to make over 200, a clear demonstration of the star's longevity). Cooper had begun as a cowboy in *The Winning of Barbara Worth* (1926) and was thought of by many as the man on horseback: in fact, cowboy gear was only a small part of the uniforms in which studios loved to dress him; through the mid-1930s he appeared far more frequently in some branch of the world's military than in chaps. And in 1936, he starred in a role that was as different for him as it was for the man who made it—Frank Capra's *Mr. Deeds Goes to Town.* Although Gary Cooper would still revert to type, that difference was symptomatic of a larger change, from type to person, that would eventually begin to alter the familiar motion picture.

Two years before, Capra had made the successful *It Happened One Night,* which linked his name with highly popular screwball comedy. Following that success he became ill and, according to his autobiography, vowed that, upon recovering, "beginning with *Mr. Deeds Goes to Town,* my films had to *say* something. . . . From then on my scripts would . . . integrate ideals and entertainment into a meaningful tale" (*The Name above the Title* [1971], p. 185). *Mr. Deeds* was the story of a small-town hick who has inherited twenty million dollars and who, upon arrival in New York, becomes the property of the press and in particular of a female reporter (Babe Bennet, played by Jean Arthur) who turns him into a quirky celebrity. But even as she continues writing derisive pieces, she begins to fall for this utterly simple and commonsensical man whose two interests in life are playing the tuba and writing doggerel—and who is already smitten with her.

As he is about to propose to Babe, Deeds learns her true identity and decides to return home. On the way down the stairs, he is confronted by an embittered dust bowl farmer who berates him for not using his millions to benefit the starving common man. Deeds is converted, decides to give away his fortune to the unfortunate, and is promptly dragged into court by those who believe his selflessness is clear evidence that he should be committed. When Babe comes back to him in the courtroom, she convinces the judge that he is "not only sane but the sanest man in the courtroom," and the picture ends on a happy clinch.

Gary Cooper in the lead role was an instance of felicitous casting. He was the image of the lanky American, spare in frame, thought, and words—the man whom Carl Sandburg called "the most beloved illiterate to appear in American history."[1] In this case, *illiterate* presumably meant someone without learning, confirming the idea that excessive mentalizing is likely to deter from common sense. Cooper was a morality figure: like the cowboy he had once been (and would be again), he was an image of purity, walking proof of virtuous asceticism. He was too spare to indulge the vices of the body, too taciturn for the deviousness of mind or speech. Instead, like other Capra models—like the Clark Gable of *It Happened One Night*—he spoke simple truths (naivete being preferable to casuistry), made good use of an unspoiled, native shrewdness (in Deeds's opinion, if the Opera House is failing it must be because it gives the wrong kind of shows), and was good with his hands (he may not have liked opera, but he played the tuba, a sure sign he could cook up as good a breakfast as Gable's Peter Warne). Gary Cooper conformed to the beliefs of the white-collar worker, whose assurance derived from a traditional morality contained within the actual social order and who was therefore suspicious of ideas that suggested change through either assault or improvement. Cooper's inarticulateness was a warrant of his basic conservatism.

If one asks how this can be, seeing as Deeds assaults the New York establishment—just as Jefferson Smith assaults the legislative establishment (*Mr. Smith Goes to Washington*)—it is that these white-collar heroes are not attempting change. They are neither crusaders nor visionaries: they are not opposed to business or government as they know it but, rather, simply want to return business and government to a moral covenant from which they have strayed—another tenet of white-collar morality being that the collectivity imposed by size is inimical to virtues that inform the individual.

In a talk given at Wake Forest in March 1978, Capra rejected the implication of a religious message in his socially conscious films; he suggested instead that all "can worship in the ecumenical church called Humanism" (quoted by Charles J. Maland, *Frank Capra* [1995], p. 92). And in a PBS television series on Hollywood directors, he once again explained that the attractiveness of that particular church was its mirth: "First I entertain, then I get them in a spirit of laughter and then, perhaps, they might be softened up to accept some kind of moral precept" (in Richard Schickel, *The Men Who Made the Movies* [1975], p. 74). It is very likely that this Christmas Catholic (as he called himself) remembered that the ecumenical message was one of joy and that it could still be spread at a time when the audience was more unified in its acceptance of common moral denominators. In the words of Maland, "Between 1936 and 1941, Capra's social vision projected a mythology to a culture that . . . hungered for the very social values Capra believed in" (*Frank Capra*, p. 93), or, very likely, Capra was conditioned in the making of films like *It Happened One Night, Mr. Deeds Goes to Town,* or *Mr. Smith Goes to Washington* by the beliefs of his audience and knew that they would laugh at his mockery of their villains even as they approved of those who articulated unquestioned credos. Capra gave the spectator a world that spectator knew, a world finally redeemed in the film, as the spectator believed his own would be, by a simple morality he could understand.

The doors to Frank Capra's particular church had most likely been opened in *It Happened One Night,* even though the fun that would establish the identity and popularity of the screwball genre had obscured the message. When Capra summarized his social philosophy for *The New Yorker,* he put it simply enough: "The people are right. People's instincts are good, never bad" ("Thinker in Hollywood," p. 24). This was a truth he would seemingly forget in pitting the people as mob against *Meet John Doe*'s wiry hero, but only seemingly, for here, too, size (the people thought of collectively) corrupts the inherent goodness of the people thought of as a constellation of individuals. In that sense, *It Happened One Night* had been a movie of the "people," with a lower-class context defining the representative but individualistic Peter Warne and effecting Ellie Andrews's salvation. Depression-era audiences were afforded comedy and access by the descent of this midsummer night's dream from the forest of Arden to backwoods beyond the depravities of Miami and New York, bringing the principals together on a bus rather than a train and having them escape to motels rather than grand hotels. This allowed the depression spectator to believe that fairy tales could occur in more recognizable and affordable settings and that even the economically destitute riding the bus might find a millionairess sleeping on his shoulder. This happened during a time when more generally held beliefs tended to inhibit questioning, when "people reared in the school of wish-fulfillment [believed] that if you stepped up to a grumpy plutocrat, who, of course, had a heart of gold despite it all, bawled him out, told him his daughter was a spoiled brat, he'd at once grow enamored of you and you'd come into millions" (Robert Stebbins, "Mr. Capra Goes to Town," pp. 117–18).

It Happened One Night was not only too funny not to blunt whatever social point it intended (the hitchhiking scene or the many motel scenes were played for laughs rather than for even sexual politics), but the picture was dominated by the star's personality—and, as such, it belonged to the thirties: the glimpses of opulence as well as the more proletarian settings did not dissipate the dominant force of Clark Gable's sexual magnetism. Gary Cooper did not assume the same power. He was too much the embodiment of the idealized American, the tall, handsome (but not aggressively handsome), "soft-spoken gentleman with unswerving integrity and sincerity, overcoming adversity regardless of the odds—or the situation" (Homer Dickens, *The Films of Gary Cooper* [1970], p. 1) (as long as the situation did not involve a woman and require him to voice feelings that made him feel uncomfortable or he was unable to express): it was an idealization whose accuracy depended on its limits.

Much of *Meet John Doe* is defined by its metacritical quality: it is a picture about image making using photography and script to create a character who demonstrates how photographs and a written text that has been memorized create that character.[2] And it focuses on the figure of Gary Cooper as a parafictional tautology. Ann Mitchell (played by Barbara Stanwyck) has lost her newspaper job at the old *Bulletin* when a new broom is brought in and writes as her final column the fictional letter of a John Doe protesting society's injustices and warranting his sincerity by promising to jump off the City Hall tower on Christmas eve. When the letter raises a potentially sales-boosting stir, Ann is re-hired to keep the letters coming, and an incarnation of John Doe must be found. Long John Willoughby (Gary Cooper) is picked from a line-up of unlikely drifters—Ann's reaction is immediate and logically so, for it echoes the spectator's: "The face is wonderful. . . . They'll believe him." That face was one familiar to the spectator, a face belonging to a body no longer dressed up by the studio to encourage the spectator's dreams of romantic escape but, rather, dressed down to extend an even more intimate familiarity. In Otis Ferguson's words, Gary Cooper was "so much an American John Doe type you could never say whether he was cast in a part or vice-versa" (in Robert Wilson, *The Film Criticism of Otis Ferguson* [1971], p. 351).

Ann Mitchell loses her job (temporarily) because the newspaper she worked on has been taken over by D. B. Norton. After a few situating shots of the town and its people, we are shown the wall of the build-ing upon which the words *The Bulletin: A Free Press Means a Free People* are being jackhammered away—though graven in stone, the words are easily removed. The plaque that goes over them says *The New Bulletin: A Streamlined Newspaper for a Streamlined Era*: a world of expediency and coercion is presumably replacing the old world of moral values and freedom. However, the immediate concern of the new editor, Henry Connell (James Gleason), is merely to raise circula-tion: he so informs Ann and tells her, in fact, that sensational journal-ism is in. Ann feels she can be as sensational as the next journalist and goes to her typewriter to dream up the first John Doe letter.

The letter is an anguished attack on hypocrisy, injustice, and cor-ruption; and though Ann's purpose in writing has been in part to vent her own anger, when Connell accepts it (even for the purpose of in-creasing circulation), he does not place the *New Bulletin* in a moral po-sition inferior to that of the old one: from the start, ethical assumptions are confused. Ann accepts vengefully the idea that sensationalism will henceforth be the *New Bulletin*'s way (playing the same dangerous game as Sartre's protagonist in "The Wall," who accidentally gives away the hiding place of a rebel leader thinking to send his pursuers on a wild goose chase). Written out of a sense of personal outrage, her let-ter strikes an indignant moral tone, but when its sensational aspects achieve the purpose for which sensationalism was devised, she returns to the newspaper and agrees to continue what is now a conscious ef-fort to maintain a higher level of sales. As for Long John, he is a baseball player whose pitching arm has failed him, and he agrees to become John Doe simply for the money.

The packaging and promoting of John Doe proceed at a frenzied pace and are freely mocked by Capra: once Long John the redneck is roped in through a white collar and tie, he is photographed holding a midget on each shoulder, "symbols of the little people," while a girl in a bathing suit is brought in alongside him ("I want a Jane Doe ready to go on if this thing fails"). The enterprise is so successful that John Doe clubs soon begin to spring up. The answer to social injustice is a Christian ethic: the clubs have as their motto and purpose "Love thy neighbor." When what had been intended as merely a publicity stunt spreads beyond the newspaper, D. B. Norton enters the picture. Hearing his servants mesmerized by the appeal of John Doe, he is able to gauge the extent of the scheme's political potential.

D. B. Norton is portrayed by Edward Arnold, a man condemned through his comfortable corpulence to play mainly bankers and other kinds of plutocratic entrepreneurs. Edward Arnold was the somatic inversion of Gary Cooper—where Cooper was too lean for the indulgence of sin and corresponded to the spectator's meager economic expectations, Arnold's double-breasted rotundity bespoke an excess of wealth (one unlikely to have been acquired within the strictest bounds of legitimacy) and cried out for a capitalist cigar. Through directorial savvy, Cooper never wore his clothes comfortably in *Meet John Doe*: his white collar was unbuttoned and his tie was loosened in order to show how uneasily he accepted his transformation; Arnold, on the other hand, remained throughout the buttoned-up villain.

Although made after Dunkerque and just before the entry of the United States into the war, *Meet John Doe* is never concerned with the war as such and never refers to it directly. Its awareness of Germany and the consequences of Nazism are manifest only indirectly: Norton has an equestrian statuette of Napoleon in evidence on his desk; a motorcycle corps performs exercises with military precision; and a nephew whose uniform, like that of the motorcyclists, is very close to those worn by the S.S. If Norton intends to go into politics, the implication is that his ideology will be totalitarian. And it is clear that Norton has political ambitions; in a film whose main characters proceed through indirection, he is the only one who knows where he is going and states his intention clearly. He also writes the ultimate script in a story whose other characters are usually providing each other with their lines—an "ad lib ventriloquizing" (Carney, p. 48) that is supposed to contrive a social consciousness.

After giving Long John the words that turn him into John Doe and a media success, Ann Mitchell runs out of steam ("Unless he says something sensational—well, it's just no good"); it is now she who must be given words: her dead father's diary will come to the rescue. That diary encapsulates a bitter wisdom: the words of hope it speaks to humanity never left the locked pages of the little book. When they are finally made public through Ann, who transcribes them, John Doe, who speaks them, and D. B. Norton, who provides the microphones, they bring Ann traditional symbols of sexual success—an expensive bracelet and a fur coat—paid for by the only one whose sight and purpose are still clear: Norton. Still muddled in her intentions, Ann accepts them.

To confuse things further, Capra has provided us with a chorus— Long John's fellow hobo, the Colonel, who is on his way to an ideal part of the country where the two of them will be able to spend the rest of their days fishing. (Here, too, the image is blurred: it locates corruption at the usual seat of power—the city. However, because it wants to state its thesis in absolute terms, distinctions are not as clear as they once were in *It Happened One Night* or *Mr. Deeds Goes to Town*. There is no longer an idyllic countryside, the fount of purity and common sense—we don't really know where the Colonel wants to take us. Nor is the city a real city: starting with its farcical mayor, it looks more like Middletown, USA.)

Repeatedly, the Colonel tries to get John to walk away from the quicksand into which he sees him sinking. When John tries to rationalize his acceptance of the money as the only way to get his pitching arm mended, the Colonel explains that money will drag him down to the depths of a quagmire. But John isn't listening: he is becoming fascinated by his own image—he senses that his audience is "hungry for something." The Colonel is able to convince him only for a while— they hop a freight train out of town, but the world into which they escape has already accepted John Doe as its emblem. The Colonel is now convinced that the damage is done and Long John is beyond redemption: after they return, the refractory hobo leaves his friend.

Meanwhile, D. B. Norton is sponsoring John Doe clubs in every state of the Union to serve as his political base. He organizes a national convention that John Doe will address. Norton intends to use the occasion to announce the foundation of the John Doe Party, a fact to which Doe is tipped off by a rival newspaperman (another instance of a good deed done for bad reasons). Finally seeing the light, Doe confronts Norton: he will not give the speech he was supposed to deliver but will denounce Norton, "in my own words this time." (Ann, confused as usual, had already lumped together her father's vision of a better world and her own career in the service of the man who wants to destroy that world and begged John to remain with the idealistic script she has prepared.) The clear-sighted Norton tells John that, one way or the other, it is too late—the publisher holds all the cards. Undercutting the picture's final scene, John's last words to Ann as he runs out of the Norton dining room are, "Nice bracelet you got there."

Having started by denouncing Nazism in the person and purpose of Norton, Capra now turns Doe into a Christlike figure of bereavement who discovers latent fascism in the American masses. At the convention, Norton reveals that Doe is an imposter. The crowd, so long swayed by John Doe, turns against him instantly: whatever decency the people may have had individually they lose as a mob that can be manipulated by any demagogue who comes along, regardless of his message. John tries to talk, but Norton's police officers cut off the microphones: he is left a lonely, hatless figure in the pelting rain, which washes one of his posters down the drain—an image that, as Maland writes, might well "serve as a logical conclusion to the film" (*Frank Capra,* p. 112).

Unfortunately, it is not the final image—Capra shifts instead to a Christian fairy tale. Because John Doe was nothing but his voice, and because that voice has now been cut off by each of its mediators, he decides to become what he never was: the actual John Doe who promised to jump to his death on Christmas eve. Dismissing logical continuity, Capra interposes a number of saviors between John and his leap of faith: he first resurrects the Colonel; he then allows Ann to see that her love for Doe is stronger than her career ambitions and that the politics of idealism can be best served by John's survival; and last, Capra plucks from the jeering mob of thousands three members of the charter club who will convey the same message as Ann. Together, the Colonel, Ann, and the John Doers prevent John from jumping and becoming something more than a figment; they offer him a promissory note: he will be able to achieve the same end if he lives.

That promissory note is not sufficient to dispel the malaise of the audience as it leaves the picture house: the image of the angry mob shouting its hatred and that of John Doe's picture floating down the gutter remain in the mind. Capra himself knew that the ending was not satisfactory: "Riskin and I had written ourselves into a corner. We had shown the rise of two powerful, opposing movements—one good, one evil. They clashed head on—and *destroyed each other!* St. George fought with the dragon, slew it, and was slain. What our film said to be-wildered people hungry for solutions was this, 'No answers this time, ladies and gentlemen. It's back to the drawing board'" (pp. 338–39). Unfortunately, Capra's explanation is hardly better than his ending: we are not left with the sense that both movements have destroyed each other—our feeling is that the angry mob has won. And the small hand-ful of people we see at the end leading away a drenched and suicidal St. George are hardly compelling evidence of his eventual resurrection, while the "Ode to Joy" to which they exit seems more in the nature of an ironic statement than a lifting of our spirits.

Capra tried four other endings besides this one. One had Ann con-vincing John not to jump because of her love for him. This would have discarded the political message in favor of one emphasizing Christian benevolence and was rejected perhaps because it would have stressed even more the in extremis nature of Ann's conversion (what Capra at-tempted was finally the awkward synthesis of both the Christian and the political messages). Another, more powerful ending gave Capra's chorus the last, cynical word: the Colonel stands over the dead body of John, who has finally jumped, and whispers, "Long John, you poor fool, you poor sucker" (Maland, *Frank Capra,* p. 112).

One is left wondering what made Capra move away from this last ending, which seems to be the one toward which the rest of the film builds most logically. Longfellow Deeds and Jefferson Smith were ide-alists from the start—Deeds because he was the incarnation of Yankee common sense, Smith because he was the incarnation of the Founding Fathers' dream. But Long John's common sense is the narrow and self-serving understanding of the redneck, not the altruist. If the act of put-ting on a white collar constrains his mental faculties for a while, his friend the Colonel is there to remind him: after John Doe has given his first speech, the one asking people to tear down the fences that sepa-rate them, the Colonel comments, "If you tore one picket off of your neighbor's fence, he'd sue you."

The difficulties Capra encountered are evidence of the fact that *Meet John Doe* was stuck midway between previous conventions and per-sonal truths subverting those conventions: spectators were joined by the universal appeal of the stars, and when that appeal faded, they were returned to their individual inwardness. In time, even the solace of a categorical morality would be unavailing.

Deeds and Smith knew from the start (and we along with them) who they were: Long John never knows who he is. He has always been someone else's creation, someone on whom a label has been put in order to designate a symbol. This happened even before we meet him, when his pitching stance in the bush leagues earned him the only other name we know him by—Long John. (And even though we know some of the Colonel's philosophy to the extent that it means escaping from the establishment, we have no way of knowing to what that dream of escape is supposed to lead, for he too can make no affirmation. He too is merely a nickname, a label, rather than a person—he is no more than the romanticized, abstract idea of personal freedom.)

John Doe is in reality John Dough[3]—putty in the hands of those who created him before we knew him and while we know him—and, indeed, putty in Capra's hands too. Therefore, as Carney suggests, we can never meet John Doe (p. 351). His single usefulness, for someone else (Ann, or Norton, or some other manager), is that he can put in a personal *appearance*—but he himself is not there (and as we have noted, even his chance to finally give substance to his shadow by jumping off City Hall is denied). An emblematic scene is that of the only game of baseball we will ever see Long John pitch—a wholly imaginary game, played in his hotel room without a ball.[4] Further evidence of his nonbeing occurs during his marriage proposal: he knows that such a proposal concerns him for a change, not his surrogate. But because he exists only as a surrogate, he does not feel that the words he can speak will be adequate to reach the proper addressee: he directs them to Ann's mother instead—asking her in fact to propose for him. But in one of the film's most poignant moments, he realizes that even this mediation must be ineffectual, for only the surrogate has the words—and by extension, the substance: "[John Doe would] know what to say. . . . He'd know how to do it."

Meet John Doe strays from predictability in a curious way. In Gary Cooper, Capra had the perfect American Everyman of the forties. It is said that he first thought of James Stewart for the role, but, as Carney suggests, "the choice of Cooper for the part seems inspired, precisely because of the difference between the central characters in this film and *Smith*. Doe is not a character with the sort of breathless, bewildered innocence and emotionality that Smith represents and that Stewart captures in his acting" (p. 357). Instead, Gary Cooper was Mr. Average Man—the one Anita Loos had used as an unfortunate yardstick against whom to measure other lacks of brilliance: "[Clark Gable is] even duller than Gary Cooper in his conversation" (quoted in Swindell, *The Last Hero,* p. 155). If not quite the fascist Andrew Sarris sees him as, his manner certainly represents the American mainstream at the time, "suspicious of all ideas and all doctrines, but believing in the innate conformism of the common man" (*The American Cinema*, p. 97).

Capra thus began with a figure whose presence was already characterization: Ferguson writes, "*Meet John Doe* has its humor, inspiration, and interest in uneven degrees; but whether you find it good, fair, or merely endurable depends more on Cooper than on what we know as sound moviemaking" (in Wilson, p. 351). And yet, this is the figure Capra chose to eviscerate: after the expectation of *Mr. Deeds* and the confirmation of *Mr. Smith,* Capra set a trap for the spectator. He gave him a hero he had already learned to recognize and then pulled the rug out from under him in order to make a point about the danger of demagoguery. This was at a time when Capra, the son of Sicilian immigrants, may have been especially sensitive to the jeopardy of any culture when its masses are carried beyond reason and humanity by the words of dangerous phrase makers. This substitution of the recognizable hero by the director's message may well have made of *Meet John Doe* the first *auteur* movie. Of course, the substitution did not work: a figure so like the spectator could be read within a symbolic social context only at a certain level of abstraction—one that the familiarity was not likely to allow.

Something about Gary Cooper always remained bemused and whimsical; perhaps it was the malaise and skepticism of the rural primitive within the realities of an industrial world. Whether as cowboy, bush league pitcher, or small-town eccentric, his occasional straying from accepted forms (but never from the common store of shared beliefs) created a distance between him and a more corrupted otherness which preserved his fundamental wisdom and Arcadian goodness while mocking the world into which he would not be assimilated. In the Clark Gable of *It Happened One Night* the same rootlessness embodied many of the same virtues, but because of his aggressive sexuality he was not simply a free-floating presence, he was a dangerously loose cannon, and the reality of his presence asserted itself in whatever space he occupied. Gary Cooper was made of less heady stuff: however much he might be rooted, he remained a drifter—some part of him continued to be the ideal cowboy, wrapped in his aura of purity, forever floating away from the corrupted present into a yet-unsullied beyond.[5]

Spencer Tracy may have been even more Mr. Average American in that he came with roots firmly planted: the presence of Spencer Tracy signified immediately a job, a home, a family. While the whimsical part of Gary Cooper, and his handsomeness, might still reach the spectator's id, allowing him fantasies of quiet, strong seduction in a minor key, Spencer Tracy could extend the male ego only as far as the good provider, the strong shoulder, the gruff and sensible man from Springfield, Massachusetts, or Springfield, Illinois—or from whatever part of the country might still be impervious to newfangled ideas or regional quirks, just so long as the town was not large enough to dilute his individuality. He was the sort of regular guy who would be as out of place in a tuxedo as Cary Grant in blue jeans.

Tracy was the quintessence of the personality actor—a solid, small-town, middle-class presence seemingly unaffected by the camera. During his Hollywood heyday, his mythology included the usual number of stories about his hard drinking and his womanizing (at least until his extended liaison with Katharine Hepburn attained the level of worshipful hagiography), but his camera image was such that, in spite of the gossip columns, it was generally seen as the extension of an exemplary private life—the kind that was the mainstay of Elm Street, USA. This contamination of life by fiction allowed Supreme Court Justice William O. Douglas to say of him, "I never knew anyone more American than he. . . . He was Thoreau, Emerson, Frost" (quoted in Donald Deschner, *The Films of Spencer Tracy* [1968], p. 1).

It is instructive to follow William O. Douglas further through his musings: "I know he never talked bunk. He thought and talked in simple terms" (quoted in Deschner, *The Films of Spencer Tracy*, p. 1). As in the case of other American prototypes (Gable or Cooper), and conforming to our deeply rooted suspicions of intellectualisms, Spencer Tracy becomes a demonstration of our belief that simple talk denotes fundamental honesty: a mind uncluttered by useless complexities confirms a Puritanical virtue because superfluities of the mind may be dangerously close to the sinful superfluities of luxury and pleasure.[6] And Douglas notes that, caught within the interreflexion of the public and private images, the actor Spencer Tracy "seldom wore makeup"—the bare face reflecting the barefaced truth.

In this circular definition, whereby art and existence fade into each other, Powers notes in the same vein that the man who seldom wore makeup, "almost alone of the great stars, did not have a personal press agent" (in Deschner, *The Films of Spencer Tracy*, p. 25) and, perhaps as a logical extension, that he was a private man (where Gary Cooper was only a taciturn man): "His private life was imperturbably his own. He was not disposed to discuss his professional life" (p. 26). To be an egghead may not be in good taste, but it is important to sense that there is nevertheless a life, that something is happening beyond the front of the strong, silent man—it is the evidence of his depth and dimension, a litotes that his close friends, and maybe a privileged woman, will be expected to read and decode.

None of this denies the fact that these interreflexions are real, nor does any of it tell us necessarily which is the reality and which is the image. Suffice it to note that Spencer Tracy the actor was to a large extent Spencer Tracy the man—a middle-class worker in his outlook and manner. Joan Bennett testifies to the fact that, "invariably, he took two hours for lunch and went home promptly at five."[7] Although directors, critics, and fellow performers thought that Tracy was a consummate actor,[8] for him acting was neither learnable nor an art: it was simply the extension of a gift. Tracy once mused, "I've never known what acting is. Who can honestly say what it is? A lot of people try, and they criticize actors, but I don't think they make sense. I wonder what actors are supposed to be, if not themselves. Even Laurence Olivier, the greatest of them all, just plays himself. I've finally narrowed it down to where, when I begin a part, I say to myself, this is Spencer Tracy as a judge, or this is Spencer Tracy as a priest or as a lawyer, and let it go at that" (in Deschner, *The Films of Spencer Tracy,* p. 23). This was so true that in the rare instances when the real-life person intruded on the legend, it came as a shock. His co-star, Joan Bennett, remembers that Tracy "was an impeccable dresser, sartorially splendid at all times, and had his clothes tailored by one of the great specialists in New York" (in Deschner, *The Films of Spencer Tracy,* p. 12). But Bennett remembers the evidence with surprise (it runs so very "counter to the image he presented on the screen"): the fact is nearly a betrayal of Elm Street's mainstream.

Finally, Spencer Tracy was right: he could play only Spencer Tracy—he was unlikely to be tempted by either Shakespeare or the Sheik. Instead, he brought to the screen someone as recognizable as the man next door, whether the spectator lived on Elm Street or wrote for *Izvestia.* It was in that sense that Tracy's acting integrity consisted of remaining as much as possible simply what he was, being the center of a story that disposed itself around his reality, and in the process became something (as he said about *Woman of the Year*) "about understandable people and their problems" (Swindell, *Spencer Tracy,* p. 180).

Perhaps because Katharine Hepburn offscreen was so difficult to fit into familiar molds, she tended to be cast in the roles of women who likewise did not fit into familiar molds. The difference with real life was that by the movie's end, she was *required* to fit into them. In *The Philadelphia Story,* she was made to discover how much more satisfactory it is to be a conventional woman rather than a goddess. In a similar vein, *Woman of the Year* (1942) was to demonstrate that the woman overachiever is basically flawed—or, in the irritated words of Spencer Tracy, "isn't a woman at all." Tess Harding (Hardy's Tess of the D'Urbervilles?) is a successful news columnist who mixes with the movers and shakers of the wartime world. Born in China, the daughter of a career diplomat, she speaks without effort every foreign language she encounters. New York is her fief—the opening shot shows us the Manhattan skyline to the jazz accompaniment of Franz Waxman's musical score: we are in the dynamic center of the world, where glitz and energy may well dim the traditional values of the hinterland.

That hinterland is preserved within Gotham by Spencer Tracy: as Sam Craig, a sports columnist on Tess's newspaper, he literally slows down the action. His world is not New York so much as that of a more universal American brotherhood—those who write about, read about, and perform sports ("I like people," says Sam with absolute self-confidence, "they're pretty unimportant people. I guess that makes me a pretty unimportant guy"). It is a world of men and an island of small-town America within the white telephone world of Manhattan. We first meet them in the bar run by "Pinky" Peters (William Bendix), listening to a quiz program on which Tess is a contestant who knows all the answers—until it comes to sports, about which she confesses knowing nothing. She considers men running around in play "a frightful loss of energy," and when the moderator asks her whether she feels we should therefore abolish baseball, she answers yes: there are more important things going on in the world right now.

Even though the picture was released two months after Pearl Harbor, Tess is the only one of the characters who acknowledges the importance of what was happening: we encounter a world at war (and merely the European part at that) only in her world—its emblem is the map on her office wall that shows in dark the hold of the Rome–Berlin axis. Sam will demonstrate his ignorance of, or indifference to, that world throughout the picture—and so will the picture itself. What arouses Sam and his pals at the bar is the suggestion that a foreign crisis might curtail baseball: "Baseball and what it represents is part of the American way of life," says Sam. In the words of Tess's aunt, Sam is "just a normal human being," and as such he reflects the values of ordinary, normal

Americans in 1941—those for whom Europe was still a relatively distant concern while the movie was being made (certainly less of a concern than sports). For such normal human beings, that portion of New York associated with the elite that commands its glamour was likely to have achieved its status at the expense of virtues that kept the virtuous from similar achievement. Only there might a woman rise to such ridiculous heights as to forget her most fundamental definitions.

When Sam's outrage over Tess's rejection of baseball threatens to become a clamorous breach within the newspaper, both are called into the editor's office for a reconciliation. Sam's first sight of Tess occurs at the moment when she is hitching her stocking: instantly, the man in Sam betrays the sports idealist and the embodiment of middle American virtues—he falls in love with the enemy. Although similarly attracted, Tess keeps her head: she is first more interested in the rebuttal article he was in the midst of typing, and later she ambushes him on his way up the stairs in order to make it clear he was following her (women lose only the wars: they win all the small skirmishes).

Tess accepts a date. Sam throws his rebuttal in the wastepaper basket and takes her to a baseball game, where both she and the film are allowed to display their respective lack of sensitivities. As she comes into the crowded stands wearing a huge sun hat, she asks (at a time when the depression wounds had still not healed), "Are all these people unemployed?" And she then obscures the view of the fans behind her by keeping on her very wide-brimmed hat. Her presence in the press box is a deliberate, alien assault on male preserves by a self-centered woman: only someone as blinded by infatuation as Sam could fail to see it. "No women in the press box," mutters Sam's partner, who had previously acknowledged, "It's our own fault. Women should be kept illiterate and clean, like canaries." He is countered by only one voice—the thoroughly confused journalist who thinks Tess should be admitted for their collective enjoyment because "she's purty" but who also states her right to be there by desexualizing her: "She's a newspaperman." His voice echoes the movie's: Tess's fault is that she is acting like a newspaper*man* when her beauty intended her for a female role (as is typical of such reversals, she employs a *male* secretary).

At the ball game, Tess confirms what her legs had first stated—that beneath all that unseemly professionalism is a genuine woman waiting to be released: she gets into the spirit of the game, ends up understanding it, and even demonstrates enjoyment. But this is only a momentary lapse: she invites Sam to a nine o'clock party at her place. Still totally under her spell, Sam arrives before nine and waits for the hands on his watch to mark one minute after nine. He is ushered into a luxurious apartment full of people (evidently even more eager than he), all of whom speak in foreign tongues. Trying to integrate Sam, Tess sighs, "I guess you don't speak Hindi," to which he replies he doesn't, "only a little broken English." Where Philip Marlowe once acknowledged that English was an idiom he had mastered but abandoned, Sam's irony suggests that it is those who do not master his own idiom who are at fault. His mere presence is an assertion of rectitude: it renders pointless any argument about middle American common sense and honesty. Tess's contrast with Sam shows the extent to which she has been corrupted by an alien world whose values she absorbed before absorbing her own (which would have prevented her from becoming so unnatural). The xenophobia that underlies these assertions is articulated by Sam: marooned on a sofa with a fat man in a turban, he confirms that the man cannot speak a word of even broken English by saying to him, "You're a pretty silly-looking little jerk sitting there with that towel wrapped around your head."

Completely unable to read the signs that he brings into such stark relief, Sam proposes marriage to Tess. She feels somewhat unsure but accepts, telling him how much she has lived with "the frightening idea of being tied down." In fact, Tess has no intention of being tied down. She forces Sam to move into her world, which she really does not change to accommodate him. Such minor accommodations as she attempts simply emphasize the ever more visible differences between their worlds. Their marriage has to be arranged between several other commitments in her schedule. When Sam protests that he had wanted to "do it right," she allows him to come to the hasty ceremony in striped pants and top hat: although it was his idea, the clothes semiotics betray Sam. What would have looked natural on Cary Grant makes the honest, simple Spencer Tracy look foolish and out of place.

At this point, Tess's father is introduced. He is the moral image of his daughter: his chauffeur tells him he has only ten minutes for the ceremony; he looks at his watch and says, "Twelve." But such defects do not show as much in a man: he and Sam are immediately linked by a bond of mutual sympathy. Anyway, he is better than his daughter for being weaker: in a subsequent moment of masculine intimacy, he will confess to Sam the misery of success purchased at the price of loneliness (and he will admit that as a lonely widower he never had the courage to propose again).

Left alone at the conclusion of the ludicrously abbreviated ceremony, Sam indulges in a parody of the traditional gesture that signifies
male despair: he drains the glasses meant for the now departed participants. His mock bereavement sets the scene for the ultimate blacken-
ing of Tess, who must be sufficiently exiled from the moral center to
allow a conclusion that will satisfy all sensitivities by pulling her only
halfway back. Just as she is named Woman of the Year, she adopts a
Greek orphan as a public relations gesture and commits the ultimate
sin: she demonstrates her failure as a mother. As they are about to leave
for the award banquet, Sam turns to Tess, asking, "They won't ask me
to make a speech, will they?" "I don't see why," answers the now utterly insensitive Tess.

Endowed with all the middle American virtues, Sam's versatility
turns him into an instant father—or at least into an instant friend: he decides not to accompany Tess to the ceremony because the kid "can do
a lot of crying in four hours." Self-centered Tess asks how she will explain his absence. He replies, "Tell them I had something important to
do." Now assuming a role that would make sense in a man only if he
were a bully, Tess shoots back, "Who would believe you had something important to do?"

Even though he has been shown as a bachelor, Sam was never a
free-floating sexual presence—his squat, solid, slow demeanor always
emphasized his center of gravity, the kind of stable mass upon which
hearth and family rest. He thus understands the orphan's need for a
home and returns the child to the Greek refugee organization from
which Tess had taken him. Deserted by her "two men" and moved by
the wedding of her father (who finally found the courage to ask her
aunt), Tess returns to Sam ready for complete capitulation: cooking,
cleaning, children, husband, and home—her ineptitude for which she
promptly demonstrates by turning Sam's kitchen into a disaster area in
an effort to fix his breakfast. When he points to the evidence of this impossibility, she rebels—still not having quite learned: "What makes you
think I can't do the ordinary things any idiot can do?" Sam patiently explains (in his own idiom), "You can't expect Sea Biscuit to stop in the
middle of the stretch, take a glass of water, and count to seven at the
same time. That takes training." Tess is a purebred horse and cannot do
what she still considers to be "ordinary things"—and which, by the
common yardstick, are not.

The final moral is spoken by commonsensical Sam: "I don't want to
be married to Tess Harding any more than I want you to be Mrs. Sam

Craig." It will thus be sufficient to rope Tess in only halfway. But the picture has undercut this benign ending: there is in fact no world in which Tess can remain. From the start we have been given the symbiotic preposterousness that links Tess and her milieu. Sam is unmoved by the fact that Tess hobnobs with Churchill and Roosevelt (as the opening shots of newspaper headlines showed us) but is impressed when her father is detained by the secretary of state: a woman who usurps a man's role is ridiculous to the point of ruining that role, even though it may be otherwise identical. Her presence even renders trivial a world crisis long in the making and about to explode—while Sam's indifference to it is given as contrasting evidence of his common sense. In her world, the Yugoslav statesman who has just escaped from a concentration camp becomes a small clown with a German accent and two gorillas as ineffectual bodyguards (good old American "Pinky" Peters knocks them down).

Sam represents common sense because he is the vox populi—it is expected that everyone else shares his sense of things. Even Tess's sweet aunt Ellen (Fay Bainter) is part of the chorus. When she tells her niece about her impending marriage, Tess expresses surprise: "You were my Woman of the Century. . . . I always felt you were above marriage." Ellen replies, "I'm tired of winning prizes," and she evokes the sexually empty bed: "They're cold comfort. . . . This time, I want to be the prize myself."

Woman of the Year told us that, in 1941, marriage was the manifest destiny of men and women—the result of an inborn dependency that makes people miserable when it is not addressed. But resisting marriage, if it was a woman resisting it, was worse than simply the assertion of a personal aberration—it became an affront against a social structure based on the natural order of things. That natural order was still understood by the ordinary people of middle America, like those in the audience, even though Megalopolis might have lost sight of it. (Typically enough, it is once again the pastoral world that affords healing: Tess's father and aunt marry away from the madding crowd, in Connecticut—the New Yorker's vision of Arden; it is also there that Tess has her epiphany.) When Sam offers to drop off Ellen Whitcomb (on their way from one of the numerous airports from which Tess keeps taking off), she tells him he can drop the Miss Whitcomb, "It sounds like a reproach": in fact, it *is* a reproach—the whole picture has made that amply evident. So at the end, when Sam allows Tess to remain what she was, it is clear that it will have to be according to the terms of his world: symbolically, she gives up her apartment for his.

Where Gary Cooper demonstrated a vulnerability that allowed romantic fantasizing, Spencer Tracy is all of a piece—"the man-as-a-rock," according to Ferguson (in Wilson, p. 415), whose physical reality asserts the acceptability of his world, alongside which Tess's is so unacceptable. He looks at his world with that steady, honest stare of his and sees that it is good: sports, a man's concern, define an essential way of life; foreign affairs become foreign for him once they are a woman's concern—and that includes speaking too many languages, giving parties for too many funny-looking people, and generally causing an outlandish (female) attention to them to make them outlandish.

There is an often told story about the initial encounter between Spencer Tracy and Katharine Hepburn just before shooting of *Woman of the Year* began:

> Mankiewicz introduced them, and Kate's first words were, "I'm afraid I'm a little tall for you, Mr. Tracy."
> They shook hands. . . . Tracy remembered that she had a handshake that didn't make the trousers she wore seem unnatural and that he remained disapproving of her clothes. He stared hard at her for a long moment and then a smile plowed its way across his strong, broad jaw. "Don't worry, Miss Hepburn," he replied. "I'll cut you down to my size." [Anne Edwards, *A Remarkable Woman: A Biography of Katharine Hepburn* (1985), pp. 194–95]

There was no need to: the picture they were about to co-star in would do it for him. Or perhaps Tracy was such a masculine evidence in a world of men (yes, and women), which still accepted such evidences, that his presence imposed itself on the picture and shaped it. That evidence and that acceptance moved the man next door ahead of the star, even if the star's radiance was to shine on for some time after its extinction.

NOTES

1. He said this in a 1960 speech at the Friars' Club (according to a letter of his to Harry Golden, 20 June 1961). The spare, lanky ideal (already apparent in the characters' names—Longfellow Deeds and Long John Willoughby in *Meet John Doe*) accounted for Capra's casting of a gangling James Stewart in a similar role, the 1939 *Mr. Smith Goes to Washington*.

2. In fact, the "technologies of [Capra's] filmmaking mirror the technologies of experience" on a grand scale, as Raymond Carney concludes in his more detailed analysis (*American Vision: The Films of Frank Capra* [1986], pp. 373, passim).

3. See Carney's comments on his "plasticity" (p. 357).

4. This contrasts interestingly with Antonioni's imaginary game of tennis at the end of *Blow-Up:* that game is mimed by the Rag Week students but actually played within the imagination or the questioning of the spectator. In *Meet John Doe* the imaginary game of baseball shows the illusory nature of the bush league pitcher whom we only know through borrowed identities.

5. This may explain why his ultimate Hollywood pairing with the leading lady never seems to be quite satisfactory.

6. Spencer Tracy confirms this part of his positioning within the mainstream: "I have no particularly joyful recollection of school, grammar school, at any rate. For some reason I just couldn't get interested in books. They bored me. I tried spasmodically to be interested. I managed to stagger along from grade to grade, just getting by on passing marks and an occasional ability to kid the teachers along. I did get a kick out of athletics" (in Deschner, *The Films of Spencer Tracy,* p. 34).

7. As James Powers said, "Quitting time was quitting time, and Tracy did not work beyond it. [He] established his own working hours early in his career. His working day ended at five, although six, seven, and on into the morning is not unusual for some movie-filming. It is said that one day, a few minutes before five, a scene ended. The director, new to Tracy, [said] 'in this next scene we will all assemble on Stage Nine.' 'You will. I won't,' responded Tracy as he tucked his gear and went home" (in Deschner, *The Films of Spencer Tracy,* p. 28).

8. George M. Cohan said, "the best damn actor I ever saw"; Humphrey Bogart, "almost the best"; Stanley Kramer, "he was a great actor"; Dore Schary, "He worked his jaw muscle in a two shot and you forgot the other person on the screen"; Sergei Gerasimov, in *Izvestia,* "Spencer Tracy opened for many persons the best traits of his people. Soviet audiences came to love him for his manly serenity, his just, kind, and somewhat sad view of the intricate world around him." These remarks are taken at random from Deschner *(The Films of Spencer Tracy)* and Swindell *(Spencer Tracy: A Biography).*

William S. Hart.

Rudolph Valentino.
Arab and torero garb were not his only exoticism, as shown by his portrayal of a French nobleman in the 1924 *Monsieur Beaucaire*.

Charles Chaplin in *City Lights* with Edna Purviance.

Charles Boyer was the film seducer of many of the screen's most
desirable women, here Jean Arthur in *History Is Made at Night*.

Clark Gable threatening to go shirtless before Claudette Colbert in *It Happened One Night.*

Edward G. Robinson.

James Cagney in the famous grapefruit scene with Mae Clarke in *The Public Enemy*.

Cary Grant, with James Stewart and Ruth Hussey, in *The Philadelphia Story.*

Gary Cooper in a studio shot that seemed out of character
for an actor whose roles were so much a function of
the clothes he wore for the parts.

Spencer Tracy, with Katharine Hepburn, who played such an important part in both his films and his life.

Marlon Brando in one of his many incarnations of animal
manliness as Stanley Kowalski in *A Streetcar Named Desire*.

James Dean in a now famous pose from *Rebel without a Cause.*

John Wayne and James Stewart in
The Man Who Shot Liberty Valence.

Woody Allen with one of his frequent costars, Diane Keaton, in *Manhattan*.

8

The Adventurer (II): Humphrey Bogart

If we look at *The Big Sleep* (1946) today, half a century after it was made, we feel there is a rather unsettling exchange between Lauren Bacall and Humphrey Bogart toward the end of the picture. They are in the car escaping from Canino, whom Marlowe-Bogart has shot. When he thanks her for her assistance (in that gritty monotone so unsuited to thanks), she confesses she loves him. He then tells her he is tired and won't tip the police off about the Sternwoods' involvements with Rusty Regan. She asks, "Why are you doing this?" and he answers, "I guess *I'm* in love with you too"—and we realize that the Bogart rasp is even less suited to such a declaration than it is to expressions of gratefulness. Though he has already told her twice that he is growing fond of "another one of the Sternwoods" (meaning her), his words seem out of character: we don't expect this self-revelation—the word *love* sounds strange in Bogart's mouth, especially when it is his own love he is referring to.

The declaration remains in our ears not only because Chandler's Marlowe never spoke it to Vivian: Bogart himself never prepared us for it. His had been a case of life imitating art, and it was an art with no place for a sentence like "I love you." If it is true that the personality actor brings more of himself to his character than does the script, then Humphrey Bogart appears to have spent a good part of his life becoming like the roles that would later make him famous. Unlike the

Cagneys and the Gables, Bogart was born into easy circumstances and a good address—New York's Riverside Drive. His father, Dr. Belmont DeForest Bogart, was a fashionable Upper West Side surgeon, and his mother, Maud Humphrey, a just as fashionable children's portraitist. Through the private Trinity School in New York and later Phillips Academy at Andover, young Humphrey was being groomed for Yale.

In the words of Alistair Cooke, it is at Andover that "the omens of his coming lapse from gentility" first became discernible (*Six Men* [1977], p. 188). When the children of the wealthy are ill-behaved, it is customary to excuse their behavior as rebellion against their parents (which is what Cooke does). If so, Bogart took out his feelings on Phillips Academy, which expelled him for "uncontrollable high spirits" and "irreverence"—two traits he would cultivate with some modifications for the rest of his life—dooming any Ivy League ambitions his parents may have entertained.

His rejection of the Upper West Side was not total: theater producer William A. Brady was a neighbor, and through him, Bogart began his life as an actor. In those days, he parted his dark, brilliantined hair down the middle and played second young leads in parts that, as Alistair Cooke or Jonah Ruddy suggests, either coined or glorified the expression "Tennis, anyone?" (Ruddy and Hill, *The Bogey Man*, p. 25). On the strength of these romantic leads, he got a first call to Hollywood in 1930 and made six pictures during what he thought of as "a very unsuccessful year at Fox" (Clifford McCarty, *Bogey,* p. 7). Until 1934, he spent time on both coasts, trying to advance his stage and film careers, drifting away from blazer–and–white flannel roles for which he was no longer sufficiently young and into hoodlum parts to which his face predisposed him (after seeing his screen test, Columbia's Harry Cohn is said to have advised him to go back to Broadway and stay there, having failed to discover anything photogenic in him).

The most successful of his hoodlum roles was that of Duke Mantee in Robert Sherwood's *The Petrified Forest.* When the play was bought by Hollywood, Bogart was given the same part thanks to the insistence of the lead, Leslie Howard. That role typed him for the better part of the thirties. It was what made Raoul Walsh say, "You can't kill Jimmy Stewart, Gary Cooper or Gregory Peck in a picture. But you can kill off Bogart. The audience does not resent it" (in Ezra Goodman, *Bogey: The Good-Bad Guy* [1965], p. 127). When he attempted to break out of the mold in a picture like *Stand-In* (1937), Walter Wanger's assistant director muttered that no one could "make a hero out of him—the son of a bitch lisps!" (Nathaniel Benchley, *Humphrey Bogart* [1975], p. 75).[1]

Bogart's private-public life confirms the fact that the ethos of the heavy was not necessarily a drawback throughout the thirties. Cagney had parlayed the fictional consequence of that awareness into stardom: Bogart borrowed it for his private life. The much quoted remark of a restaurateur named David Chasen ("the trouble with Bogart is that he thinks he's Bogart") is confirmed by most biographers. Peter Bogdanovich remembers Joseph L. Mankiewicz saying that if someone would approach the table at which Bogart was sitting, you could feel the heavy rising in him (quoted by Bernard Eisenschitz, *Humphrey Bogart* [1967], p. 21). Goodman puts it this way, "On the screen, Bogart is a tough, trench-coated character usually sporting a gat and a growl. He shoves around everybody, from the leading louse to the leading lady. Off the screen, Bogart may not be quite as tough, but he tries his darndest to act so, [as when] barging into the chi-chi premises of Romanoff's hashhouse in Beverly Hills unshaven and minus a cravat, spouting profanity, and in general behaving like a middle-aged Dead End kid" (p. 22).

Bogart's simplistic iconoclasm was an attempt to give himself the dimension of his screen image—a dimension easily recognized and readily accepted: "doing and relishing doing something we might secretly like to try ourselves," as Ian C. Jarvie sees it (*Movies and Society* [1970], p. 153). Bogart reversed Cagney, who drew on his roots in the roles he played while distancing himself from them in actual life, but both Cagney's and Bogart's instincts reveal an identical truth about the thirties—the need on the part of the American male (or at least of sufficiently large numbers to make stars of Cagney and Bogart) to meet a perceived threat through counterthreat and to be quick in perceiving it. That counterthreat was physical in Cagney and not incompatible with a smile. It was more likely to be a sneer in the early Bogart.

The perceived threat could be of several kinds, starting with the malaise of an endless depression that, toward the end of the decade, was deepened by fear of an impending war. Sociopolitical structures within which the average man had found little material solace, and that now appeared unable to protect him from the turmoil already gripping Europe, were unlikely to be trusted. A screen outsider like Cagney, who was pitted against the system, articulated for the spectator an adversary position that was essentially his own. It is possible that Cagney represented the earlier and more optimistic part of the decade, when a lingering belief in the self-made man still gave the hood's physical onslaught the appearance of an immediate, if temporary, solution.

For someone like De Becker, Bogart represents the death of the American male: "The Bogart hero looks on without surprise as his dreams collapse and he tries to adjust, if one might put it that way, to his maladjustment" (p. 172). Certainly, he does not rebel with the kind of gusto that would bring Cagney at least momentary success. In a picture like *The Maltese Falcon* (1941), Bogart plays a man several times defeated even in victory: his partner is killed, the precious statuette of the falcon turns out to be a fake, the woman he was falling for is his partner's murderer, and, when he hands her over to the police, he completes his absolute isolation.

The war brought to an end social structures that had been maintained largely on faith but whose questioning could be seen, before their collapse, in the spectator's readiness to accept the gangster as hero. Now, knowing how irremediable was the loss of possibilities, the Bogart character could move out of the hoodlum parts of the thirties into the lawful Marlowe of the forties without any real change.[2] His brooding presence throughout the second half of the thirties emerged as the definitive Bogart of the forties, an image of progressive disenchantment in which resignation disguised as cynicism tended to replace the solace, however brief, of physical violence.

Cynicism, however, requires a certain kind of purity: where Cagney's audience might root for him as the gangster rat-tat-tatting the plate glass that law and order are supposed to protect, Bogart could remain scornful of law and order's motives only if he did not share in their corruption. Moral decency overwhelmed Cagney on his hospital bed or as he finally tumbled into the wicked streets, but Bogart had to preserve a more difficult balance, never departing from the rough manner and scowl that warranted his toughness, yet never allowing that manner to draw the scowler into the evil world of those he resembled because of it. He demonstrated the city's corruption even though he remained scarcely distinguishable from it. As long as he did not cross that line, he could stay (in fact it was important for him to stay) within the mainstream of his audience's most visceral prejudices and beliefs.

Bogart was to the manner born, but in moving from the Upper West Side to the Hollywood sets of lower east sides, he shifted to another kind of manner. His interview with Ezra Goodman for *Time* magazine shows how much he eventually made mainstream prejudices and beliefs his own—among them the sense that drinking is a manly virtue (as is male companionship: "My friends are people like Nunally [Johnson], [Peter] Lorre, [John] Huston. They must . . . never be dull or bores. If possible, they should drink a little"); that virility is demonstrated by fighting ("I used to get loaded in New York and one night, years ago, when I was playing juveniles, I and another guy decided to throw all the fags out of Tony's [speakeasy]. We got the hell beat out of us"); that men capitulated too soon in the war of the sexes ("about women: we've lost the war, they've got us. I feel we never should have set them free"); and that it is necessary to badmouth those in charge ("The ignorant s.o.b.'s who should be behind soda fountains or gas stations mess up Hollywood").

There is a picture of Humphrey Bogart arriving at the Ritz, Place Vendôme, with Lauren Bacall; he is wearing the same kind of sailor sweater he wore in *Passage to Marseille* (1944) and which he continued wearing to the Paris races—he felt entitled to the Ritz and Longchamp but felt it necessary to show his contempt for them.

There seems to be little doubt that Bogart became a huge box office success by the forties because he had more than his finger on the common pulse: that pulse had by then become his. It is therefore hazardous to confine him within the definition of a personal psychology (however much his words may tempt us to do so: "I'm not at ease with women, really. I must obviously like certain women. I've certainly married enough of them. But I don't like collective [*sic*] women")—whatever sexual insecurity his words and his various definitions of masculinity may convey, it appears to have been at least as much that of an age as his own. But his words link the on-screen and offscreen images: "Love on the screen is not for me. It is just terrible. I have a personal phobia maybe because I don't do it very well." Clark Gable personified the masculine love-'em-and-leave-'em fantasy. Bogart encountered a more rugged kind of woman—the kind who may have fallen for him but who sassed him as well. "You know you don't have to act with me, Steve. You don't have to say anything and you don't have to do anything. Not a thing. Or maybe just whistle. You know how to whistle, don't you Steve? You just put your lips together—and blow" (Bacall, in *To Have and Have Not,* 1945): that kind of invitation was calculated to remove from whistling just about all of its assertiveness. Typically, Bogart seldom whistled; it simply remained as a given that women were charmed by his cragginess and drawn to what Alistair Cooke called the curious animal magnetism of an attractive armadillo (p. 186), an assertion for which no evidence was adduced: "His general view of women implies that he was brought up, sexually speaking, no earlier than the twenties. Hence, he is unshockable and offhand, and, one gathers, a very devil with the women, [but someone] who is saved from absurdity by never having time to prove it. ('Sorry, angel, I have a pressing date with a fat man')" (p. 198).

The fantasy of the Gable encounter was one that entailed no aftereffects; the Bogart kind of irresponsibility was more complicated. It is set down in *Dead Reckoning* (1947): the ideal woman is only a few inches tall so that a man can tuck her away in his pocket. But when he needs her, he can bring her back to the splendor of full size. That dream states once again the man's need and his desire to be free of its consequences—but minus the self-confidence that informed Clark Gable's character. Because he cannot contrive a portable woman, he contrives a sordid office or the transient's hotel room: his is the dream of independence (freedom from the clutches of "love," for example) reduced to the dimensions of Marlowe's sleazy world.[3] All of which brings us back to *The Big Sleep* and explains why we feel a little awkward when Bogart turns even momentarily into a swain.

In 1946, the year of *The Big Sleep*'s release, Bogart was at the height of his long career (over seventy-five pictures). He had been among the top ten moneymakers for three years; he would remain in that exclusive group for another three. The preceding year he had married Lauren Bacall "after a well-publicized courtship" (Clifford McCarty, p. 8).[4] The two of them were thus a hot item distilling a special chemistry—or whatever Hollywood labels highly advertised and well-received pairs whose combined appeal is the promise of a film's success. But in order to take advantage of that appeal, the film had to link them romantically. To that end, *The Big Sleep*'s screenwriters (William Faulkner, Leigh Brackett, and Jules Furthman) rewrote Chandler's story. Chandler's Marlowe is attracted to the woman he calls Silver-Wig, the wife of underworld gambler Eddie Mars—which is a love that, according to the canons of the genre, cannot develop. Marlowe can keep her only in memory, as the book's final sentence confirms when, having swigged two double scotches at a bar, he concludes, "They didn't do me any good. All they did was make me think of Silver-Wig, and I never saw her again." The screen version just about cut out Mrs. Eddie Mars, shifted most of her role to that of Vivian, and allowed the real-life Mrs. Bogart to drive off with Marlowe into the promise of a final union.

The box office considerations that required this kind of ending when the Bogart–Bacall team was featured (the year before, in *To Have and Have Not*, or later in *Dark Passage*, 1947, and *Key Largo*, 1948) ran counter to conventions that were as readily accepted by films as by the novels from which so many were drawn: the intervening *Dead Reckoning* or the subsequent *Tokyo Joe* (1949) found no compelling reason for Humphrey Bogart to be finally united with Lizabeth Scott or Florence Marly. In those pictures, Bogart remained to the end the usual outsider—a tough loner whose image would have been impaired by the domesticating presence of a woman and who was better dead than wed by the time the lights went on.

The Bogart films that define him, those of the forties, reflect the American male's lingering sense of inadaptability. When Alistair Cooke opposes the view of later French critics who might be tempted to see Bogart as the marginal Outsider and argues that he is the embodiment of a social truth ("the Insider gone sour, all the more convincingly because the disillusion grew from his own background and the unknown cause of his protest against it" [p. 196]), he merely confirms the sense one has that American society comprised many who felt themselves to be outsiders.[5] The difference is that, by the forties, the expression of that alienation had become more internalized than in the preceding decade, most likely reflecting a growing sense that little could be done about it, a pessimism that replaced the 1930s fist or machine gun with the sneering utterance of the undeceived.

In his eulogy published by *Cahiers du cinéma* (1957), Bazin recalls that Bogart image as it stands out at the end of the picture, "pathetically victorious in his struggle with the angel, all he knows" (p. 3). The cult status Bogart enjoyed later may be due to the fact that younger audiences identified with his resignation: Belmondo is "breathless" in Godard's first film (1959) because he cannot stop running—away from the law, after the money owed him, after the woman he wants. His dream is one of rest: to be Bogart, the outsider who has not been turned into a jumping jack by others. Unfortunately, until he is shot in the final scene, he can only acquire Bogart's mannerisms, not what he believes to be his inner peace.

Raymond Chandler pays Bogart an ambiguous compliment on his interpretation of Marlowe: "Bogart is always superb as Bogart" (quoted by Ruddy and Hill, p. 95). The accolade would ring true for most personality actors—it rings especially true for Bogart, who, when he attempted not to be Bogart, showed "the strain of deliberate 'acting'" (Cooke, p. 200). To reread *The Big Sleep* after having seen the picture is to replace the face of Marlowe with that of Bogart. It is worth noting that even though the camera eye of the 1978 remake with Robert Mitchum is closer to the book in its unblinking look at the grim city, it leaves an impression of color-processed slickness alongside the gritty memory one has of the Howard Hawks picture. This is the more surprising when one notes that Hawks keeps the camera far from sweaty urban armpits: most of his outdoor action occurs in what look like middle-class Los Angeles neighborhoods. It is Bogart who nearly single-handedly conveys Chandler's sense of corruption.[6] Chandler's ineffectual redeemer takes on the coloring of the urban wasteland, while in Hawks the hero's grittiness rubs off on his surroundings: within the seven-year span that separates book and film, and across the bridge that links popular literature with popular motion pictures, both document the continuum of a social truth emblematic of the times.

Marlowe's is the voice that speaks Chandler's story—it is tough from the start, and from the start it makes, even when it does not state them, a number of assumptions: "It was about eleven o'clock in the morning, mid October, with the sun not shining and a look of hard wet rain in the clearness of the foothills. I was wearing my powder-blue suit, with dark blue shirt, tie and display handkerchief, black brogues, black wool socks with dark blue clocks on them. I was neat, clean, shaved and sober, and I didn't care who knew it. I was everything the well-dressed private detective ought to be. I was calling on four million dollars" (Chandler, p. 1). The aura of this redeemer is one of gloom (against every expectation of a Southern California Chamber of Commerce, the October sun will not shine on Marlowe). He is clothes-wise (the socks that would be otherwise too dark are brought into the color scheme through their "dark blue clocks"). But, well dressed, he becomes self-conscious, mocking his finery through the "display handkerchief" and the "brogues," and preserves the chip on his shoulder with the assertion that he "was neat, clean, shaved and sober, and . . . didn't care who knew it." His ironic self-distance echoes Cooke's appraisal of Bogart, "showily neglecting the outward forms of grace" even when he is forced to assume them. Marlowe is only masquerading as the "well-dressed private detective." His toughness being commensurate with the city's, he is more likely to be less than neat (though he will always remain emblematically clean, for cleanliness is next to godliness). Nor does he need to obey the social code that imposes shaving: he does not tolerate such impositions on himself. And as for being sober, we have already seen the equation that the Bogart male (along with so many other males) establishes between drink and manliness.

This dress-up is necessitated by the fact that Marlowe is "calling on four million dollars," a reason that should not arrest the reader too long, lest he wonder why money has such powers of coercion. But, of course, the reader is no more likely to spot a contradiction here than is the spectator: money *is* important. Its possession is evidence of the underdog's emancipation, and as such it cannot force him to shave or to remain sober any more than it can change a Rico Bandello or a Tom Powers—you check in at the Ritz, but you do so unshaven if it works out that way and wearing a proletarian sweater for good measure.[7]

What is hidden by the unshaven appearance of Marlowe, when that appearance is not itself disguised, is what Cooke sees in Bogart as "the rather shameful secret in the realistic world we inhabit of being an incurable puritan" (p. 205). Marlowe is the redeemer—the cynic whose fundamental honesty (his "cleanliness") allows him to be a cynic. His definition, and that of the very few other loners that are to be found in Gomorrah, is spoken in Chandler's novel by Captain Gregory of the Missing Persons Bureau:

> "I'm a copper," he said. "Just a plain ordinary copper. Reasonably honest. As honest as you could expect a man to be in a world where it's out of style. That's mainly why I asked you to come in this morning. I'd like you to believe that. Being a copper I like to see the law win. I'd like to see the flashy well-dressed mugs like Eddie Mars [those who *always* dress well] spoiling their manicures in the rock quarry at Folsom, alongside the poor little slum-bred hard guys that got knocked over on their first caper and never had a break since. That's what I'd like. You and me both lived too long to think I'm likely to see it happen. Not in this town, not in any town half this size, in any part of this wide, green and beautiful U.S.A. We just don't run our country that way." [p. 191]

The cop who is as honest as one can be in a world where honesty has gone out of style is cut of the same cloth as Cooke's Bogart, "a touchy man who found the world more corrupt than he had hoped; a man with a tough shell hiding a fine core [who] transmuted his own character into a film persona and imposed it on a world impatient of men more obviously good" (p. 205). And the cop's sympathy for the poor little slum-bred hard guys that never had a break acknowledges that whatever side of the law they happen to be on, each feels equally outcast within that flawed society: "We just don't run our country that way." You play by the rules of that society only if it's important—only if your cynic's definition is in jeopardy. Otherwise, it is sheer hypocrisy to do so, and the refusal to shave or to dress is raised to the level of a political statement.

Marlowe, whose name reminds us of the Cambridge-educated, hard-drinking, iconoclastic poet and dramatist, was never one of the little slum-bred hard guys who now people most of his world. Like Bogart, he left some upper west side a long time ago because he wasn't comfortable there. But, as he says in the picture, he can still speak English if he has to. In the book, that part of his portrayal is similar. Vivian casts a disapproving glance at his office and remarks, "I was beginning to think perhaps you worked in bed, like Marcel Proust." Marlowe puts a cigarette in his mouth and asks, "Who's he?" She tells him, "A French writer, a connoisseur in degenerates." Then she makes the mistake of adding, "You wouldn't know him." "Tut, tut," answers Marlowe. Culture becomes objectionable when it is acquired only for its own sake: it then becomes a frivolous luxury and a pose. Other than that, it remains in the public domain: Marlowe does his research at the public library in order to trap Geiger because he belongs to a culture that prizes knowledge of facts above imagination. Culture as a useful acquisition is an additional attribute of the all-around man (it can help trap Geiger in the same way as knowing how to handle a gun or fix a car engine)—the all-around man is also a good tinkerer. But culture with a capital "C" is suspect, not something the he-man would like to be caught indulging. Finally, it is not so different from the powder-blue suit you put on when the four-million-dollar circumstance requires it: you know how to wear it, but you don't make a habit of it, like the phony Eddie Mars.

Captain Gregory knows that Marlowe will be defeated in the end, as he himself will be. Both of them will continue to put criminals behind bars, but they will do it largely as catharsis, to preserve a self-image; within the corruption of the city, a criminal more or less makes very little difference. Anyway, they cannot fool themselves, they are too much like the small-time hoods whose kinship they acknowledge to dream of the golden city on the hill. The quiet disenchantment of the forties will not allow it.

Having solved one more case, Marlowe leaves the Sternwood hill for the last time. On that hill, an emblematic sun shines, the same sun that withdrew itself emblematically from the hero. It is a queer sun—"the bright gardens had a haunted look, as though small wild eyes were watching me from behind the bushes, as though the sunshine itself had a mysterious something in its light"—but still, it is a kind of sunshine and, therefore, the luminescence of a place that Marlowe must leave: "I got into my car and drove off down the hill." And as he descends into the grimness of his city, Marlowe is overwhelmed by thoughts of death that begin with the image of Rusty Regan's "horrible, decayed body" rotting in the cesspool: "What did it matter where you lay once you were dead? In a dirty sump or in a marble tower on top of a high hill? You were dead, you were sleeping the big sleep, you were not bothered by things like that. Oil and water were the same as wind and air to you. You just slept the big sleep, not caring about the nastiness of how you died or where you fell. Me, I was part of the nastiness now. Far more a part of it than Rusty Regan was." Thoughts of Rusty Regan, whom he never saw, may have caused Marlowe's extended and uncharacteristic introspection, but he had been a part of that nastiness since before he ever put on his Sunday best to meet General Sternwood.

Chandler's novel is about death and the wicked city—the wicked city to whose back alleys and brutality Marlowe returns after leaving the Sternwood gardens. As for death, it is prefigured in the isolation of the loner: as in *The Maltese Falcon,* he is allowed for a brief moment to come close to a woman who might have been a companion. It is a brief moment indeed, for he knows all the while that their relation, like any other, is stillborn. There is no other human outreach: typically, when Captain Gregory is through with his little speech, Marlowe remains silent—"I didn't say anything"—even though Gregory has laid bare both their souls. The ideal of the strong silent man—the man of few words who in the Western spoke mainly with his gun in order to avoid yet another form of contaminating intercourse—has now been silenced by the futility of serious utterance. Marlowe's silence is a sign of his friendship, of the intensity with which he has heard Gregory. Someone more dismissible would have elicited a scowl or at best a sarcastic response.

Close to the last of her exchanges with Marlowe, Vivian still misunderstands him: "You son of a bitch!" she says. He explains patiently, though sarcastically, why he is not a son of a bitch, and then they part. In the motion picture they come together—the spectator is allowed to superimpose on the fictional Marlowe and Vivian the real-life romance of Bogart and Bacall—making of the film what Heidi Dawidoff sees today as an obsolescence "where heroism and love still have a chance" (*Between the Frames,* p. 92). Yet it is doubtful whether the spectator believes in that ultimate reunion any more than Chandler's Marlowe believes in an eventual union with Silver-Wig. The spectator senses that to the extent Bogart is real, his unlikely declaration of love is fiction. The film's hopeful ending does not dispel the image of the male who dreams of a portable woman but knows that, because she does not exist, women as presently constituted are simply not an adequate hedge against the wretched city, the harshness of a culture gone wrong, the irremediable loneliness of being a man—something only

other men can understand, which accounts for the cold and brief nature of their bonding.

The silence of the Bogart man is the start of a new era in American
motion pictures. It comes at the end of several kinds of enthusiasm.
What begins to fade in the forties along with the raucous energy of previous decades is the enjoyment of what was once the exclusive magic
of moving pictures—their ability to capture human motion. With the
downgrading of human motion, the motion picture turns to human
emotion, but even that will very likely be subdued as "the rather
shameful secret in the realistic world we inhabit of being an incurable
puritan": the male spectator who sees himself in Bogart is divided—a
puritan by necessity; luxury and pleasure are as sinful as only that from
which you are cut off can be. But the reality of removal does not alle-
viate desire; he rejects the objects of that desire as effete—or more precisely, he rejects their active quest—and replaces them with more at-
tainable and safer virtues: drinking with other men, and as he drinks,
talking tough—about the shortcomings of women, the boss, the long-
hairs, the unfairness of life. That talk sublimates action, whether sexual
or political, and does not regenerate the loner, but it does become
through a sterile tautology the virile mask of those who have so defined it, and the loner is able to glory in the bittersweet awareness of
his isolation.

Bogart is evidence of a coming inwardness. After him, the picture that
sees the man as a loner, whether heavy or hero, will tend to be more in-
trospective. By midcentury, the very mask that allows men to know
each other starts falling into disuse, and the spectator's immediate and
comforting recognition of familiar codes is lost within the peculiarities
of individuals—the Weltschmerz of even the criminal becoming more
important than his rebellion, giving birth to the thinking man's heavy.
This new dawn rising will dim the stars' luster, one by one.

NOTES

1. That famous lisp was the result of an accident ("a piece of wood lodged
in my lip") on board *The Leviathan*, a troop ship on which Bogart served
briefly at the end of World War I. More than anything else, that little piece of
wood may have accounted for Bogart's subsequent casting: it also left a scar
and turned his smile into something like a sneer.

2. We have already seen that Cagney was able to effect the same shift as effortlessly. Alistair Cooke sees here an instance of the kind of conflation we will

examine later between the private and fictional Bogarts. He believes that Bogart deliberately kicked "the pedestrian old-school virtues" because he mourned their passing, and gives as evidence his growling awareness of change: "I came out here with one suit and everybody thought I was a bum; when Brando came out with one sweat shirt, the town drooled over him" (p. 202).

3. This was a world to which the male spectator nevertheless relates, if Cooke is right: his only domestic base may be a fairly seedy hotel bedroom with an unmade bed, but "this is called audience identification, and to tell the truth is the sort of independent base of operations most college boys and many rueful husbands would like to have" (pp. 198–99).

4. Critics more exclusively interested in the sexual politics of our society see *The Big Sleep* mainly as "a celebration of the Bogart–Bacall romance" (Sklar, p. 174).

5. Bogart had long understood the appeal of the loner—even the criminal loner: "When the heavy, full of crime and bitterness, grabs his wounds and talks about death and taxes in a husky voice, the audience is his and his alone" (quoted by McCarty, p. 8).

6. He does so even if, in the words of Annette Kuhn, there is a "degeneracy pervading the film [that] takes the form of various kinds of 'abnormal'—perverted, excessive or threatening—sexuality" (*The Power of the Image*, p. 94). And because she has conceded that the "only normal relation" is that "between Marlowe and Vivian" (p. 89) and that Bogart so dominates the picture, we must look to him for the seeds of that degeneracy.

7. If Alistair Cooke is right and the transient's hotel room represents the freedom every rueful husband would like to have, it is at least as true that the room at the Ritz represents the affluence that every small wage earner would desire—if for no other reason than that he could read into it the erotics of freedom and power. When you have money, you don't have to justify your claim to the Ritz.

9

Midcentury Icons:
Marlon Brando, James Dean

In 1946, Dr. Benjamin Spock published *The Common Sense Book of Baby and Child Care*. The book became hugely successful—in a short time, the U.S. paperback edition passed the half million mark—and, like the Bible it was, became known by a generic title: few had read *The Common Sense Book*, everyone had read Dr. Spock. It is likely that its success was not due so much to its medical advice as to the guidelines it gave middle-class parents on the rearing of children. Common sense, prior to Spock's, had seen the child as Locke's tabula rasa; that view implied the presence of parents was primarily responsible for shaping the experience to be inscribed. But Spock saw the child nearly from birth as an individual whose development depended on space—which responsible parents had to avoid crowding.

It is possible that Spock recommended this kind of distancing because the times encouraged it: parents of the Great Depression and World War II were anxious to spare their children the privations they themselves had experienced and within the relative affluence of the postwar years may have given their sons and daughters more than was good for them. If this translated as a sense of something they were due, those parents may have read in Spock an encouragement to equate materialism and freedom to the extent of jeopardizing traditional discipline.[1] Whether or not that is so, the generation gap between children and parents grew. Ten years after the book's first appearance, children were starting to show unmistakable signs of rebellion. And throughout the next decade, that rebellion gathered strength, perhaps in large part because parents had grown timid and unsure. In due time, their children's revolt included that very timidity in its list of grievances.

The young moved quickly into the areas ceded to them by adults and awakened nearly as quickly to the disillusionment of hastened maturity: "Teen-agers in the mid-fifties experienced a level of autonomy which had not been possible for previous generations. As teen-agers at the time realized, they were the first generation of young people who seized the opportunity to be different from their parents, but it was an act fraught with moral and psychological dangers" (Terence Pettigrew, *Raising Hell: The Rebel in the Movies* [1986], p. 98). They were twice vulnerable—being unaware that freedom (termed by Mircea Eliade "one of man's essential nostalgias") was not the absolute they had expected it to be and having had so little time to prepare for its consequences.

Meanwhile, Hollywood kept a shrewd business eye on the changing social scene. It knew that, in the fifties, by far the greatest proportion of the motion picture audience was under twenty-four and that of these the majority were in their late teens.[2] There ensued a steady production of films meant to satisfy those who wanted the screen to reflect their boundlessness, their anger, their anxiety, and, paradoxically, their sense of persecution. Montgomery Clift in *From Here to Eternity* (1953), Sidney Poitier in *The Defiant Ones* (1954, as opposed to his softer role in the 1955 *Blackboard Jungle*), and Paul Newman in *The Left-Handed Gun* (1958) were a few of the more notable loners and losers at odds with conventions, the law, their parents, or society as a whole. Two figures emerged during the decade that seemed especially able to capture this specific aspect of the popular imagination: Marlon Brando, the brutish, lower-class loner-subverter; and James Dean, the loner-subverter with Weltschmerz.

Marlon Brando was a star before he came to Hollywood: he had appeared in Elia Kazan's Broadway production of *A Streetcar Named Desire*. There is some significance to the juncture of that actor and his role: Kazan had belonged to the now defunct Group Theater whose patron saint was Constantin Stanislavsky and whose "Method" required the actor to become his character by understanding the submerged psychological reasons for his words rather than simply their interconnections at the level of manifest action.[3] There was, thus, an even greater temptation than usual for the actor to behave as his character did. This presented few problems when stars of a previous time incarnated glamorous stage or screen figures. Expressing the deep-seated emotions of a scruffier character involved a certain risk—there was nothing to say that an offputting surface might not discourage further exploration. Luckily, times were becoming scruffier too, and, by the fifties, there was even some expectation that an unprepossessing surface was likely to hide more interesting depths.

Half a dozen years after the demise of the Group Theater, Elia Kazan reemerged with the Actors' Studio, and the Stanislavsky Method was revived. One of its first pupils was Marlon Brando, and one of its first productions was *Streetcar*. As the primitive Stanley Kowalski (the part that had first been meant for another Method actor, John Garfield), Brando was the raging sexual force that finally shatters the genteel construct into which Blanche du Bois had turned her life. How much Brando contributed to Kowalski and how much Kowalski contributed to the image of Brando is hard to gauge. But when he was called to Hollywood because of his success in Tennessee Williams's play, it is not particularly surprising that some of Kowalski rubbed off on him.[4] He preserved Kowalski's sweaty T-shirt personality, prompting *Time* magazine to suggest that "where John Barrymore was the Great Profile, Rudolph Valentino the Sheik, Clark Gable the King, Marlon Brando was the Slob" (Gary Carey, *Marlon Brando* [1985], p. 71). And whether out of social consciousness, posturing, natural diffidence, or a combination of all three, he acted the part of the proletarian rebel. He either carried on the inarticulate mumbling of Method acting or gave disdainfully outrageous answers during interviews and, in addition to his dress and unshaven manner, maintained a purposefully anti-establishmentarian way of life. Even his nearsightedness (and his refusal to wear glasses) contributed to his image: the relatives with whom he first roomed in Los Angeles remembered that "he doesn't bring the food to his face. He brings his face to the food" (Carey, p. 62). And, of course, the sexual core of Stanley Kowalski was preserved in "his sullen looks and in every line of his sculptured body" (Pettigrew, p. 77).

But in his demeanor and beliefs, Brando was also intuitively in step with his times (perhaps no less than Tennessee Williams). As a child, he had already shown the sensitivity and rebelliousness that would be the conscious self-definition of the young some years later: "He was noted for his energy, his competitiveness, his general refusal to conform, and his intuitive feeling for the underdog. He brought home wounded animals and, in at least one instance, a 'wounded' person. At school he was considered as bright as he was irresponsible" (David Downing, *Marlon Brando* [1984], pp. 11–12).

Expulsion ended a year and a half at a military academy in Minnesota to which his father had sent him in the hope that he would acquire some discipline—the same father toward whom he remembered nurturing a sense of violence and anticipated the posture that would one day make James Dean famous: "I once tried to kill my father. Really" (Thomas, *Marlon,* p. 83).[5] However much posturing there might have been in the defiance of young Brando in Hollywood, it did not wholly disguise the resentment at a world judged to be corrupt or the malaise at not being able to cope with it: "He was regarded as a loner. . . . That he had, beneath the bonhomie and practical joking, problems, was evident to Kazan, who sent him to his own analyst" (David Shipman, *Brando* [1974], p. 14).

It was this mix of hostility, distrustfulness, and vulnerability that Brando brought to his first Hollywood picture, *The Men* (1950), the story of a paraplegic veteran attempting a return to the world designated by the title. Brando agreed to leave the stage for motion pictures because he believed in their power to effect social change: "The films are, I think, the most powerful single influence available to the American public today—much more than either the church or formal education. I do not think that anybody connected with the films in the United States has ever made a sincere effort to avail himself of their fullest potentialities" (in Thomas, *Marlon,* p. 51). *The Men* was to be produced by Stanley Kramer, whose socially conscious *Home of the Brave* (1949) Brando admired.[6] And, indeed, the story could be read as an anti-war statement. But it was finally shaped by the presence of Brando: the subtlety of the script, or the increasingly skeptical times, let the hero's bitterness and self-irony cast doubt on the promissory ending of a successful marriage.

The following year, in the filmed version of *Streetcar,* Brando preserved *The Men*'s vulnerability only in the final acknowledgment of his need for Stella, whom the Breen Office had forced to leave Kowalski in repayment for the rape scene it had grudgingly allowed Williams to keep.[7] With *Streetcar* Brando achieved superstardom, and his next two pictures reflected that status. In Kazan's *Viva Zapata!* he played the role of the Indian peasant who was able to formulate a new agrarian policy for Mexico and became with Francisco Villa one of the most influential revolutionaries in that country's history (the motion picture's name was derived from a novel by Edgcumb Pinchon, *Viva Villa!*). The film gave Brando the kind of socially significant role he desired, but the requirements of the disguise that changed the young man from Omaha into a fierce Indian who was part bandit, part idealist, altered the nature of his hot-bloodedness. The part was lusty enough, but the brown contact lenses he was required to wear, the plastic rings to enlarge his nostrils, the black mustache all constrained the inner man at the heart of any Method role.

Method disappeared altogether in his next vehicle, his part as Mark Antony in Mankiewicz's *Julius Caesar* (1953). Brando, who had lived among paraplegics for *Men* and Mexicans for *Zapata,* now immersed himself in recordings of Shakespeare by John Barrymore, Maurice Evans, Laurence Olivier, and Ralph Richardson. After two weeks of osmosis, he made his own recording of the text. When he took it to Mankiewicz for his appreciation, the director told him that he sounded just like June Allyson (Thomas, *Marlon,* p. 72). The idea was to reintroduce Brando into the character of Antony, but in the first reading Brando submerged the character with disastrous results: "He sat hunched over the script, both elbows on the table, his eyes eight inches from the page. Ears strained to hear his words. Only the faintest of sounds emerged. Producer Houseman later termed it 'Marlon's secret performance'" (Thomas, *Marlon,* p. 73).

Brando's Mark Antony was studio casting capitalizing on box office reputation—a role in which the soldier unavoidably dominated the politician[8]—in a reversal of Shakespeare, who makes the character a man of inspired words. But by all accounts, and in spite of moments when vernacular rhythms slipped in, Brando the superstar was sufficiently able to tame the Method actor. On an NBC *Today Show,* Laurence Olivier concurred: "Don't tell me he searches inside himself for everything. He looks out, too. He's peripheral, just as any other character actor is peripheral" (Shipman, p. 37). Nevertheless, Brando the superstar, who could do Mexican characters and Shakespeare, was neither the real nor the full Brando: no other proof needs be adduced than to note that *Zapata* and *Caesar* breezed through the Hollywood Production Code. It was in his next picture that both Brando and the Breen Office would resurface. Although Otto Preminger's *The Moon Is Blue* (1953) had been the first major Hollywood picture ever to be released without the office's approval, *The Wild One* (1953) and the pictures it spawned hastened the dumping of the Production Code into the ash bin of history.

The Wild One was a sign of the times—an actual occurrence made into a short story (Frank Rooney's "The Cyclist's Raid"): in the late forties, thousands of motorcyclists had descended on a small California town, which they pretty much destroyed throughout the night. For the socially conscious Brando, the story was of interest: "There are so many kids who are confused today, and the problem hasn't yet been intelligently articulated in entertainment" (Carey, pp. 90–91). He also anticipated the gist of the case study by the psychiatrist who would give his title to *Rebel without a Cause* in his questioning of "why young people tend to bunch into groups that seek expression in violence" (Carey, pp. 90–91).

Brando was thus sympathetic to the members of the gang—more interested in exploring the reasons for their actions than in condemning them. The story intended to be equally sympathetic and ran into immediate problems with the censors, forcing Stanley Kramer to place the same kind of disclaimer Warner Brothers had found necessary for *Public Enemy:* "This is a shocking story. . . . It is a public challenge not to let it happen again."

The disclaimer was projected against an infinitely receding shot of what would soon be Kerouac's *Road,* while Brando's voice-over said, "This is where it begins for me." With the disappearance of the disclaimer, that road becomes the channel for the forward surge of the motorcycles—the powerful assault on the 1953 spectator of the brutal and aimless young on the phallic beasts between their legs. They are the ones bereft of the father Brando had killed only in press interviews. That loss releases them as a dangerous force but also turns them into waifs—and having shown their threatening charge of sexual energy, the picture begins the analysis that is to articulate the bipolar vision of youth during the fifties: the gang is evicted from a town where tame motorcyclists are contained within the circular track of an ordered race. They leave, having stolen a race trophy one of the gang members gives Johnny (Marlon Brando), the gang leader. Symbolically, it is a second-place prize, but Johnny treasures it and straps it to his handlebars.

The small town they move to next is sleepy and dull. The gang is amazed by its sterility and boredom and counterstates it by sassing its respectability, whooping it up in the streets, and having some beers at the local bar—activities that the town does not discourage: the beauty salon operator, whose off-the-shoulder dress is an indication of relaxed morals, and her assistant enter into a flirtatious barroom relation with the gang members, and the bar owner is delighted at the unexpected business.

In his voice-over, Brando says, "Mostly I remember the girl. . . . Something changed in me. She got to me." That girl is the policeman's daughter, Kathie (Mary Murphy). She is the good girl in white but nevertheless a kindred spirit to Johnny: she confesses her feelings of closure and constraint and her dreams about one day escaping with a stranger who would be passing through. (The theme of impossible escape recurs: when Johnny is accused of attempting to harm Kathie, who was "trying to get away from him," she answers, "*He* was trying to get away.") Before the policeman is turned into the benign surrogate for the missing father, he is the symbol of constraint and the reason for the dream of escape. "I don't like cops," says Johnny, "I made a deal with a cop once . . .": the cop enforces a life judged to be untenable by the young. And, beyond the fiction, other cops maintained that enforcement: when Kathie asks Johnny why he is on the road and aimless, the censors deleted the justification that only mainstream Kathie was allowed—Johnny's explanation that his motorcycle afforded him weekend release from a meaningless job.

The diligence of the Breen Office thus removed the explanation of rebellion and justified the gang's name: the Blind Rebels Motorcycle Club. When the beautician asks, "Whaddya rebelling against, Johnny?" he confirms the name: "Whaddya got?" But the censors still could not alter the fact that the picture intended to emphasize that these Hell's Angels were not wholly hellish—their black leather jackets, soon to become the national uniform of the young, emphasize the shadows cast over them rather than their evil (Kathie understands: she will tell Johnny, "You're afraid of me. . . . I'm not afraid of you"). They engage in disrespectful but not criminal behavior (when an elderly man with poor driving habits breaks the leg of one of the gang members, they try to straighten and start his car for him). And when the rival gang led by Chino (Lee Marvin) shows up, its outlandish shabbiness shows by contrast a certain neatness and innocence in the Blind Rebels' uniform (the insensitivity of even the socially conscious fifties allows us to assume that Chino may quite possibly be twice an outsider—a Chicano).

It is paradoxically the town that is turned into the villain—the town bully (he's been that way ever since he was a child) gets a gun and gathers together a vigilante group: those people are out for blood (even Chino's group was little more than a drunken bunch whose leader is effortlessly led to jail in order to sleep off his binge). And it is at the hands of the respectable vigilantes that Johnny suffers his Gethsemane—he is nearly killed by them (they actually do kill someone when they throw a piece of metal at Johnny, who falls off his motorcycle, which then careens into the path of an old man).

The picture allows a just few to come forward and exonerate Johnny: the girl and her policeman father enable the sheriff who has been called

in to become the missing father figure ("I don't know what you're trying to do, son. I don't think you know"). But all this figure of authority
can do is turn Johnny loose and return him to what he was. Kathie
knows this—Johnny cannot be the stranger who will take her away because he must persist in the martyrdom of the loner: when the sheriff
asks Johnny if he doesn't want to thank his witnesses, Kathie anticipates
Johnny's silence: "That's all right. He doesn't know how." Kathie may
have gotten to him (he leaves her a smile and the second-prize trophy
he had treasured so much only to make it a valuable gift), but he cannot get to her: if something changed in him, it will be simply one more
wound he must carry in him. The final shot inverts the threat of the
opening: Johnny disappears down the long, empty road alone.

Brando was disappointed in the picture: "We started out to do something worthwhile, to explain the psychology of the hipster. But somewhere along the way we went off the track. The result was that instead
of finding why young people tend to bunch into groups that seek expression in violence, all that we did was show the violence" (in
Thomas, *Marlon,* p. 83). This was not quite so, as we have shown. But
in showing more of the violence and less of the reasons for it, the
movie was developing an idiom to which the young responded: for
them the message was quickly becoming the rebellious act; soon, they
would be beyond reasons. *The Wild One* was a shocker and therefore
not the immediate success its producers had hoped for; in England, it
was banned until 1968. Before *The Wild One,* rebellion represented an
attempt to return to what the object of the rebellion had obscured—it
took place within the memory of a paradise lost. Now, rebellion was
becoming a fever in the blood, an opposition without justification.

After *The Wild One,* Marlon Brando went on to the spectacular triumph of *On the Waterfront* (1954) and other major pictures that kept
him in the public eye as one of America's foremost screen actors. But
that was later, when he fell into a more public domain. *The Wild One*
was one of the sluice gates of the fifties: its tone and its idiom would
belong to the young for the next twenty years.

Perhaps because the figure of marginal and defiant youth was so readily accepted in many forms, it took some time to differentiate the loners. At the start, James Dean was thought of as the new Marlon Brando.
It was Brando whom Elia Kazan had wanted for *East of Eden* (1954),
the picture that made an overnight star of the previously unknown
Dean. And, for a while, Dean patterned himself on the already estab-

lished Brando, understanding early on that the separation between the cinema actor and his role (a separation seldom encouraged by Hollywood) had to be merged in an act of social consciousness: "He dressed sloppier than Brando, was even more tactless, and, with his all-night carousing, motorcycle riding and race-car driving, was considered even wilder than Brando" (Morella and Epstein, p. 86). When Bosley Crowther of the *New York Times* first saw *East of Eden,* he noted that Dean "scuffs his feet, he whirls, he pouts, he sputters, he leans against walls, he rolls his eyes, he swallows his words, he ambles slack-kneed—all like Marlon Brando used to. Never have we seen a performer so clearly follow another's style" (in Morella and Epstein, p. 88). What Crowther did not see at the time was that with only three motion pictures to his credit, this forlorn figure would establish himself as a universal emblem—perhaps, indeed, because he was *not* imitating anyone but was the look-alike of an entire generation. Shortly after James Dean's fatal accident, Edgar Morin noted,

> There is a legend that he miraculously survived his accident, that it was a hitch-hiker who was killed, that James Dean was disfigured, unrecognizable, perhaps unconscious; that he has been shut up in an insane asylum or a hospital. Every week, 2,000 letters are mailed to a living James Dean. Living where? In a no-man's land between life and death. . . . This is why one young girl cried out: "Come back, Jimmy, I love you! We're waiting for you!" during a showing of *Giant.* . . . That is why *James Dean Returns* by Joan Collins has sold more than 500,000 copies. [*The Stars* (1960), p. 132]

Before the young won their battles, the characters defined by John Garfield in the forties, and the Newmans, Clifts, Brandos, or Deans in the fifties, were called juvenile delinquents. In 1954, Elia Kazan, with "his finger quite shrewdly on the pulse of contemporary thinking" (Pettigrew, p. 103), had taken Steinbeck's reworking of biblical themes and condensed them into the generational conflict between a father and his angry, destructive son; Kazan's *East of Eden* made of James Dean in his very first picture the mirror image of the young who felt but could not articulate what they perceived as their parents' misunderstanding and the world's wrongheadedness.[9] Even though James Dean was an unknown among well-established actors (his father was played by Raymond Massey), his instant popularity showed the large number of those hungering for a symbol.

The numbers were so large that, by the mid-1950s, "juvenile delinquency had become a social issue, and the movie business, always the first to exploit cultural trends, began to produce low-budget, high gross films" on the subject (David Dalton, *James Dean: The Mutant King* [1974], p. 224) (there is no doubt that *East of Eden* was one of the motion pictures that capitalized on that awareness). Ten years before, Warner Brothers had purchased a book by a criminal psychologist, Dr. Robert M. Lindner. It was the case history of a young psychopath named Harold who was being treated at the Lewisburg Federal Penitentiary. The property finally devolved to a young director who had previously worked with Kazan, Nicholas Ray. Ray remembered the author and his purpose: "His own book, he told me, contained the most searching basis possible for any film on delinquency. 'You must do it this way. You must make a developmental film.' In his lectures he was going to discuss *the conflict between protest and conformity* that faced young people today. The problem of the individual's desire to preserve himself in the face of overwhelming demands for social conformism was, he felt convinced, at the heart of the subject" (in John Francis Kreidl, *Nicholas Ray* [1977], p. 88). But Ray was marching to the tune of an entirely different drummer. As Kreidl notes, it would be "thirteen years before the debunking documentary approach even had a chance against the youth myth, and eighteen years before debunking it became popular" (p. 88). Not only was Ray going to fuel the youth myth, he was going to provide it with its most visible and lasting symbol.

Lindner was aware of the repressive and deleterious effects of conformity. He saw the young of his time as being different from those of previous ones: they acted out their feelings of isolation but did so, paradoxically, by "running in packs." This, he felt, robbed them of their identity and submitted them to yet another kind of compliance. Ray departed completely from Lindner's thesis by keeping that rebellion individualistic and by providing the rebel with a framework to which he might return. The character of Harold was thus replaced by that of Jimmy Stark, a substitution that privileged the myth over the clinical study—the first name being Dean's and the second an anagram of Trask, the family name of Dean's character in *East of Eden*.

The film became James Dean's in other ways as well and reflected his world closely. Leonard Rosenman, who had written the music for *East of Eden* and was by now a close friend of Dean, said, "Nick Ray didn't know anything about Jim Stark. It was up to Jimmy Dean to find out" (in Dalton, p. 232). As a result, Ray allowed Dean "to improvise acting and dialogue" (Kreidl, p. 81). It is clear that part of the director's intention was to make the picture as true to life as possible by injecting real, parafictional life into it. Ray put out a casting call for the gang members and asked questions like, "How did you get along with your mother?" to the hundreds of youngsters who responded (Dalton, p. 227): in that way, he ended up with nine actors who were nonprofessional but who had presumably unhappy family relations. Even Natalie Wood was cast for reasons that had little to do with her acting ability:

> I wasn't going to cast Natalie Wood in the picture because she's a child actress, and the only child actress who ever made it as far as I'm concerned was Helen Hayes. But after Nat's interview, she left, and outside waiting for her was this kid with a fresh scar across his face, so I said, "Let's talk again." She seemed to be on that kind of trip. [And, a little while later at a police station, after Natalie suffered a concussion in a car accident] she grabbed me and pulled me close to her and whispered in my ear, "You see that son of a bitch?" and she pointed to the precinct doctor. "Well, he called me a juvenile delinquent. Now do I get the part?" [in Dalton, pp. 227–28]

Stewart Stern, who authored the final script, was also generationally right—in his early twenties. His notes for the characters read in part, "Jim (James Dean): The angry victim and the result. At seventeen, he is filled with confusion about his role in life. Because of his 'nowhere' father, he does not know how to be a man. Because of his wounding mother, he anticipates destruction in all women. And yet he wants to find a girl who will be willing to receive his tenderness" (in Dalton, p. 228). It is in the casting of the "nowhere" father and the wounding mother that the attempt to preserve "real" characters broke down. Ray was so intent on having the father contribute justification to the son's revolt that he gave Jim Backus the part, the comic actor known for his roles in *I Married Joan* and *Gilligan's Island*—credentials that cast some doubt on the character's seriousness. The mother's definition was even more a caricature: she was the woman as bitch, an overly emphatic cliché of the castrating female. This combination resulted in a man so emasculated as to be inarticulate and indecisive in any exchange with his son (and wearing a frilly apron to drive home the point), while the woman was little more than a self-centered neurotic filtering every human crisis through concerns for her own well-being. These two alone belied the title because they gave Jim Stark more than ample cause to be a rebel (and suggested that when Ray abandoned Lindner's story, he should have jettisoned the title as well: it identified only the psychologist's book).

In reviewing *The James Dean Story,* a compendium of photographs, film clips, letters, and interviews released by Warner Brothers in 1957, the London *Times* saw "a lonely young man, haunted by insecurity, longing for affection yet thrusting it away from him, gifted yet suspecting his gifts, ambitious yet preferring to live like a tramp, in love, like T. E. Lawrence, with speed, and hugging a surly manner around him like a protecting cloak" (Morella and Epstein, pp. 94–95). Though accurate as far as it goes, this conflation of the fictional and real-life persons does not compose the total picture. The myth was made up of many more elements that may have added up to a more simplistic picture.

The definition of juvenile delinquency was first the antisocial or criminal behavior of adolescents. When the problem became widespread, it was necessary to determine its causes, but once the youth cult had fully blossomed, causes were no longer sufficient—culprits had to be found for the anger, destructiveness, and self-pity of the young: parents and society as a whole were discovered to be guilty. It was within this structure of guilt that the young defined themselves. They felt themselves to be, as Lindner had surmised, a society within society, with special clothes (blue jeans, leather jackets), emblems, hairstyles (the slightly pompadoured look of the boys that had already helped defined a first group of postwar marginals—the zoot suiters— contrasting themselves to the short hair and even the crew cuts of the more regimented). It is very possible that this peer recognition allowed the Brandos and Deans of the fifties to find their character so accurately and for the spectators to accept them so readily. And at this point, a natural symbiosis produced the faltering speech of Method acting, denoting both a suspicion of words and an inability or reluctance to articulate suffering (thus the inarticulateness of Johnny, unable to say thank you in *The Wild One*).

That suffering was first the child's at the hands of unfeeling parents and a repressive society. The initial shot of Jim Stark in *Rebel* shows him crawling on the ground, playing with a toy monkey, while the sound of police sirens is heard. He is also playing at being more drunk than he is—a sense he dispels at the police station when he soberly demands the return of his toy. Dean was the perfect representation of someone caught between two worlds—half child, half adult, brutal and tender, masculine and not quite masculine. He drinks milk rather than the alcohol we thought of during the first scene (absence of the mother? need for nurturing?). When he hides in the abandoned mansion of Plato (Sal Mineo) with Judy (Natalie Wood), the three compose an imitation family but avoid the sexuality of the couple: there is as much bonding between Jim and Judy as there is between Jim and Plato (whose locker pinup is Alan Ladd). Morin has noted that in *Rebel* (as in *East of Eden* and *Giant*) the woman sought by James Dean is the woman-sister: "Sexual love is still enclosed within a sororal-maternal love" (*The Stars,* p. 127).

The hero's childlike suffering is also Christlike: unable to get his parents' attention, Jim says, "I don't know what to do . . . except die on them." In fact, death remains throughout a threat and a wish (as had been, in a way, the terrible speed of the huge Harleys in *The Wild One*): when Jim's father tries to make light of his son's predicaments by telling him that in ten years they will have faded into proper perspective, Jim spits out, "Ten years!" He repeats the words later as if they were the evidence of someone who cannot understand that there is no future. But the death wish is a rage to destroy more than just the self, and the hero's innocence contrasts shockingly with his brutality: the gang plays a game of chicken, driving cars at full speed toward the edge of a cliff, and Buzz, the gang leader, dies. Jim, unable to die in order to get his parents' attention (he jumps out of the car before it goes over the cliff), tries to strangle his father and destroys the painting of his mother by kicking it.

Nicholas Ray had documented that brutality firsthand with the co-operation of the Culver City Police, social workers, and psychiatrists: "In listening to these adolescents talk about their lives and their acts, two impressions always recurred. What they did had a terrifying, morose aimlessness—like the sixteen-year-old boy who ran his car into a group of young children 'just for fun'—and a feeling of bitter isolation and resentment about their families" (in Dalton, p. 225). It is to be noted that in his research, as in his picture, Ray remained nonjudgmental, but Stern did encapsulate the bonding death wish and emptiness of these rebels in a scene between the gang leader and Jim, whom he has previously ostracized but who, he now knows, will participate with him in the death run (which is a central moment—the working title of the picture was *The Blind Run*):

Buzz: This is the edge, boy. This is the end.
Jim: Yea.
Buzz: I like you, you know?
Jim: What are we doing this for?
Buzz: We got to do *something*. Don't we?

Strangely, after these intransigently one-sided portrayals, the picture offers its principals a haven. The intimacy between Jim and Plato has been symbolized throughout by Jim's jacket, with which he tries to keep Plato warm.[10] At the end, Plato shoots a member of the gang, panics, and is shot by the police. Jim's father, mistaking him for Jim because of the jacket, thinks that his son has died: when he discovers that Jim is alive, the parents are reconciled with their son and his girl in a final scene of smiling tenderness.

Rebel without a Cause was made ten years after the end of the war. The country still enjoyed a relative, war-induced affluence: the emptiness and the corruption identified by the picture are in the suburbs, the kids are all from well-to-do homes (they have something to be saved for—Brando's Johnny was too proletarian for salvation). But as in the case of Johnny and his gang, their emptiness is manifest in the missing father: each of the juveniles we know—Jim, Judy, Plato—is looking for a father (Jim: "Can I talk to you, Dad? . . . I have to talk to somebody. *Dad?*" Judy, whose father would not let her kiss him: "He looked at me like I was the ugliest thing in the world. He doesn't like my friends. He doesn't like anything about me. . . .—my own father!" Plato, whose absent father sends him only checks, hears the astronomer talk about the extinction of the planet and whispers, "What do they know about man alone?").

The absence of the father is not only the absence of love (the mothers are conveniently absent or conveniently castrating): it is the absence of the role model, the missing authority figure (Jim: "If I felt I belonged some place"; or trying to make his father understand the gravity of Buzz's death: "You better give me something, Dad. You better *give* me something fast. . . . Dad? Aren't you going to stand up for me? [Screams.] *Dad?*"). The single congenial adult in *Rebel* is proof of this need: that adult, the role model par excellence and the official superego, is the police officer who heads the Juvenile Precinct, Detective Ray Framek.[11] His door is always open; he will not only listen, he will actively save his wards by not allowing them to retreat into themselves (Jim: "Leave me alone." Ray: "No."). Symbolically, he rubs off even on Jim's father, who is sitting next to him in the squad car just before the final reconciliation.

Detective Ray's is but one of a number of strange metamorphoses in *Rebel without a Cause*. In addition to the police detective who becomes a father, the castrated man who is turned into both a man and a father (father to Jim: "I'll try to be as strong as you want me to be"), the

castrating woman who is altered into a mother,[12] there is the police itself. As in *The Wild One* (in the figures of the town's policeman and the
sheriff), it ends up being the superego rather than the repressive
agency whose ominous sirens we heard as the film opened (that superego was useless for Johnny: here, we are given implausible hope). And
in killing Plato, the police bullet removes the homosexual temptation
so that in the final apotheosis the hero can claim the rebellious daughter now transformed into the girl next door.

Judy's transformation is perhaps the most puzzling of all: when she
contributes to the illusory picture of the ideal family in Plato's abandoned mansion, she counterstates Jim's real parents, who want him to
leave his dangerous world and reenter theirs (Mother: "I don't want
him to go to the police! There were other people involved and why
should he be the only one involved!" Jim: "A boy was *killed!* You don't
get out of that by pretending it didn't happen." Father: "You know you
did wrong. That's the main thing, isn't it?"). But when Jim attempts to
save Plato, who is running toward his own death, Judy tries to restrain
him in exactly the same way—she admits that Plato needs him but insists, "I need you too!" There is no understanding the ending of *Rebel
without a Cause* unless one is to assume on the part of Nicholas Ray a
bitter irony that the rest of the picture fails to demonstrate. Stewart
Stern said that the purpose of his script "was to tell the story of a generation growing up—in one night" (in Dalton, p. 258): he did not say
that this implied a return to the fold.

But no one was listening to the picture's end: in the idiom of *Rebel
without a Cause,* happy endings were out of style by 1955. The film
was already an archaism: it achieved its success only because of the selective response of its audiences.

Dean had done his own research: "The thing that interested me in
Rebel was doing something that would counteract *The Wild One.* I
went out and hung around with kids in Los Angeles before making the
movie. Some of them even call themselves 'wild ones.' They wear
leather jackets, go out looking for somebody to rough up a little. These
aren't poor kids you know. Lots of them have money, grow up and become pillars of the community! Boy, they scare me!" (in Dalton, pp.
262–63). As it turned out, Ray and Dean did not counteract Brando.
What the audience picked up in *Rebel* was neither the unlikely ending
nor the probing that led up to it; they responded instead to the rebellious gesture, to the hurt and desire to hurt that had been *The Wild*

One's less mediated gist. *Rebel* suggested through Detective Ray the possibility of dialogue and affirmed the success of that dialogue in the final reconciliation. This limited the absolute nature of the rebels' intransigence: the audience thus limited its attention to the film's anger and its apocalyptic moments.

When it opened in October, *Rebel without a Cause* was stuck in the wake of history. To Marlon Brando, himself stranded on a reef of sanity from which the difference between art and life was still apparent, Dean had already outstripped his movie: "I spoke to [Dean]. I took him aside and asked him didn't he know he was sick? That he needed help?" (in Dalton, p. 195). Events were moving too fast for even the very tenuous line that still separated the characters of *Rebel* from their real selves. The picture that had been so much James Dean's failed to keep up with him: unable to contemplate happy endings, the hero had already found his absolute—he had killed himself in a car crash a few weeks before the film was released.[13] And beyond the blandishments of the silver screen, the dialogue proposed by Detective Ray had already been stilled in the rebels' deafness. What resonated within them was not salvation through the goodwill of an authority figure but, rather, the Music of the Spheres and the astronomer's voice concluding, "Destroyed as we began, in a burst of gas and fire." What they saw was the savagery of Jim's rebellion against his parents; what they heard was, "This is the edge, boy. This is the end." The late sixties and early seventies were on the horizon.

The rebel's gesture was by now a gratuitous act: it aimed at neither catharsis nor social improvement; it was a sounding board that was made to vibrate for the sheer bittersweet pleasure of its amplification. As such, it did not disturb the capitalist monster that had presumably engendered the suburbs, their ills and their rebels: for about two years, James Dean had it all—the fame, the money, *and* the anarchic life that fame and money allowed him to live. In so doing, he combined the American Dream with the more modish dream of rebellion. But the American Dream as big money outlived him: even though he was already gone by the time *Rebel without a Cause* came out, one last James Dean picture would feed box office receipts—the following year's *Giant*.

NOTES

1. David M. Potter (*People of Plenty,* 1954) notes how "economic abundance" allowed the postwar growth of families and their paradoxical under-

mining. Something as simple as the possibility for the middle class to afford the luxury of space in its housing "destroyed the extended family" as it gave the child a sense of "his separateness as an individual" (p. 195).

2. This was true not only in the United States but in Europe as well. See the close correlation of the comparative charts and figures in Jacques Durand's *Le Cinéma et son public* (1958).

3. Harold Clurman explains, "The purpose of the Stanislavsky Method is to teach the actor to put the whole gamut of his physical and emotional being into the service of the dramatist's meaning" (*The Collected Works of Harold Clurman* [1994], p. 371).

4. The part fit, even though he had first turned down the role in the play because he felt "it was a size too large for me" (in Bob Thomas, *Marlon* [1973], p. 40).

5. The statement is topical enough, but the "really" takes something away from its conviction, especially as Brando went out of his way to be as outrageous as possible in his interviews—and also in view of the fact that, very early on, he had made his father his investment counselor and never discontinued that trust.

6. Nevertheless, he refused to do the picture for less than forty thousand dollars, a substantial sum for a first picture in 1950. And he turned down Kazan on the filming of *Streetcar* until he had raised the initial offer of fifty thousand dollars to seventy-five.

7. The same censors worked to attenuate the sexual rawness implicit in the Brando–Leigh encounter by forcing Williams to pencil out the play's reference to the homosexuality that led to the death of her husband.

8. Otis Guernsey noted in the New York *Herald Tribune* the bursting forth of Brando's "animal vigor" (quoted by Joe Morella and Edward Z. Epstein, *Rebels* [1971], p. 71).

9. Pauline Kael writes, "The romance of human desperation is ravishing for those who wish to identify with the hero's amoral victory: everything he does is forgivable, his crimes are not crimes at all, because he was so terribly *misunderstood*" (*I Lost It at the Movies* [1965], p. 56).

10. That symbolic jacket survived along with other symbols. A 1991 catalogue (The J. Peterman Co.) features a James Dean Jacket: "How did it happen? Unknown kid from Indiana. Only three movies. Immediately, overwhelmingly famous. Then dead. Dead in a car crash. Aged 24. Killed but unkillable. 36 years later he's everywhere. Alive in a million grainy black and white posters. There's his face right now looking at you along mean streets in Paris, in Dublin, in Greenwich Village. . . . James Dean Jacket. Classic American windbreaker. No better, no worse."

11. In a picture in which so many of the characters are supposed to be playing themselves, Nicholas Ray's sympathetic ear is called Detective Ray.

12. Representations of male impotence via the castrating woman are inscribed within a specific acceptance of gender relations: reversal of the tradi-

tional binary opposition (men over women) signifies disorder and male weakness (if the presumption of order were not assumed within this binary opposition, the castrating woman would not threaten disorder).

13. Morin writes, "The mythological hero encounters death in his quest for the absolute. His death signifies that he is broken by the hostile forces of the world, but at the same time, in his very defeat, he ultimately gains the absolute: immortality" (*The Stars,* p. 123).

10

The Western in an Age of Suspicion: John Wayne, James Stewart

Because Hollywood is on the Pacific—that is to say on the western-most edge of the country—and because that is where motion pictures grew up, the movie Western comes into being at the end of the frontier dream and nurtures even at its birth an inescapable nostalgia. The last big cattle drives had run their course half a dozen years before Thomas Edison applied for patents on the Kinetograph and, even earlier, the standard-gauge track had been adopted, allowing the rapid develop-ment of railroad networks around the transcontinental lines shrinking the distance between East and West: in a sense, every Western from the very first is in some way about the ending of the West.

Still, nostalgia can be many kinds of longing: it may recall the sunrise as well as the twilight. As we have seen (chapter 1), the earliest Westerns were still informed with the westward project: they moved the city dweller *outward*, through them he relived the enthusiasm of an impossi-ble adventure and an impossible escape. Being obsolete at the start, the genre was able to endure as a constantly renewed archaism. After the new loners, the Brandos and the Deans, had become emblems for large segments of the viewing public, Westerns continued to be made—and more or less within still-accepted traditions. The cowboy remained the loner he had always been, but he was different from the new loners: even though he was rootless like them, he believed in roots—and in a code. He did not wear his Weltschmerz as openly as those who turned their very essence into protest, nor did he display suicidal tendencies, being, in

Warshow's words, a creature of "style, concerned with harmonious appearances as much as with desirable consequences" (p. 141).

But even though Westerns continued to be made, and continued to be made within a recognizable convention, the contrast of the mid-century Western clearly showed the extent to which it had been affected by several kinds of aging. One of the names most commonly associated with the genre is John Ford. When he had to identify himself for a court stenographer during the McCarthy era, he said, "My name's John Ford. I make westerns" (Peter Bogdanovich, *John Ford* [1978], p. 19). Even though his name was associated with important pictures of a different kind, like *The Informer* (1935), *The Grapes of Wrath* (1940), or *How Green Was My Valley* (1941), by far the greatest number of his films had been Westerns and would continue to be throughout his active, sixty-year career. When Peter Bogdanovich suggested to him, "Your picture of the West has become increasingly sad over the years— like the difference in mood, for example, between *Wagon Master* and *Liberty Valance*," Ford replied, "Possibly—I don't know—I'm not a psychologist. Maybe I'm getting older" (Bogdanovich, p. 100).

There is no doubt that Ford was getting older—he was sixty-seven when he made *The Man Who Shot Liberty Valance* (1962), and because Ford's career in films began in 1914, only very few years after the Westerns did, there was a parallel aging. The film to which Bogdanovich refers, *Wagon Master*, was made in 1950. It was similar in its story line to the most famous of all Ford's pictures, *Stagecoach* (1939)—the westward trek of a group through character-testing danger. The Mormon pioneers to whom *Wagon Master* paid tribute allowed Ford a simple affirmation: "His values were clear-cut. The good people outlasted and destroyed the evil ones. Even in a Cold War there were lines to be drawn between virtue and sin—at least in the past" (Andrew Sinclair, *John Ford* [1979], p. 155). The symbolic Mormons are headed for the San Juan, a valley "that's been reserved for us by the Lord, been reserved for His people, so we can plough it and seed it and make it fruitful in His eyes." Astride their path are the Cleggs, representations of absolute evil (John Ford was not one to complicate psychologically what was bad about his bad guys): they are murderous and very likely insane. But the covered wagons cannot be stopped; in Tag Gallagher's words, this "is a movie about *passage*," about faith "in the forward movement of life" (*John Ford: The Man and His Films* [1986], p. 267).

More than through its refusal to use color, *Wagon Master* was in many ways a black-and-white movie. A dozen years later, *Liberty*

Valance was still black and white:[1] John Ford was continuing to emphasize, sometimes with annoying insistence, truths to which he was deeply committed. But ambiguity modulates the black-and-white assertions of *Liberty Valance,* and that ambiguity may have caused Ford to think of his own aging: the picture is that of a man meditating over past enthusiasms.

Primarily a flashback, *Liberty Valance* is framed by the image of a train spewing smoke as it winds across the prairie: we are at the Iron (Horse) Age of the West. The train brings to the town of Shinbone the aging Senator Ransom Stoddard (James Stewart) and his wife Hallie (Vera Miles). Through the questioning of the newspaper editor, we learn why Ransom Stoddard has returned to Shinbone: he has come for the burial of an old friend, Tom Doniphon—whom no one in the town seems to know. Pressed to reveal his connection, Stoddard reluctantly begins the story that will lead us through flashbacks that begin when Ranse, as a young lawyer, heeded Greeley's advice to go west.

The stage bringing young Ranse to Shinbone is held up by the gang belonging to Liberty Valance (Lee Marvin). When Ranse tries to oppose the illegality of Liberty Valance's action, he is severely beaten by Valance, who also rips up his law books. Tom Doniphon (John Wayne) brings the wounded Ranse into Shinbone and calls on his girlfriend Hallie for assistance. When Ranse recovers, he works in Hallie's restaurant kitchen while waiting for customers to take note of the shingle he brought with him from back East, "Ransom Stoddard: Attorney at Law": he has patched together his law books and is now teaching Hallie to read.

Eventually, Ranse hangs out his shingle while in his spare time he conducts reading classes. He has written on the blackboard, "Education is the basis of law and order." But law and order are under attack: anti-statehood cattlemen have hired Liberty Valance to terrorize voters. As Shinbone and Ranse start to integrate their respective views, Ranse accepts a gun, and the townsfolk gather to choose representatives for the statehood convention. Liberty Valance tries to disrupt the meeting, but Ranse wins the nomination. Although advised to leave town, Ranse decides he has no choice but to confront a drunken Valance: there is a shoot-out, and Valance is killed while Ranse is wounded in the arm. And having understood by now that Hallie has fallen in love with Ranse, a drunken Tom returns to his ranch and sets fire to the room he was building for her.

Haloed as the man who killed Liberty Valance, Ranse sees his political fortunes rise and feels progressively less comfortable. He decides to leave Shinbone: "I'm going home, Tom. I'm going back East where I belong. . . . Isn't it enough to kill a man, without trying to build a life on it?" But Tom will prevent him from leaving: he discloses that it was he, not Ranse, who shot Liberty Valance and adds, "Hallie's your girl now. You taught her how to read and write. Now give her something to read and write about." What she will read and write about is history, which is what takes us back into the present. Ranse asks the journalist whether he is going to use the story and gets an unequivocal response: "No sir! This is the West. When the legend becomes fact, print the legend." The time has come for Ranse and Hallie to get back into their railroad car for the return trip. The final shot is of the train winding its way through the prairie, headed back East.

A narrative synopsis of most pictures, and of this one in particular—a translation into words—misses the essential: the statement of the image, starting with the principals. "Wayne actually played the lead," said Ford to Bogdanovich; "Jimmy Stewart had most of the scenes, but Wayne was the central character, the motivation for the whole thing. I don't know— I liked them both—I think they were both good characters and I rather liked the story" (Bogdanovich, p. 99). A reference to Tom Doniphon without the physical presence of John Wayne robs the character of his density: by 1962, the realism of motion pictures had long since replaced the ritual gesture (that once encoded a message) by the actor whose meaning derived from the layering of his previous roles.

Prior to *Liberty Valance,* Wayne had already made a dozen pictures with Ford, most of them Westerns. The "individual films of John Ford are inextricably linked in an awesome network of meanings and associations. When we realize that the man in the coffin is John Wayne, [it is] the John Wayne of *Stagecoach, The Long Voyage Home, They Were Expendable, Fort Apache, She Wore a Yellow Ribbon, Rio Grande, Three Godfathers, The Quiet Man*" (Andrew Sarris, *The John Ford Movie Mystery* [1976], pp. 177–78). John Wayne is self-referential within the tradition of the Western: the (unlikely) spectator who sees him in *Liberty Valance* for the first time will miss the depth that Tom Doniphon derives from Wayne's previous roles and his semimythic presence. If, as Renoir said, "The marvelous thing about westerns is that they're all the same film" (quoted by Joseph McBride and Michael Wilmington, *John Ford* [1975], p. 180), then the Western spectator is in the position of his Greek counterpart, who once came to the theater in order to rehearse personal emotions rather than to witness the unfolding of a plot he already knew. John Wayne's spectator reawakens his own understanding of "the archetypal hero of the West and of certain aspects of the American character" (Gallagher, p. 390).[2]

Once we know it is John Wayne lying in that coffin, we know that more than simply a character in a yet-unfamiliar story has died. But the stable with the coffin contains more than one death: in an adjoining room, there is the carcass of a dusty old stagecoach without wheels. When Stoddard wipes away the dust, he reveals the name *Overland Stage Line*—it is the same coach that once brought him to Shinbone; it is also the vehicle that had brought Wayne to stardom a quarter of a century earlier in *Stagecoach* (1939). But in 1939, the coach was moving westward, through the epic grandeur of Monument Valley, and Wayne was the faithful outlaw—faithful to ideals of justice and personal integrity, faithful to the Western's tradition (redeemed and redeeming, riding away at the end, beyond the place of his redemption). This is the dead figure of our first encounter: again as in Greek tragedy, we know how things will end; it is expected that our private rehearsals will be more important than the story.

The coach moves us into the story—the flashback that is supposed to tell us how we got here. The coach riding as it should, westward, contrasts forcefully with the alien train,[3] and it is fittingly held up by the mythical villain Liberty Valance, who introduces us to the picture's other star, James Stewart. In contrast to Wayne's rough-hewn traits, "Stewart's is a smooth face that wouldn't stand out in a crowd, gentle and full of good will, but ordinary" (Jean Roy, *Pour John Ford* [1976], p. 131). Stewart has his own mythology: we know him as well as we do John Wayne because we have met him as often before. Among others, he was the small-town idealist in *Mr. Smith Goes to Washington* and the poet-reporter in *The Philadelphia Story*.

In many of his previous incarnations, James Stewart had also been a cowboy. But he was not John Wayne, the West incarnate. However, in their emblematic roles both have the same mission—each brings his incorruptibility to a place of corruption in order to cleanse it.[4] That place of corruption is a town to which, by definition, the redeemer cannot belong. The westerner's town is smaller because it needs to contrast only with what is left of the still-pure wilderness. Away from the frontier, the center of corruption is a large city because the redeemer comes from a proportionally virtuous small town. The westerner is quiet. He leads a primitive life in an as-yet-primitive part of the land—he still has attributes of the noble savage. He is, therefore, a man of deeds rather than of words. The city dweller is already a man of words: even if the small town is not yet corrupt, it has at least domesticated the one who stands as its representative.[5]

Because the westerner comes from and returns to such a very different world, he has few illusions. He knows what corruption is and expects it. The one we may term by contrast the eastern redeemer may well appear innocent: he is likely to be surprised by the difference between his town and the one that should have been like it in spite of its larger size. In this sense, the tough skin of the westerner and the smooth face of the easterner become emblematic within a visual medium. John Ford relies extensively on this visual mythology. McBride and Wilmington have analyzed a segment of the action (as when Liberty Valance and his henchmen invade Hallie's eating place, where Ranse is helping serve the meals) in the following way:

> Valance laughs giddily at Stoddard's appearance in an apron, and trips him to the floor. Doniphon suddenly appears on the right of the screen: "That's my steak, Valance." Valance jumps up and announces, "Three against one, Doniphon." "My boy, Pompey, in the kitchen door," Doniphon replies, and Pompey is shown cocking his shotgun. . . . Doniphon, his eyes riveted on Valance, moves towards him and the two men freeze into a tableau. . . . Stoddard, who cannot abide a transgression against his moral system, breaks the impasse by "rising out of the gravy and the mashed potatoes" (as [the editor] Peabody puts it), slamming the steak on the plate, and screeching, "What's the matter? Everybody in this country *kill*-crazy?" [pp. 183–84]

The innocence of Ranse is evident here—in the feminizing apron that causes Valance's hilarity, in his sense that a steak is not worth a recourse to guns, in his *articulation* of that belief (note the spare, essential speech of the others), and finally in the fact that this man of words does not have much of a voice: he *screeches*.[6]

Because the easterner is not the man of action but the one who cerebrates, it is fitting that *The Man Who Shot Liberty Valance* should be the recollection of Ransom Stoddard. However, that also means we will see not the myth but, rather, its translation into eastern terms. Typically, the action will reverse the westward trek and make it, as in *Easy Rider,* the story of a return east. Ranse's memories are those of a man who has left Washington, D.C., briefly and experiences a sense of involuntary memory because of where he finds himself for a few hours. The genius of John Ford shows us this in the figures that people Ranse's recollection:

they are not the ones they would have been had they been shown in the proper time frame; they are older than they should be, more like the grizzled figures of the present than the young people they were at the moment the narrative describes (John Wayne was fifty-five at the time the film was released, James Stewart was a year younger, and Vera Miles was thirty-three). Though Ranse knows how remote are the events he translates, it is his present awareness that filters his perception.

Ranse is a creature of words. In his present incarnation as Senator Stoddard, he is insufferably the politician, as talky as he is pompous. Though his stodginess contrasts the ingenuousness of young Ranse, he confirms the loquaciousness of the man who first boarded the Overland Stage Line because he was heeding the *words* of Horace Greeley—the one who meant to replace the tangible western gun with the intangible words of eastern books (the blackboard emphasizes the verbal weight in this confrontation: "Education is the basis of law and order"). He brings with him his law books and his shingle: Liberty Valance will rip up the first (saying savagely, "Books? Law? Lawyer, eh? Well, I'll teach you law—Western law") and later will use his gun to eliminate from Ranse's shingle the title "Attorney at Law." But the dynamics of history are on Ranse's side. Tom tries to tell him while he is still wounded that words are no good—people like Liberty Valance understand only the gun—to which Stoddard replies, "I don't want a gun. I don't want to kill him. I want to put him in jail." Doniphon does not feel that this is a correct response: it does not show in Ranse a gut revulsion against injustice, the defining necessity of immediate naysaying (because this film is in part about the lukewarmness of civilization, Tom will be shown to be fundamentally right even though, in the case of Ranse, he is partially wrong). When Doniphon responds, "Out here a man solves his own problems," Stoddard feels that Doniphon is as bad as Valance: "What kind of a community have I come to here?"

He has indeed come to a community—but not one informed by his communal values. It is a community in which there is a place for a Liberty Valance as well as for a Tom Doniphon. But only later will Ranse realize this: this is the community of legend. In the story and in his reminiscence, Ranse has entered the West as it used to be, a place where, in a very real way, Tom is as bad as Liberty—or as good. The mythological West is a place of tradition or clichés, according to whether one accepts or does not these larger-than-life figures—the brutal outlaw against whom is measured the equally raw but moral redeemer,[7] the cowardly town marshal, the drunken newspaper editor (the custodian of words who, in the reality of the Old West, could not remain faithful to his trust). In Ranse's memory, the cliché endures even though the principals have not: Liberty and Tom are dead, the drunken editor has been replaced by a businesslike journalist, and the town marshal who survived, Link Appleyard (Andy Devine), is not anything like the cowardly buffoon Ranse remembers—we see him in the present, dignified and serene, smoking a pipe.

Even though Ranse sees them in a stagy and exaggerated way (because they are already the exaggerated stereotypes around whom stories are spun), they compose a world with its own structures and values—values that are not so very different from the bookish values that Ranse brings with him but which are preserved through individualism rather than through communal purpose. If Ford thought of John Wayne as "the central character, the motivation for the whole thing," it is because he is the one "to whom Ford assigns all the indications of worth and virtue—courtliness, skill, courage, a devotion to community principles" (John Baxter, *The Cinema of John Ford* [1971], p. 166). But in order for those virtues to be appreciated, they must be understood within the codes of a particular structure, one that has room for a Liberty Valance as well as a Link Appleyard or a Tom Doniphon. And that is precisely the structure that words, within the inflexible inscription of books, cannot accept.

When Liberty Valance tears up (but, symbolically, cannot destroy) Ranse's books, he is being true to his name—Liberty—and he is destroying them just as much for his own sake as for the sake of Tom Doniphon. It is he who is the valence of liberty[8]—the one who allows the interaction of the others, the one because of whom Tom Doniphon carries within himself (rather than within a set of books) his own moral principles. Stoddard has come to replace this balance of individualisms, Liberty's and Tom's, with an acceptance of law and order; it is the price of civilization.

As usual in the Western, a woman is the civilizing force incarnate. Though Ford thought of John Wayne as the central figure, he is only the (dead) effigy of a romantic past: the moving force at the center of this meditation on the past is Hallie. When the newspaperman asks Stoddard for his story, he glances over to Hallie, and only in response to her affirmative nod does he proceed: she is, and has been for some time, the regulating authority.

Originally, we see Hallie as Tom's girl, but she is soon seduced by the words (and books) of Ranse. "Do you think I *could?* Do you think

I *could* learn to read?" she asks Ranse, who drawls back with all the ingenuous conviction we expect of James Stewart, "Why *sure* you can,
Hallie!" But once she overcomes her diffidence, Hallie is changed from
the more primitive creature who could see no sense in Peabody's attention to the placement of table settings.[9] More precisely, she leaves
the cast of mythic characters to become the traditional woman whose
rooting instincts arrest the westward advance. In her particular case,
she reverses it: instead of the sexual rawness represented by the gun,
she chooses rational stability and will end up severing her roots in
order to move eastward.

Hallie does not turn suddenly into what she will become: even while
she remains a part of the myth, the latency of her civilizing power is
felt. She has already awakened rooting concerns in Tom, as evidenced
by the extension he is building on his ranch, a sartorial awareness
("Why, Tom, look at you! You're all dressed up!"), and the flower he
brings her. But Tom is in fact suspended between two worlds: he will
never finish his building project, the dress-up clothes are a temporary
constraint, and the flower is a cactus rose, a bloom that is both rare and
a natural part of the western landscape—and one that he brings Hallie
with its roots. Even so, Hallie will not be satisfied with such conces-
sions. Her conversion is the more visible in contrast with Ranse's: she
now helps teach class while he leaves to practice shooting, having
been sufficiently threatened by the reality of Valance to know that a
less theoretical response than law books is required. (As he goes out of
the classroom, he erases "Education is the basis of law and order.") But
each character plays out the conversion in different ways: when Hallie
hears about Ranse's acquisition of a gun, she is horrified, while out at
Tom's place, Ranse misses the target at which he aims and is made
good-natured fun of by the well-intentioned Tom.[10]

The cactus rose, like Tom, is halfway between two worlds. Even
though it is a part of the desert, its flowering denies the arid waste and
prefigures other denials. When Hallie shows Ranse the desert flower,
he understands how much he is still living in someone else's myth:
"Hallie, did you ever see a real rose?" "No," says Hallie, who then
shows the extent to which she already strains against the myth—"but
maybe some day, if they ever dam the river, we'll have lots of water,
and all kinds of flowers!"

Alongside these optimists, Tom Doniphon is a tragic figure, unwill-
ing to accept what Hallie now looks forward to, and knowing that it
must inevitably happen. He walks in the shadow of Cooper's Natty

Bumppo: like the legendary Leatherstocking, he is running out of space. But he is also cursed with clear sight: because he cannot forestall an inexorable progress, he bitterly agrees to become its agency—and as that progress is reflected in Hallie's choice, Tom's acceptance becomes intimate. He determines to save Ranse from Liberty Valance by shooting the outlaw—an act that will shatter the myth; Tom kills a part of the Old West. In fact, he shatters the myth twice: he also shoots Valance the wrong way—"Cold-blooded murder," he will say later. (As Lee Marvin recollected, "It was the only time John Wayne ever shot anybody in the back of the head" [in Sinclair, p. 196].) His dignity and allegiance to a bygone order will claim only one last ironic comment: he will let the legend say it was Stoddard, the man of words, who shot Liberty Valance. Having upset the balance of which he was a part, he continues his self-destruction by burning down the structure intended for Hallie (after having bowed to the requirement of drinking as an expression of masculine grief).

Ford uses the rugged and rare cactus rose as an emblem for Tom Doniphon: like him, it is doomed because so many threaten its survival. Ranse and Hallie are not the only ones who see its eventual replacement: the reach of (eastern) federal control grows with each declaration of statehood. Moreover, state government is little more than the legal equivalent of the ruthless anti-statehood cattlemen who also want control of the land: every powerful force conspires against the freedom of the West, and Ransom Stoddard is an active part of it. Having clearly read the handwriting on the wall, Tom seconds Ranse's nomination as representative to the territorial convention (still ironically inverting Ranse's priorities: "not only because he knows the law, but because he throws a good punch"). He himself declines the nomination (he remains with arms folded while the others in the hall are cheering wildly): the bullet in Liberty's head may have shattered the myth of which Tom was a part, but he remains too much a figure of the Old West—he looks too much like John Wayne—to help midwife the new.

Once the old structures are torn down, a dialogue of the deaf ensues that engenders only further ironies. In response to Ranse's discouragement at the seeming triumph of the gun over the book ("I'm going back East where I belong"), Tom voids the legend: he tells Ranse the truth—Ranse did not kill Liberty Valance and need not worry about "trying to build a life" on a murder. Ranse is now free to start climbing the political ladder. But only the endurance of the myth makes it possible for Ranse to start that climb—he is elected as "the man who shot Liberty

Valance." And when Ranse is finally given his mandate, it sends him east and requires that he help further destroy Doniphon's West.[11]

Now Ransom tries once more to lay the old myth to rest, even though he has become a politician, a pretentious figure of words. The Shinbone to which he has returned shows small signs of corruption inherent in its growth (Hallie says, "The place has sure changed. Churches, high school, shops") and its valorizing of goods and services: the journalist who phones his story into the *Shinbone Star* is asked for a nickel by the station master (and charges it to his boss); the undertaker steals dead Tom's boots, spurs, and gun belt. But the final irony is provided by the voice of the new Shinbone, the editor who will *not* print Ranse's story: "No sir! This is the West. When the legend becomes fact, print the legend." The legend will be preserved by a community starting to show signs of corruption—one willing to treasure the myth, not the individuals that made it.

Shinbone shortchanges itself in choosing the legend over the people in the legends. To start with, it is many times fraudulent: the man it honors contributed only words, while the man it should have honored knew his act was one of "cold-blooded murder." Still, Doniphon's lucidity was inseparable from a fundamental morality: "Cold-blooded murder. But I can live with it." In contrast, the present Shinbone has laws, set down in books, which (because of and thanks to their codifying) people are learning to get around: its law no longer rests on the personal, undeceived integrity of the enforcer. The process is unavoidable: looking at it through Doniphon's eyes, John Ford simply raises questions about its consequences.

In the compartment on the return journey, Ranse asks softly, "Hallie, would you be sorry if, once I get the new irrigation bill through, would you be too sorry if we just up and left Washington? 'Cause I, I sort of have a hankering to come back here to live, maybe open up a law office." And Hallie answers, "Ranse, if you knew how often I dreamed of it. My roots are here. I guess my heart is here. Yes, let's come back." But as she gazes out the window, Hallie knows she is indulging memory; there is in fact no return. "Look at it," she says; "It was once a wilderness, now it's a garden." Presumably, she now knows what a "real" rose is. And when she adds, "Aren't you proud?" the sentence is fraught with irony: Ransom Stoddard's words have indeed wrought a tangible change—an irrigation bill and the transformation of the land.

The necessity of that progress is played out against a variety of personal nostalgias. Somewhere, beyond Shinbone, there is still a trace of what once was. The surviving link between the old and new—Link Appleyard—had already told the returning Hallie, "Desert's still the same," and suggested, "Maybe you'd like to take a ride out desert way an' maybe look around." The symbol of that desert is the yet-enduring cactus rose. As Link and Hallie gaze at the ruins of Doniphon's ranch, she acknowledges the unspoken kinship of memory:[12]

"You knew where I wanted to go, didn't you?"
"Well, you said you wanted to see the cactus blossoms. There's his house down there, what's left of it, blossoms all around it."
"He never did finish that room he started to build on, did he?"
"No. Oh well, you know all about that."
"There's a lovely one there."

That lovely blossom is the one Hallie will place on Tom's coffin before they leave: now that there is no Shinbone left, no Tom Doniphon, Hallie is free to confess her love and the error of her choice. Like Tom before him, Ranse will have to translate into more intimate terms the meaning of those deaths in order to understand them. "Hallie," he asks, "who put the cactus rose on Tom's coffin?" Her answer intensifies the heavy silence between them: "I did." That echoing silence will last until the ironic intrusion of the conductor, who comes to assure Ranse that he will have no trouble making his connection to Washington, D.C.: "Nothing's too good for the man who shot Liberty Valance." The words arrest Ranse, who was about to bring a lit match to his smoke: it is our last image of him. As the train winds its way across the prairie, the black letters of "THE END" appear on the screen and emphasize our awareness of several kinds of death. And we realize that we have seen only twice the great outdoors for which the John Ford of Monument Valley was so famous, and each time they were streaked by the smoke-belching locomotive. We have been scrutinizing the sadness of individual faces instead of racing through the open land.

We are back in 1962. We are more distant from the new Shinbone than it was from its legend. The new Shinbone could not create legend but, rather, nurtured its memory. We now live in a time of debunking: editor Scott did not use Ranse's story—"When the legend becomes fact, print the legend." But John Ford, in 1962, prints the fact. Outliving himself, living beyond the time of even cinematic myths, John Wayne is used for the purpose of exposing a lie. Even the ingenuous James Stewart—"unfailingly nice, unwaveringly honest" (Bingham, p. 41)—once the idealistic innocent of *Mr. Smith* and a dozen similar pictures, becomes the politician whose mythical reputation we know to be fraudulent. Cinema is on its way to becoming cinéma vérité—an attempt to penetrate in the name of truth the ordinariness of what once was the myth; and the mythic figure of the star, once a self-sufficient evidence, is now questioned for the sake of a spectator more inclined to question.

NOTES

1. This gave it what Peter Stowell calls "a dark and anachronistic look" (*John Ford* [1986], p. 108).

2. Andrew Sarris adds, "There is also the pastness of Ford's own old movies, a pastness reflected in Wayne's first entrance in the film, on horseback, and adorned with the very tall hat of the earliest cowboy heroes. For a film historian with any kind of visual memory, the effect of Wayne's headgear is electrifying" (*The John Ford Movie Mystery*, p. 180).

3. This is another sign of Ford's and the Western's aging: his *Iron Horse* (1924) was infused with the enthusiasm of the westward surge; but now, Link comments ambiguously on Hallie's observation of Shinbone's growth: "Well, the railroad's done that."

4. James Stewart could therefore also be cast in Westerns, but as the "gentle" persona imposed itself, he played a more innocent westerner.

5. Of course, a part of his virtue is likely to be his manual or other skills, as demonstrated by the tinkerer Clark Gable in *It Happened One Night*, the tuba-playing Gary Cooper in *Mr. Deeds Goes to Town*, or the Spencer Tracy who can show a delinquent female the way around a kitchen in *Woman of the Year*.

6. This is one of the many Stewart traits we already know from other films—the drawling, unevenly pitched speech and diffident manner, continued evidence of a nonassertive, "non-threatening masculinity" (Bingham, p. 83).

7. When Liberty Valance tells Ranse to stop hiding behind Tom's gun, the spectator is meant to realize that these figures are bigger than life: it is at the camera, and in close-up, that Liberty spits out, "You be there, and don't make us come get ya!"

8. For a more extended discussion of this metaphor, see Gallagher, pp. 392 ff.

9. Even though her glances in the direction of Ranse sometimes confuse the man and his books (she desires both), she will still see for a while the devitalizing effect of words: "What has [legal education] done for you? Look at you, you're in an apron."

10. Of course, Ranse is not wholly an abstraction: when Tom demonstrates what real shooting is by hitting some paint cans and splattering Ranse, the frustrated easterner lands a single, incredible haymaker and floors Tom. Macho America still required in 1962 that in becoming the new incarnation of Tom Doniphon, Ransom Stoddard not lose *all* of his manly virtues—under that feminizing apron, there beats a virile heart. (This does not prevent Tom from remaining ironic: he knows that just one punch is an inadequate statement and smiles it off as, symbolically, he tosses Ranse his gun.)

11. When Wayne walks out of the building, he passes a torn, anti-statehood poster: it is like Arthur Penn's faded posters, pinned to the desolate clapboard, which comment on the Great Depression with such poignant irony in the opening scenes of *Bonnie and Clyde*.

12. The two had already been shown linked by a silent and tender glance: Link is the remaining vessel of Hallie's true love. Symbolically, when they sit down in the funeral parlor, Link, Hallie, and Pompey occupy one bench; Ranse is left alone on another.

11

The Star as Anti-Hero: Dustin Hoffman, Jack Nicholson

The fact that Westerns continued to be made right through the youth revolution documents the endurance of certain values even during times that are severely perturbed. Perhaps the link between those values is proven through the specificity of their inversion: ideas seem to be governed by the same laws that apply to the conservation of energy, frequently deriving their strength from a sensed resistance. Dean's rebel was the reverse of Wayne's Doniphon: Jim was twice a victim of society—the more so for having allowed it to dictate the terms of his rebellion—while Doniphon had little use for Stoddard's books because the code he carried within him was imprinted at least as indelibly as written words. *Liberty Valance* may have been the lament over a passing, but that very lament implied a persistence of memory in the spectator and suggested that the passing was not yet complete: in order to understand the film, the 1962 viewer required an inner reference similar to Doniphon's. The success of *Liberty Valance*, even during a time of surging opposition, allows one to assume that many did.

When the film came out, Charles R. Webb was putting the finishing touches on a manuscript he would publish the following year, *The Graduate*. Its hero, Benjamin, was about Webb's age and just out of college. His "graduation" is an initiation into the real world beyond ivy walls—first into sexual maturity by the wife of his father's business partner, later into the bliss of true love when he falls for her daughter Elaine, whom he saves from a conventional marriage and with whom he escapes into a better world. Perhaps because Webb was twenty-three as he gave his book to the publishers, he felt that Benjamin (and no less Elaine) was a rebel in the current mode, the two of them being driven by a "desire to upset things" (F. A. Macklin, "Benjamin Will Survive," p. 2). He believed "Ben is both heroic and effective" (p. 3) and that the ending was optimistic rather than ironic.

The question about the ending was put to Webb presumably because the film's resolution was less clear than the novel's—even though it left many viewers, like Stanley Kauffmann, feeling "very, very good" (*Figures of Light* [1971], p. 41). It is not unlikely that the film's ambiguity began with the persona of Dustin Hoffman—with the kind of actor he was, with what was happening to motion pictures that brought this particular actor to that particular role, and with the consequences of this sort of casting. A month after *The Graduate* was released, Adelaide Comerford praised it in her review, "despite an uninteresting and untalented actor in the title role" (p. 55)—and the following month *Films in Review* placed *The Graduate* among the ten best films for 1967. Comerford may not have known that Hoffman, who had no previous motion pictures to his credit, had made his mark on Broadway—"a young actor already known in the theater as an exceptional talent" (Kauffmann, p. 36). Comerford may have been confusing surface and substance.

The fact of the matter is that Hoffman lacked the mien and manner of the traditional young lead; he lacked even those of the heroic anti-hero of the fifties. He was neither handsome nor tall; he did not have the good looks of Gary Cooper, the mythic depths of John Wayne, the muscular sexuality of Marlon Brando, the angry and wistful alternations of James Dean—and contrary to the latter, he looked like only himself. Dustin Hoffman eventually became one of the enduring fixtures of the American screen, his acting disciplined by his undistinguished features. Where Brando and Dean had been flattering emblems for the young in midcentury who felt themselves to be disenfranchised, Hoffman was the faceless man (or better, one whose face was his own instead of being, like the star's, public property), with the kind of facelessness that would articulate individual and private concerns in the second half of the century. With Dustin Hoffman, generalized appeal fades—whether of sexuality or of political statement: he is *a* man, not a projection of *the* man. Later, the Rambos, Rockys, and others would still try to retrieve a more generalized appeal, but it was now possible for the screen male to be an entity that was both common (unexceptional) and yet peculiarly personal. In that sense, the end of stars with the passing of the studio system is more a matter of individual perception and response than an actuality: the loss of the studios' former ascendancy is less interesting than the loss of a former audience whose homogeneity would not allow this kind of perception.

Thus, at the height of the youth cult, Dustin Hoffman was not a likely (or likeable) emblem—especially if, as Pauline Kael suggests, the young were looking to movies as "part of the soap opera of their lives" (*Going Steady* [1970], p. 125). She compares them to those who once "used to live and breathe with the Joan Crawford–working girl and worry about whether that rich boy would really make her happy" (p. 125)—but the point is that Joan Crawford was the myth of Joan Crawford, an unmistakable divinity in Hollywood's pantheon, whose aura alone guaranteed that she would transcend her working-girl character and could *only* marry that rich boy. But there was no comparable aura or mythology to redeem the schlimazel in Dustin Hoffman. So that when Kael suggests that "the inarticulate dull boy becomes a romantic hero for the audience to project into" (p. 126), she is referring to a different time, when the exceptional figure was becoming the exception and when that unique, yet unexceptional person was certainly more than simply the young's vision of themselves (after all, both Brando and Dean had been inarticulate in their words but had demonstrated other kinds of articulateness that the late sixties no longer felt necessary to project).

Still, there is no doubt that *The Graduate* became one of the shrines at which the young worshipped: "If [Antonioni's] *Blow-up* was instrumental in attracting young people to film, the equivalent American landmark was Mike Nichols's *The Graduate*" (Larry Cohen, quoted by Kauffmann, p. 46). But their attraction had to do with more than simply the dumb inarticulateness of the hero. If Kael is right in surmising that *The Graduate* was evidence of the young going "back over and over to the same movies, mooning away in fixation on themselves" (p. 127), it is likely that they were doing so because it allowed them to applaud Benjamin enacting in the film, as in the book, a sense of their unhappiness, their hostility against the establishment, and their angry delight at its mockery or humiliation. Ben's father (William Daniels) and his father's friends are caricatures that help turn the first half of the film into farce. The hero screws the establishment in the person of Mrs. Robinson (Anne Bancroft), allowing himself to be seduced but abandoning her—leaving the one who is over thirty for Elaine (Katharine Ross), one of those who are more trustworthy for being well under thirty (continuing, by the way, to degrade even Elaine for as long as he sees her as an extension of his parents' world). And, finally, the discredited institution of marriage is flouted when Elaine and Benjamin run away together right after she has wed another man.

So viewed, *The Graduate* played well to the under-thirty crowd of the late sixties. But Charles Webb knew that something of his book had been lost in translation:[1] he seemed no more satisfied with the film than Nichols had evidently been with the original text. For Mike Nichols, the gestures of rebellion were gestures of futility: he did not intend them to raise "a not particularly bright, not particularly remarkable, but worthy kid, drowning. . . . Just drowning" (in Joseph Gelmis, *The Film Director as Superstar* [1970], p. 284). What the enthusiastic audience of the late sixties seems not to have seen is the insistence with which Nichols repeated images of drowning, or of imprisonment, throughout his picture. As the camera pulls away from the first shot, a close-up of Dustin Hoffman's face, he is shown to be within the crowded and narrow confines of a plane. He is returning home from college, but he does so to the notes of Simon and Garfunkel's "The Sound of Silence" ("Hello darkness, my old friend, / I've come to talk with you again").

In the airport, while loudspeakers bark commands (voices of authority that add noise and intensify a fundamental silence; one hears in the same song, "People talking without speaking / People hearing without listening"), Benjamin is carried along a blank wall by a conveyor belt, the image anticipating what he will later say to Elaine when he tries to explain himself: "It just happened. Along with everything else." He has a brief smile that is summarily extinguished: right from the start, the young were given a character out of their folklore, whom they could recognize without any explanation—someone adrift, unsure, and unhappy, as if such a state were defining. Benjamin himself asserts that definition, and the self-absorption of the me-generation, but does not explain it either: "I'm worried about my future"; and later to Mrs. Robinson, in a near repetition, "I'm a little upset about my future"; or "I'm disturbed about things."

In his room, he is shown against the walls of a large aquarium. When he is prodded downstairs to the lavish party given by his parents for his graduation (but which, judging from the guests, is really for his father's clients and cronies), he is in another kind of aquarium: the faces coming toward the subjective camera are crowding and cornering him. When he escapes to his room, he is photographed once more against the prominent aquarium. It is into that same water that Mrs. Robinson

(Anne Bancroft) will drop the Freudian keys of the car that leads him into her sexual web: Benjamin is everybody's prisoner. During the first seduction scene, the portrait of Elaine intrudes briefly between her mother and Benjamin: it is seen in passing, but as Benjamin looks at it, we note the glassed-in frame and soon the reflected image of Mrs. Robinson obscures her daughter's. Elaine, whom we have not yet met, is a kindred spirit—she too is a prisoner in many worlds.

Nichols then repeats Benjamin's sense of an imprisoning world through the subjective camera (much of the picture is Benjamin's: our point of vantage is largely his). Very soon after the homecoming party, another identical party marks Benjamin's coming of age: he is twenty-one. Behind the diver's mask he has been given as a present, Benjamin is once again caught within the enclosing, aquatic picture of his parents' guests, this time in an intensified form: the subjective camera is imprisoned within the mask. As he tries to rise to the surface of the pool into which he reluctantly dived, his father's hand pushes him down: the world of his parents is trying to drown him. (The camera follows on him as he sinks, erect, to the depths of the pool, where he remains standing like the rigid, unmoving plastic figure at the bottom of an aquarium.)

Benjamin seeks escape from this world by reentering Mrs. Robinson's, forgetting that there, too, someone else holds the keys. That her world affords as little solace is underscored by a repetition of "The Sound of Silence." Benjamin is caught between his pool-and-aquarium world and the predatory Mrs. Robinson (she wears a metallic black-and-white sheath whose tiger striping can be seen through a soft, delicate fabric: only for a while does her femininity not mask a cold, animal nature; her underwear displays the same feline patterns, and later, when they meet at the hotel, she is wearing a leopard-skin coat). Benjamin's batting back and forth is stressed by the increasingly rapid intercutting of the film. And interspersed within these scenes is the image of Benjamin's mother (Elizabeth Wilson), the black-and-white stripes of her own dress suggesting the extent to which Benjamin's escapade may be an attempt to return to the womb (a suggestion stressed by the especially compelling scene in Benjamin's bedroom, in which his mother enters wearing an open, black-and-white negligee).

As Benjamin's affair with Mrs. Robinson drags on, roles are reversed. Her need for him grows while he tires. Their rift is occasioned by the return of her daughter Elaine, in whom the mother senses a threat. (Mrs. Robinson, for all her domineering coldness, has given Benjamin ample evidence of her insecurity: she has confessed her unhappiness to him—

"Did you know I was an alcoholic?" And in a scene in which the tiring Benjamin tries to make talk, suggesting art as a topic, she tells him she knows nothing about art; still trying to find a subject, he asks her about her major college interest: the camera focuses on her distressed face as she tells him, art. But Benjamin is too self-centered to be sympathetic.) When Mrs. Robinson forbids him to see her daughter, he feels debased by the woman who used him for her own needs but does not find him good enough for her daughter; he is brutal in his anger ("You go to hell, Mrs. Robinson!") and spits out his disgust at "spending my life with a broken-down alcoholic." She is now the weaker one and apologizes; he responds, "Let's not talk about it. Let's not talk at all."

The young audience of the late sixties may have treated Mrs. Robinson with the same kind of dismissive rage as Benjamin—but Nichols did not. Her refusal to allow Benjamin to date her daughter stresses her jealousy occasioned by the fear of loneliness (she had already told him ruefully, "I'm twice your age"). Benjamin's brutal response may have been cheered by the generation that started cheering when Jim kicked his mother's portrait, but at a distance it emphasizes the extent to which this hungry woman is forlorn (when later she tries to come between Elaine and Benjamin, she is caught in a driving rain and shown in the destroyed sheathing that had symbolized her strength and disguised her aging: the image of drowning is not reserved for Benjamin alone).

Nor is she able to prevent the intrusion of her daughter: coerced by insensitive parents, Benjamin dates Elaine and makes her suffer for being an extension of their world. While he drives with vengeful recklessness, it is she who tries to make talk:

"Do you know what you're going to do?"
"No."
"Are you going to graduate school?"
"No."
"Do you always drive like this?"
"Yes."

He then takes her to a strip joint and makes remarks that are deliberately degrading. It is only after this extended show of resentment that he at last removes his dark glasses and sees the real rather than the symbolic Elaine—a young girl crying. Now he can explain that, since he graduated, "it's a sort of compulsion. I have to be rude the whole time": his is the meager revolt of a kid who, in Nichols's words, did not have the stuff "to rebel, to march, to demonstrate, to turn on" (in Gelmis, p. 284). Though Benjamin says to Elaine, "You're the first person I could stand to be with," and starts dating her, the sounds of Simon and Garfunkel's "April Come She Will" assert in counterpoint the decay of love: the very music of the young is thrust into an ironic commentary.

In an act of desperation, Mrs. Robinson destroys herself in order to drive a wedge between the young people: she forces Benjamin to tell Elaine about their liaison. Elaine is disgusted, and the camera moves between two kinds of desolation, from Mrs. Robinson, in her black dress soaked by the downpour, to Benjamin, once again before the large aquarium. Eventually, Benjamin tears himself away from this image of imprisonment and leaves in pursuit of Elaine, first to the Berkeley campus; then to Mrs. Robinson's, where in frustration at finding the mother rather than the daughter, he overturns the furniture; and, in due time, to the church where Elaine is going to be married to the kind of man her parents would approve of—a preppy type, complete with sports clothes and pipe. Benjamin's race to the church is photographed in part through a 600-mm lens: although he is running as fast as he can toward the camera, the powerful telephoto flattens distance and gives him the appearance of being once again on a treadmill.

Blind (as was a good part of the audience) to Nichols's symbolism, Benjamin—still imprisoned by glass—bangs on a church window while Elaine and Carl recite their marriage vows. Benjamin succeeds in getting her attention—and her: she rushes toward him screaming, "Ben!" And to her mother's "It's too late," she answers, "But not for me!"[2] That assertion may turn Mrs. Robinson's admonition into self-commentary; if so, it emphasizes further her distress and explains the predatory woman as someone who is both desperate and pathetic. But it certainly does not free the young people. Benjamin, who has no will "to rebel, to march, to demonstrate, to turn on," becomes physically brutal once again: he uses a huge crucifix as a scythe to ward off the members of the wedding party and then locks them in the church by using the crucifix as a bolt. But flouting religious interdicts allows the young couple to escape only long enough for Nichols to imprison them once again and finally: we see them cornered in the backseat of a departing bus and pick up images from the film's opening moments. The passengers in front turn to stare at them: they are the same grotesques as at the party (though seedier), composing a wall of uncomprehending eyes. Realization of her entrapment seems to show on the face of Elaine. The camera moves to Benjamin: he is smiling. The camera moves back to Elaine's face—her expression has not changed. When the camera swings back to Benjamin, his smile has disappeared. Our last image is that of the bus pulling away from us, with the two figures behind the glass of the rear window. And so that there will be no mistaking this last image of entrapment, "The Sound of Silence" accompanies their departure.

The critics and rebels of 1967 may have felt elated by *The Graduate*'s ending, but Mike Nichols did not share their euphoria. In speaking to Gelmis, Nichols said, "When I saw those rushes [of the ending] I thought: 'That's the end of the picture. They don't know what the hell to do, or think, or say to each other. . . . in five miles she's going to say, 'My God, I haven't got any clothes'" (p. 283). In the audience, the rebels' response was triggered by the immediacy of certain images; but the critics should have been mindful of Nichols's *Who's Afraid of Virginia Woolf?*, the Albee play he had turned into a motion picture the year before. There, too, an outwardly hopeful ending had been subverted: when Martha (Elizabeth Taylor) puts her hand on George's as the sun rises and she admits her need for the structures she has attacked so savagely throughout the night ("Who's afraid of Virginia Woolf?" "I am, George, I am"), George (Richard Burton) is given the last word: "Sunday tomorrow, all day"—an acknowledgment of recurrence and staleness, whose subversive resonance is emphasized through the camera's focus on the lyric light beyond the window and the loving touch of Martha's hand.

This nearly metaphysical sense of the individual's inability to break free continued to be at the center of Nichols's pictures. It is true of *Carnal Knowledge* (1971), in which Jonathan (Jack Nicholson) and Sandy (Arthur Garfunkel) are left at the end with only the words of their masculine definition, the same words that were once going to propel them (like Martha) into their glowing vision of the future. It is as true of *Working Girl* (1988), when, after Melanie Griffith has clawed her way to the top, the camera slowly pulls back from her managerial office, through the window, to show that her new world is caught within a multitude of others with identical spaces in the huge blank face of the skyscraper. "I'm not sure my pictures need to be linked together," Nichols told Frank Rich, "but in my mind they're almost the same picture over and over again" ("The Misfortune of Mike Nichols").

Those who would be a part of the often violent confrontations that were to start a year or so later could only approve of the picture of Benjamin's world and the gestures of his rebellion against it. His parents, the Robinsons, and their common friends were all caricatures of affluence, mendacity, and shallowness. *The Graduate* did not even attempt to show them as truly dangerous—they were no more than punching bags created for the pleasure of hitting them: no one asked whether such insubstantial figures even warranted the commitment of genuine anger. But having put in place this largely farcical cast (in a film that is also very funny), Nichols used the subtlety of his camera, the irony of his distance from a modish idiom, and the emergence of a new kind of actor to create a character whose dramatic texture was entirely different. Benjamin was supposed to be the suffering victim of these puppets: the expensive cloth that gave them their shape and their hollow heads was somehow able to do him harm.

Like Benjamin, Brando and Dean had been at war with their parents, with accepted conventions, with a society judged to be stifling. But they were flamboyant in their rejection and carried their pain like a trophy: their gesture of revolt may have been doomed, but that was unimportant alongside the flourish of its enactment. Dustin Hoffman belonged to a different time, when grand gestures and charismatic figures were obsolescent: Mike Nichols could no longer emphasize, as Nicholas Ray had, the epic postures of nonconformists. Because he had to work with more common clay, Nichols chose instead to focus on the reality of defeat. Young spectators may still have cheered the actions of the rebel, but Nichols was concentrating on their futility. (It is possible that *The Graduate* was a huge box office success because each segment of the audience was listening to the message it wanted to hear.)

Nichols summarized the character of Benjamin as that of a young man "finding part of himself that he hadn't found through connection with a girl. Finding passion because of impossibility. Impossibility always leads to passion and vice versa. Going from passion to a kind of insanity. Saving himself temporarily from being an object, through the passion and insanity. Getting what he thinks he wanted and beginning to subside back into the same world in which he has to live, with not enough changed. I think that's the story" (in Gelmis, p. 284). Those words of Nichols were most likely writing more than simply Benjamin's epitaph. Nichols was also writing the eventual epitaph of the youth revolution that had not yet reached its climax. He was writing finally the epitaph of a certain kind of picture, the one whose human dimension was magnified by the presence of the star. With *The Graduate,* Mike Nichols enters a workaday world whose people are so ordinary

and undistinguished that they require close scrutiny to understand the
reason for their existence.

Three and a half years after *The Graduate,* Nichols's *Carnal Knowledge,* a story about the disintegration in middle age of college-day
dreams, had its premiere at the Cinema I in New York. From the opening credits on, the picture centered on the principals' obsessions with
male–female relations: Jonathan and Sandy are first the voice-over of
college students—the battle of the sexes is the prattle of sex. Sandy,
played by an awkward-looking Arthur Garfunkel, dwells on the success of what is an abortive sexual encounter with Susan—Candice
Bergen—who appears dominant alongside him. Encouraged by
Sandy's verbal triumph, Jonathan (Jack Nicholson) assumes a "sensitive" role in his own attempt to seduce Susan: he talks about his father,
a failure under whose thumb he still lives. Because Jack Nicholson
looks older and stronger than Jonathan's words would suggest, his tac-
tical speech turns into an unintended admission of weakness—he has
already confessed to Sandy that he is afraid of being hurt.

His strategy is successful to the extent of getting Susan to have sex
with him—another abortive experience in which neither one of them
takes pleasure but which affords Jonathan the same kind of verbal triumph Sandy had previously enjoyed. Susan herself is caught up in this
initiatory ritual: it is an act she performs (with Jonathan "standing, sitting, in the car, under the car") while worrying about the safety of con-
traceptives and trying to sort out her conflicting feelings for both
men—or rather, both half men, for each provides her with only a part
of what she wants. Jonathan insists that she choose between them: she
is unable to and they break up. All he will have had of her is their sexual encounters, an awareness whose unsatisfactory nature Nichols
stresses in the solarized scene of a woman in white skating against a
white background—Jonathan's dream of the primeval virgin, the center of his sexual obsession, the idealized Susan who will be missing
from all his future encounters.

The fade-out of that image introduces an actual skater in Rockefeller
Center, where Sandy and Jonathan, now middle-aged, have met. It is
fifteen years later, in the sixties. Their talk is still what it was in college
(as a woman walks by, we learn that Jonathan "fucked her once"): they
are still exorcising what Rosalind Miles terms "the naïve faith in penis-
power . . . , the existential dread of the fallible phallus" (*The Rites of
Man,* p. 1). Sandy's life is no better: he has settled into the doldrums of

matrimony with a boring Susan; he sighs, "Maybe it's just not meant to be enjoyable with women you love." Even as grown men they still have only carnal knowledge of any relationship with women and are equally empty. At every moment when talk with a woman might turn serious, Jonathan seeks refuge in the shower, interrupting the drift he fears and allowing him to try washing away the soiling encounter to which he restricts himself. As a result, he fails to hear the pleas of Bobbie (Ann-Margret), the model with whom he is presently sleeping: she tries to commit suicide. He is forced into a brief marriage, from which he will conclude only that "she conned me into marrying her, and now she's killing me with alimony."

The next decade finds both men still analyzing their lives as sexual incidents. By this time, Sandy too has become a philanderer: the two are looking at Jonathan's slide show, "Ball Busters on Parade" (which includes Susan). Shortly after, they drift apart: even they have tired of their single topic and have nothing more to say to each other. Our last view of Jonathan is with a prostitute telling him how virile he is: he has sunk to the very bottom of a wholly verbal world—the only one he knows. Carnal knowledge is not knowledge at all. Sandy and Jonathan have become demonstrations of Joe Orton's man, a life-support system for his penis.[3]

Because our final image is of Jonathan, we assume that Jack Nicholson is the main actor in the picture: Sandy, who was never more than a part of their talk, has now gone off; Susan disappears completely during the second part of the film. But with Susan's disappearance, first from Jonathan's life and then from the film itself, the men are reduced to their words. Nicholson, who looks like an acceptable man, is, as a character, nothing more than an impotent talker—someone who first substitutes sex for other human dimensions and finally substitutes words for sex. Alongside him, the slim, athletic, slightly mannish Candice Bergen seems especially *real*. The reductive Jonathan and Sandy (with the androgynous name) make her look alive even during the dilemmas of her initiatory alternations. But she is even more a presence when she disappears: she is the core of reality that has been removed from both men, who now compose the sham of their being around her absence.

It is as difficult to envision a star of the past in Jonathan's role as it is to understand critics who allow their social consciousness to read the same message in whatever motion picture they see.[4] Stars commanded the screen, and it shone with their radiance. They could be as self-centered and destructive as Jonathan but never as petty. Cary Grant shoved

Katharine Hepburn to the ground, Clark Gable spanked Claudette Colbert, and James Cagney squashed a grapefruit into Mae Clarke's face—acts of male brutality that Jack Nicholson never indulged—but the times and the stars' charisma allowed us to think the women either deserved or actually enjoyed the punishment. The male star may have been roped in eventually by the subterranean persistence of the female (who anyway turned into a compliant wife), but his entrapment signaled the end of the movie: until then, as long as he remained within the spectators' sight, his glamour informed even his distasteful acts.

Hollywood's success in pushing technology to mirror surfaces ever more faithfully left little room for the kind of star that was born in a former time and a different world—a mythological creature now as out of place as James Thurber's unicorn in a suburban backyard. Jack Nicholson would achieve stardom through a variety of other roles and is, as such, the modern star. But in the vast majority of those roles, being a modern star meant that he was not a star at all: like Dustin Hoffman, his surface was ordinary and his substance had to be sought within that ordinariness. In 1986, Mike Nichols cast him as the husband opposite Meryl Streep in his film of Nora Ephron's *Heartburn*. The 1983 novel had been the fictional account of her own unsuccessful marriage to Carl Bernstein, the investigative reporter of Watergate days and the author of *All the President's Men*.

Ephron's novel was evidence of a self-conscious time. The story is about a divorcee who marries warily, discovers her husband is unfaithful, leaves him, returns when he promises to amend, discovers he didn't, and leaves him for good—that story could be either tragedy or farce. This one's modesty blushed at naming pain and disguised it as indigestion. Likewise, the Nichols and Ephron screen adaptation turned heartache into heartburn by keeping a scrim of one-liners, gossip fun, and incongruous gourmet preparations (Rachel is a food writer) between her distress and the spectator. The novel's descent from suffering to sarcasm reflected to a certain extent the descent of films from glamour to graffito—the desire to impose a common mask on loftier emotions. But both were products of the eighties, a time when the mask itself had become sophisticated.

In *Carnal Knowledge,* Nicholson was the eternal college sophomore who cannot grow up. His plain face bespoke a commonplace failure: he resembled all those in the audience who had similarly failed but for whom the film was not intended. *Carnal Knowledge* was meant for those who would reflect on, rather than identify with, the drastic reduction of relationships to sex. In *Heartburn,* the same Jack Nicholson brought the same absence of allure to the portrayal of a successful Washington columnist. It was the same face, grown older: thinning and receding hair that refused to be managed for very long, quirkier eyebrows, a heavier body. Age had made Nicholson distinct, not distinguished. Where *Carnal Knowledge* chronicled an uncomplicated process of decadence, *Heartburn* sent out mixed signals. Rachel is a neurotic. Even though she is seduced by Mark on their very first meeting (and they meet in the very first scene), her previous marriage has made her terribly skittish. Mark has a lousy reputation as a womanizer: "Is he single?" asks the obviously interested Rachel two minutes after sighting him. "He's famous for it," answers one of her friends. "Very famous," adds another. Yet it is Mark who will propose marriage and Rachel who, in spite of these clear warnings, will accept. Their first meeting is at someone else's wedding: not anticipating what we will learn of her, she is moved by the ceremony; he, meanwhile, is falling asleep. When, after that, she tells him, "I don't believe in marriage," her words do not ring quite true. He answers cheerfully, "Neither do I." And as if to confirm (too late) the futility of those words, she remarries only with utmost reluctance (a parade of people, including her father, her therapist, her friends, and finally Mark himself, must try coaxing her out of her bedroom before she will agree to go through with the ceremony).

Once they are married, Rachel continues being the self-conscious Jewish neurotic worried about everything from her nose (in answer to Mark's reassurance she says, "It goes with my face," then relapses, "I always say that but it isn't true") to the dust in the unfinished apartment, her anxious experimentation with recipes, or Mark tearing off a chicken wing at a picnic before the appointed time (a part of Mark's failure is that he is only verbally appreciative of the finer cuisine Rachel produces). It is Mark who absorbs these neurotic thrusts, showing himself to be a patient husband and, later, a good father: he sees Rachel through a difficult birth; enjoys playing with his little girl; and, when Rachel discovers he is having an affair and leaves him, is the one who follows her to New York and asks her to return. Meanwhile, she spends the New York part of her second pregnancy moping in front of the television, imagining that Alistair Cooke is presenting her pathetic existence on *Masterpiece Theater.*

Although Mark is able to talk Rachel into coming back to Washington, she never really reenters the marriage. She remains suspicious and tense. After giving birth to her second child, she confirms her suspicions, finding the proof she has been looking for after going through his papers, his wallet, and his clothes: Mark has not broken off the affair as he promised he would. She has one final gastronomic evening at their friends' house during which she twists the lime pie she had prepared into her husband's face and leaves him—we assume once and for all.

The signals remain confusing during the second half of the picture. Rachel seems to compensate for her lack of self-confidence through a kind of irritable indifference. She comes back from an evening out with Mark, blurting, "That was really fun, wasn't it?" in a voice so close to hysterics that even Mark is undeceived. But meanwhile, it is Mark who cries at the second birth, remembering the time of the first—while Rachel no longer seems to care (when she is told, as she had not been the first time, that the baby is fine, she turns her head away with indifference). Long before acquiring proof of Mark's continued infidelity, she appears to have remembered her own earlier words: "Marriage doesn't work. Only divorce works."

In the hospital room, her visiting friends (once Mark's friends), she, and her housekeeper leave him out of their circle. Eventually, he too grows edgier, but only after she has given him ample cause. It is difficult to reconcile his dogged devotion, especially when it contrasts so constantly with Rachel's self-centeredness and her insecurity. (She is seemingly put upon by the whole world: her father, to whom she returns after her first escape, sees her only as someone to be hastily comforted during a short hiatus in one of his own affairs. And when her therapy group is robbed by a young gangster who followed her, her therapist [Maureen Stapleton] tells her, "This robbery was not your fault." Rachel answers, "It probably was my fault." "I know," says the therapist.)

In an actor evidencing a tragic split, one would read Mark's putting up with Rachel's neuroses as the love of someone who feels good within the warmth of family and friends but whose fatal flaw is his inability to give up an affair, however much he knows he should and however much he tries. But the role was given to Jack Nicholson and treated in a comic mode with the result that the suffering Mark and the philandering Mark remain distinct people whose conjoining we never quite understand. Nicholson's Mephistophelian eyebrows and receding hairline stress the philanderer but detract from the pained and loving Mark: he has not been given sufficient soul to contain both. Finally we tend to feel, in spite of evidence to the contrary, that he is as plain inside as out, robbing the waspish Mark Forman (who had been Mark Feldman in the book) of his depth and the film of its purpose.[5] In *Car-*

nal Knowledge, Jonathan's callous womanizing was rife with consequences; in *Heartburn,* a supposedly loving Mark is finally just an adulterer, an empty figure into which the rest of the picture disappears, dragging with it what might have been Rachel's pain. The marriage ends when Rachel is able for once to assert herself and even sacrifice a gourmet recipe in order to punish Mark with the pie. In farce, pleasure at this kind of mindless aggression derives from our knowledge that the victim was discomfited, not hurt, because the farce character is not made of sensitive flesh. It was fitting that Nicholson should be treated similarly in a picture that reduced his recognizable individuality to a level of mere insensitivity.[6]

Stardom once imposed on the character general traits that turned the star into a morality figure: he was goodness, evil, daring, strength, charm, from role to role, *before* stepping into the story that required his personification. The character who was not endowed with the star's exclusiveness was able to enact a private and unique concern— one the star did not need: spectators were more likely to be attracted by Joan Crawford than by Mildred Pierce. While the star remained the spectator's lodestar, that spectator got what he wanted: he came for Joan Crawford, he got Joan Crawford; disappointment was unlikely. With the disappearance of the stars, attention was shifted to the character and his story, problematic points of reference that might well result in a better picture (a less necessary consideration for the star) but might as easily result in disappointment (if the character did not live up to the spectator's expectations, there was no longer a Joan Crawford to make up for the lack). After realistic surfaces forced the exile of the star, those surfaces tended to assume more importance, sometimes to the extent of becoming the picture's substitute stars, moving from precision to a new form of glamour that could now exile even those plain figures who replaced the stars. Pauline Kael experienced that feeling with *Heartburn*: "The physical surfaces are so exact and polished that you feel as if you'd been brought into a special, artificial world. . . . Here you get packaging with visibly skimpy insides" (*Hooked* [1989], p. 189). Ironically, most of this happens in a house that is a shambles when we first enter it, and it is never fully restored. But lacking an everyday character who dominates those surfaces and commands our interest, we tend to be seduced by them—the house, for example, becomes more interesting than its people: Will they ever find the right contractor to finish it? What dilemmas will it force them into next? Once we ask those questions, we are concerned with plot— we have left the world in which questions about marriage, divorce, or fidelity are important.

Having lost his glamour, the principal's more specific and limited definition is jeopardized by slick packaging. No longer simply a beautiful but generic signifier, his commonplace distinctiveness may be insufficient to avoid his absorption within the sheen of other surfaces. That absorption turns the actor into another kind of object: he stops being a character and becomes a performance (Kael notes, "Streep can't chew a bite of food without acting out chewing" [*Hooked,* p. 192]). Such are the risks and rewards films face once glamour ceases being Hollywood's main industry, once spectators gradually move out of their worshipful posture (which tended to be pleasurable) into a time of analysis (which tends to be grim).

Ever looking like the redneck next door, Jack Nicholson remained one of Hollywood's foremost actors throughout the eighties in such pictures as *Terms of Endearment* (1983) or *Ironweed* (1987), when his familiar face compelled us beyond its surface. When it didn't, we were left with mere vacuousness, as in *The Shining* (1980). By 1989, he was the top moneymaker in Hollywood.

NOTES

1. As a matter of fact, through an ironic reversal of moral perspectives, Webb had allowed Benjamin to reach Elaine and run away with her *before* she was married.

2. H. Wayne Schuth notes, "During some screenings, audiences have cheered at this point" (*Mike Nichols* [1978], p. 59).

3. And so they have in fact remained children. Fenichel says, "The boy at the phallic phase has identified himself with his penis. The high narcissistic evaluation of the organ can be explained by the fact that just at this period it becomes so rich in sensations" (quoted in Arnold M. Cooper, "What Men Fear: The Façade of Castration Anxiety," p. 119).

4. Bingham actually sees the picture as an instance, not a mockery, of "phallocentrism" (*Acting Male,* p. 113).

5. That Nicholson could play roles that did not remain on the surface of his quirks had been amply shown in such pictures as *The Passenger* (1975) and even through the madness of *One Flew over the Cuckoo's Nest* (1976).

6. Embattled critics, who will go as far as to redeem a former view of the world in order to show how bad things have become, overlook a film like

Heartburn when they deplore the loss of irony "classical" romantic comedies achieved at the expense of the presumptuous male (Kathleen Rowe, "Melodrama and Men in Post-Classical Romantic Comedy"). *Heartburn* is a modern romantic comedy in that the woman ends fulfilled, and because she does so through emancipation rather than marriage, the story is more than able to heap ironic scorn on the male hero.

12

Conclusion: Woody Allen

Were it not for their high salaries, it would be tempting to refer to those who come after the stars as proletarian actors—those whose idiom, whose outward style, corresponds to that of the greater number of spectators. Yesterday's stars transcended boundaries, courting the spectator's self-projection through dreams of charm, affluence, power, beauty. In contrast, the proletarian actor is selective: though he looks familiar, he may well disclose an inner life of no interest to a proletarian audience; or he may put off a spectator otherwise interested in that inner life—a spectator who will never get to it, believing that the actor's familiarity can only breed contempt.

The predominance of such actors leads to a gradual fragmentation of the audience: while something of Spencer Tracy's magnetism remained in his workaday roles and thus invited attention to those roles, Jack Nicholson was practically nothing but his role. But at least Jack Nicholson was the redneck next door—there was a good chance most spectators had already met him. By the time Woody Allen appeared, there was an equally good chance most spectators had never met anyone like this curious alien: important pictures steeped in a quintessentially American idiom, such as *Annie Hall* (1977) or *Manhattan* (1979), were better box office draws in Europe—a fact that cannot be explained away entirely through European love of exoticism.

Woody Allen was first a gag writer, working in the fifties on Sid Caesar's *Show of Shows*. Starting in 1962, he branched out on his own as a

191

nightclub comic. This genealogy is evident in his early films, whose plots are contrivances intended to more or less link together a stand-up comedian's routines. The style of Woody Allen, which survived to a certain extent in even his mature period, derived from a spare small body supporting a thin, Jewish face whose owlish eyes behind heavily rimmed glasses bespoke innocence and confusion while suggesting intellectual topics—Sex, Death, Life, God, Art, and the like. The comic mechanism consisted of reducing these topics to trivial or nonsensical associations: in *Sleeper* (1973), one of the last of his first-period movies, the hero's girlfriend says to him, "You don't believe in science, or political systems, or God. What do you believe in?" To which he answers, "Sex and death, things which come once in a lifetime. At least after death you're not nauseous."

The answer contains germs of the later Allen: an anxiety underlies its nonsense. Sex and death are indeed serious beliefs; in fact, they are obsessions far more immediate than systems, political or theological. To the Woody Allen incarnation, sex remains a danger and a mystery—it may happen more than once in a lifetime, but it is constantly an imminent risk that jeopardizes the ideal realization. And as for death, there is nothing one can finally say about it: it can be verbally reduced but not dismissed. As Woody Allen said to Frank Rich, "The fundamental thing behind *all* motivation and *all* activity is the constant struggle against annihilation and against death" ("Woody Allen Wipes the Smile off His Face," p. 76). When the anxiety lifts, a more aggressive note is struck, and one hears echoes of an intellectual Groucho Marx: "Those Greeks were all homosexuals. They must have had wild parties and taken a house together for the summer in Crete: (*a*) Socrates is a man; (*b*) all men are mortal; (*c*) all men are Socrates. That means all men are homosexuals. . . . I'm not. Some are heterosexual, some bisexual, and some don't think about it at all and become lawyers" (*Love and Death,* 1975).

In the aggregate, the sheer piling up of mad inversions achieves a lyrical flow:

A rabbi who leaps on top of a man in a frenzy and carves the story of Ruth on his nose with a stylus; a girl who looks like a herring; a man wandering the Urals and emotionally involved with a panda; a man who stutters, but not when he speaks, only when he writes; a doctor who attends a seance at which a table not only rises but excuses itself and goes upstairs to sleep; a man who dates a Cornish hen; a beagle who goes to a Park Avenue Jungian veterinarian who, for fifty dollars a session, "labors valiantly to convince him that jowls are not a social drawback"; a goldfish who sings "I Got Rhythm"; a horse that can recite the Gettysburg Address; a pope who talks like a gangster; a sea monster with the body of a crab and the head of a certified public accountant. [Foster Hirsch, *Love, Sex, Death, and the Meaning of Life: Woody Allen's Comedy* (1981), p. 164][1]

This lyric flow reminds us to what extent movies have become talkies and how much comedy was altered as a result. The Chaplin gag was nearly always visual (even in the later pictures that use speech): the gestures of childhood delight the spectator who luxuriates in their freedom, and then they avenge him of the adult's constraints (now the constraints of the spectator's own oppressive world) by striking out successfully against them. But because Chaplin is essentially a mime in a silent world, he dances the forms of that freedom as well as the manner of his subversion, and the spectator participates in that dance before he mentalizes its implications. Only at a second and retrospective level does he *think* about what all this means.

When words become an integral part of the motion picture, the immediacy of sight competes with the immediacy of words and loses. The Marx Brothers represent a splintering of the mime into the transitional figures of comics halfway between the old silents and a modern world of words: Harpo is mute and so remains largely a mime; all three are figures of physical subversion, but in Chico and Groucho that comic subversion is primarily linguistic. By the time we get to Woody Allen, the subversion is wholly linguistic, and for a while the pictures he makes allow him merely to *speak* his gags.[2]

But Charlie Chaplin also has a darker side; the child is sometimes defeated—he remains alone, bereft of love, distraught. That darker side is apparent in Woody Allen as well: his comic anxiety and neuroses have their roots in Allen Stewart Konigsberg, the Jewish kid from Brooklyn, before he became Woody Allen, and sooner or later all metaphysical questions become acute at a personal level. Sex is not the only problem, though it remains central. For Allen, interpersonal relationships are an intimate and vexing quandary: "When it comes to relationships with women, I'm the winner of the August Strindberg award." Another of the critics who deplore bygone times, Heidi Dawidoff sees Allen as emblematic of those who now "can't work or wait for a relationship" (*Between the Frames,* p. 16).

Women, at the center of his puzzlement over sex and relationships, take on curious and sometimes contradictory roles. In the earliest *What's New, Pussycat?* (1965), women are simply the objects of schoolboy jokes, frightening and desirable creatures created by someone who "is both enchanted by and fearful of women" (Hirsch, p. 30). That enchantment and that fear account for his vision of the female in later pictures as well. In the mature *Manhattan,* they can be the virginal dream of the Jewish kid who wants to pass in a non-Jewish and sexual world (Tracy is played by Mariel Hemingway, the granddaughter of the emblematically American author), or they can be lesbians whom he finds both fearsome and hateful. At other times, the woman is the healer: for the man who once said he could not conceive of "living without analysis" (Hirsch, p. 13), she may be the psychiatrist, as in *Another Woman*; or she can offer even more complex solace, as psychiatrist and mother, saving *both* him and herself in *Zelig*—Allen biting the hand that strokes him as he urges the physician to heal (her)self. Or again, at the other end of the scale, she achieves character status as a kindred spirit—the complementary neurotic in a picture like *Annie Hall.*

Because all metaphysics sooner or later founder upon more intimate physics, concerns about relationships that are already entangled with worries over analysis soon give way to even more mundane distractions: having cornered the desirable Mary (Diane Keaton) in a cab speeding him through *Manhattan* toward unknown delights, Allen pants, "You look so beautiful, I can hardly keep my eyes on the meter." And the very bleakness of life, seen from the abstraction of moral high ground ("Mankind faces a crossroads. One path leads to despair and utter hopelessness, the other, to total extinction. Let us pray we have the wisdom to choose correctly"), becomes the awareness that opportunity can never be grasped as anything more than a personal loss: "Why did I quit college? I was in black studies. By now, I could have been black."

After *Sleeper* (1973), Woody Allen's skill in crafting motion pictures turns them into a psychoanalyst's couch: he drops the disguise the stand-up comedian had previously interposed between the source of his gags and their articulation and creates instead characters with roots deep in the same subsoil. In *Zelig* (1983), he uses his cinematic virtuosity to examine the loss of selfhood: his very Allen-like hero, the traditional Jewish nebbish, tries to participate in significant moments of history by entering the newsreel clips that preserved them.[3] (While the satirist mocks Warren Beatty's *Reds,* no less an expert than Bruno Bettelheim comes onscreen to assert of Leonard Zelig that he was "the ultimate conformist." And Irving Howe corroborates: "[He] wanted to assimilate like crazy"). In *Broadway Danny Rose* (1984), Allen turns Fellini, remembering his own days on the seamier inside of the entertainment world—a vision that is sometimes so personal that it seems accessible only to those who are a part of it (characters playing themselves, in-jokes, etc.).[4]

Like Fellini again, Woody Allen is at his best when he allows his memories, his loves, and his nostalgia to inform his filmic world—along with his angst. His love of movies, evident in many of his pictures, contributes frequently to his characterizations, as often as not his own (e.g., *Stardust Memories* or *Hannah and Her Sisters* in 1986), and gives movies like *Play It Again, Sam* (1972) or *The Purple Rose of Cairo* just about their entire raison d'être. This clarinet player, who for so many years did a Monday night gig at Michael's Pub on 55th Street, brings the sweet remembrance of big band melodies to his recollection of things past. And when the score is Gershwin's, as in *Manhattan,* it intensifies the paean he addresses to the object of his undying affection, New York.

The film as confessional occasionally propels Allen beyond comedy. *Stardust Memories* (1980) lashes out at spectators and critics who were disappointed by *Interiors* (1978), his attempt to give an inner angst to the objective dimensions of Ingmar Bergman and Eugene O'Neill. Nor did the failure of *Interiors* deter him: in 1988, *September* told the story of a family haunted by the memory of a teenager killed by her mother's lover. This time Allen did more than merely hide his gloom within female characters; reentering the world of O'Neill or Chekhov, he went beyond restating their kind of location—here the stifling interior of a Vermont country house. Still experimenting with the possibilities of film, he turned his picture into a deliberate play, the single setting and the curtain drops of the blackouts between scenes contributing to the drama's confining mood. He repeated the experiment the following year with *Another Woman,* objectifying himself once again within a female projection—as he had done in a comic mode in *The Purple Rose of Cairo* and would again do in *Alice* (1990).

Critics took unkindly to Woody Allen's disguises and his feeling that he could be more penetrating in gloom than in comedy; they turned against him the line he had contemptuously given them in *Stardust Memories,* "Why doesn't he make movies like he used to do, you know, those early funny ones?" Allen's point was well taken, nevertheless: his early "funny" movies were hardly movies at all—little more than extensions of his nightclub acts. Nor can he be faulted for attempting different ways of approaching the human quandary, pushing his imagination and his camera to new limits. But the critics are also right in suggesting that a film like *Annie Hall* is more complex in its style and more searching in its analysis than those that banished laughter in the belief that it would interfere with the seriousness of his project.

Annie Hall takes as a springboard for its fiction the biographical equivalent of what newsreel clips would be in the later *Zelig*—the irrefutable evidence of reality, and that reality is once again Woody Allen's own existence. The opening shot shows him doing a nightclub bit close up to the camera: he is not in a nightclub, but he is talking in the idiom of the entertainer directly to the audience. However, Allen *also* proposes to tell the story of a comedian (and one who was first a gag writer for others), turning forty and in the midst of another of his life crises—a crisis he suffers even though he is in analysis and has been for the last fifteen years.

Woody Allen underscores the routine nature of his patter with a cliché: "I would never want to belong to any club that would have someone like me for a member" (which he personalizes when he tries to explain why he is rejecting a woman who wants him). Having resurrected the stand-up comedian who once appeared at New York's Blue Angel and San Francisco's Hungry I, Allen turns away from this parafictional opening by introducing the fictional Alvy Singer, who cannot get his "mind around" the fact that Annie and he have broken up. The fiction will now take us in flashback through the rise of Annie Hall (Diane Keaton), someone who for once matches the male lead's neuroses. Guided by Singer, she emerges from nervous nonentity to accomplished performer—a singer sufficiently well known to break away from him and go her own way.[5]

But even as he moves into the fiction of his narrative, Woody Allen keeps it within a biographical proximity: years later, *Celebrity* (1998) is partly informed by the press-hyped account of the lurid events leading to his breakup with Mia Farrow. But this was so much earlier. Diane Keaton, who was Woody Allen's lover before *they* broke up and whose career Allen nurtured since *Play It Again, Sam,* was first Diane (if not Annie) Hall.[6] Further turning the fiction on itself, Allen has Alvy writing his first play after the end of the fictional affair (Allen was the playwright who had already written *Death, Death Knocks, Don't Drink the Water, God,* and the stage original of *Play It Again, Sam*). The very play he writes will be, like the picture that contains it, the story of their love affair—we will even see the actors (who play Alvy and Annie playing Woody and Diane) as they perform the scene of their final breakup. This play, however, will have an upbeat ending: Alvy leaves his fictionalized Annie with more grace and less pain—"You want things to come out perfect in art because it's real difficult in life": confessional to the end (Alvie has already confided to us, "I'm obsessed with death"), the picture even tells us about the extent to which art is therapy for its author.[7] It also tells us about the sad distance between art and existence.

Part of *Annie Hall* was accessible to all: it allowed those who felt they had loved and lost to rehearse bittersweet memories. And the songs Annie sings, "It Had to Be You" and "Seems Like Old Times," could still stir in some recollections of a past that had not yet died. But identification required getting past the persona of Woody Allen and understanding his idiom: while it is true that being Jewish and being a New Yorker are not absolutely necessary to enjoy Woody Allen, it certainly helps (vide Annie's Los Angeles, a strange and alien place seen through the eyes of the kid from Brooklyn rather than through hers; or the way in which he puts down Annie the shiksa by having her order "pastrami on white bread with tomatoes and lettuce").[8] Being Jewish undoubtedly helps to sense as well that there is more than fun when Alvy feels himself turning into a bearded rabbi at the Halls' Easter dinner, just as being an intellectual most likely helps understand the savage pleasure Allen derives from conjuring up Marshall McLuhan to put down the spouter of McLuhanite profundities who criticizes Fellini while they are waiting in line to see a film at the New Yorker.[9]

It is at the end of *Annie Hall* that the stand-up comedian tells the one about the man confiding in his shrink that his brother believes himself to be a chicken. When the shrink asks him why he doesn't do something about it, the patient responds, "I would, but I need the eggs." Allen derives his final comment about relationships from this vaudeville chestnut: "They're totally irrational, and crazy, and absurd, but I guess we keep going through them because most of us need the eggs"—suggesting in no uncertain terms that what we derive from our relationships is utterly illusory and that we must be crazy to indulge even that illusion. This is finally not a philosophical comment but the tragicomic vision of a particular sensitivity: it may resonate within a number of spectators, but it is especially evidence of the fact that we lost long ago the single audience that stars commanded. Woody Allen is a fragmented voice speaking to a few in an age of fragmentation.

With Woody Allen, Vishnu comes down to earth in a disastrous incarnation. Seeking an exceptional avatar, he consults Siva, who, as the

Lord of All, combines both destructive power and the power of reproduction, as well as being the God of Dancing and the Arts ("Some Gods
overreach—I mean, he's already the Lord of reproduction"). Siva tells
him that because he wishes to appear on earth as either a teacher or a
fertility god, he can feed him a magic delicacy that will change him into
Durga, the Destroyer: "As Durga, you can work just about any kind of
miracle you want." The food, still unknown along the Ganges, is lox
and bagels with cream cheese. He soon detects in it a delicate aroma
and great potency: before even the Turkish coffee, he finds himself
with the eight arms and the magnificent raiment of Durga. But lacking
a mirror (a useless device anyway, as divine radiance is known to dis-
integrate such artifacts), he does not know he still has the face of
Woody Allen. So when he comes down to earth he frightens away the
maidens he wanted to emancipate by unifying flesh and spirit through
the ritual satisfaction of lust. After he has spent seven days and seven
nights trying to liberate souls with sufficient karma, the potency of the
lox and bagels wears off together with its ability to preserve the shape
of Durga the Destroyer: he is now wholly Woody Allen. And as he
wonders how he will get back to heaven, he thinks ruefully, "When the
Supreme Being gets knocked off, *somebody's* got to take the rap," but
then remembers—and this is the end—that he has already spoken
those words to Heather Butkiss in a short essay called "Mr. Big."

NOTES

1. One can note shades of Ionesco's Orator in the man who stutters when
he writes: Woody Allen is obviously well read.

2. Woody Allen said to David Sterritt, "Years ago, . . . people saw the world
in largely physical terms, and movies reflected that view[, but] our world seems
more internalized, less concrete" (*The Christian Science Monitor,* 21 July 1983).
Or even earlier, "when Chaplin and Keaton were making films, the world was
very physical. Now things are electronic, not so physically oriented. The con-
flicts have moved from the exterior to the interior" (Hirsch, p. 110).

3. Such is Allen's cinematic skill that he sometimes enjoys it primarily for its
own sake: the 1985 *Purple Rose of Cairo*'s heroine repeats Buster Keaton's feat
in *Sherlock Jr.* by physically entering the motion pictures that so entrance her.
And in *Annie Hall,* Allen keeps stepping out of character to become Woody
Allen as he addresses the audience or casual passersby, moves into flashbacks,
loses himself in a cartoon that features him, and so on.

4. Burns Raushenbush writes, "One leaves the theater with the feeling that [the sequestered, in-joke quality of the film] wasn't intended, primarily, for a wider audience" (p. 40).

5. Each character is a singer: not only the principals in their fiction but the author as well—Allen himself, the bard whose very intimate song this is.

6. This was an ongoing process within the hothouse world of Woody Allen's films: women he was involved with on-screen—Louise Lasser (his second wife), Diane Keaton, Mia Farrow—were the ones he was involved with in life. In *Hannah and Her Sisters* (1986), the family on the set was enlarged to include Maureen Sullivan, Mia Farrow's mother, and her children.

7. Some, like Maurice Yacowar, have thought this was indeed the picture's central message: "The power of art to compensate for the limitations of life is the primary theme of *Annie Hall*" (*Loser Take All: The Comic Art of Woody Allen* [1979], p. 179).

8. This was a put-down meant to be understood by only a small number—even fewer than will fathom *his* discomfort (more than simply the New Yorkers in Healthfood land) when he is reduced to ordering alfalfa sprouts with mashed yeast. (He emphasizes the cultural distance of foods in *Hannah and Her Sisters* when, as a Jew, he tries conversion by shopping for white bread and mayonnaise.) Even New York is shrunk to Woody Allen's dimension: Annie tells him that, like Manhattan, he is enclosed within himself (a fact he readily admits when he tells her not to knock masturbation, which, he feels, means making love to someone he loves).

9. This is a reminder of the nasty Woody Allen—for there is also, since his nightclub birth, a part of him that lashes out. Comedy is usually at someone's expense: even the bemused waif in Charlie Chaplin could become vengeful. Anyway, how could Allen forgive the pontificator for having complained that the Italian was "one of the most self-indulgent filmmakers."

Bibliography

Agee, James. *Agee on Film.* New York: McDowell, 1958.

Agel, Henri. *Le Western.* Paris: Lettres Modernes, 1961.

Alexander, Paul. *Boulevard of Broken Dreams: The Life, Times, and Legend of James Dean.* New York: Viking, 1994.

Allan, Blaine. *Nicholas Ray: A Guide to Reference and Sources.* Boston: G. K. Hall and Co., 1984.

Apslund, Uno. *Chaplin's Films: A Filmography.* Trans. Paul Britten Austin. Newton Abbot, U.K.: David and Charles, 1973.

Arendt, Hannah. "The Jew as Pariah." *Jewish Social Studies* 6 (2 April 1944): 99–122.

Barthes, Roland. *Mythologies.* Trans. Annette Lavers. New York: Farrar, Straus and Giroux, 1990.

Baxter, John. *The Cinema of John Ford.* New York: A. S. Barnes and Co., 1971.

Bazin, André. "Mort d'Humphrey Bogart." *Cahiers du cinéma* 68 (1957): 3–8.

———. *Qu'est-ce que le cinéma?* 4 vols. Paris: Editions du Cerf, 1958–62.

Bazin, André, and Eric Rohmer. *Charlie Chaplin.* Paris: Editions du Cerf, 1972.

Bellour, Raymond. *Le Western: Sources, mythes, auteurs, acteurs, filmographies.* Paris: Union Générale d'Éditions, 1968.

Benchley, Nathaniel. *Humphrey Bogart.* Boston and Toronto: Little, Brown and Co., 1975.

Bergson, Henri. *Laughter: An Essay on the Meaning of the Comic.* New York: Macmillan Co., 1911.

Bingham, Dennis. *Acting Male: Masculinities in the Films of James Stewart, Jack Nicholson, and Clint Eastwood.* New Brunswick, N.J.: Rutgers University Press, 1994.

Björkman, Stig. *Woody Allen on Woody Allen*. New York: Grove/Atlantic, Inc., 1995.

Blake, Richard A. *Woody Allen: Profane and Sacred*. Lanham, Md.: Scarecrow Press, 1995.

Bogdanovich, Peter. *John Ford*. Berkeley: University of California Press, 1978.

Bordat, Francis. *Chaplin Cinéaste*. Paris: Editions du Cerf, 1998.

Cagney, James. *Cagney by Cagney*. Garden City, N.Y.: Doubleday and Co., 1976.

Capra, Frank. *The Name above the Title*. New York: Macmillan, 1971.

——. "Thinker in Hollywood." Interview by Geoffrey T. Hellman. *The New Yorker*, 24 February 1940: 23–28.

Carey, Gary. *Marlon Brando: The Only Contender*. New York: St. Martin's Press, 1985.

Carney, Raymond. *American Vision: The Films of Frank Capra*. New York: Cambridge University Press, 1986.

Cawelti, John G. *Adventure, Mystery, and Romance*. Chicago: University of Chicago Press, 1976.

Chandler, Raymond. *The Big Sleep*. New York: Ballantine Books, Inc., 1973.

Chaplin, Charles S. *My Autobiography*. New York: Simon and Schuster, 1964.

——. "Pantomime and Comedy." *The New York Times*, 26 January 1931.

——. "What People Laugh At." *American Magazine* 86 (November 1918): 108–14.

Chasseguet-Smirgel, Janine. *Female Sexuality: New Psychoanalytic Views*. Ann Arbor: University of Michigan Press, 1970.

Clurman, Harold. *The Collected Works of Harold Clurman*. New York: Applause Theatre Books, 1994.

Cohan, Steven, and Ina Rae Hark, eds. *Screening the Male: Exploring Masculinities in Hollywood Cinema*. London and New York: Routledge, 1993.

Comerford, Adelaide. "The Graduate." *Films in Review* 19, no. 1 (January 1968): 55.

Cooke, Alistair. *Six Men*. New York: Alfred A. Knopf, 1977.

Cooper, Arnold M. "What Men Fear: The Façade of Castration Anxiety." *The Psychology of Men: New Psychoanalytic Perspectives*. Ed. Gerald I. Fogel, Frederick M. Lane, and Robert S. Liebert. Pp. 113–30. New York: Basic Books, 1986.

Curry, Renée R., ed. *Perspectives on Woody Allen*. New York: G. K. Hall, 1996.

Dalton, David. *James Dean: The Mutant King*. San Francisco: Straight Arrow Books, 1974.

Dante Alighieri. *La Divina Commedia*. Ed. Tommasso di Salvo. Bologna: Zanichelli, 1987.

Davis, Ronald L. *Duke: The Life and Image of John Wayne*. Norman: University of Oklahoma Press, 1998.

Dawbarn, Charles. *France and the French*. New York: Macmillan Co., 1911.

Dawidoff, Heidi. *Between the Frames: Thinking about Movies*. Hamden, Conn.: Archon Books, 1989.

De Becker, Raymond. *De Tom Mix à James Dean*. Paris: Arthème Fayard, 1959.

de Lauretis, Teresa. *Alice Doesn't: Feminism, Semiotics, Cinema*. Bloomington and Indianapolis: Indiana University Press, 1982.

Deschner, Donald. *The Films of Cary Grant*. Secaucus, N.J.: The Citadel Press, 1973.

———. *The Films of Spencer Tracy*. New York: The Citadel Press, 1968.

Dickens, Homer. *The Films of Gary Cooper*. New York: The Citadel Press, 1970.

———. *The Films of Katharine Hepburn*. New York: The Citadel Press, 1971.

Doane, Mary Ann. *The Desire to Desire: The Woman's Film of the 1940's*. Bloomington and Indianapolis: Indiana University Press, 1987.

Downing, David. *Marlon Brando*. New York: Stein and Day, 1984.

Duchovnay, Gerald. *Humphrey Bogart: A Bio-Bibliography*. Westport, Conn.: Greenwood Press, 1999.

Durand, Jacques. *Le Cinéma et son public*. Paris: Cirey, 1958.

Edwards, Anne. *A Remarkable Woman: A Biography of Katharine Hepburn*. New York: William Morrow and Co., 1985.

Eisenschitz, Bernard. *Humphrey Bogart*. Paris: Le Terrain Vague, 1967.

Eisenstein, Sergei M. *Film Essays*. Ed. Jay Leyda. London: Dennis Dobson, 1968.

Elliot, Patricia. *From Mastery to Analysis: Theories of Gender in Psychoanalytic Feminism*. Ithaca: Cornell University Press, 1991.

Essoe, Gabe. *The Films of Clark Gable*. New York: The Citadel Press, 1970.

Eyles, Allen. *The Western: An Illustrated Guide*. New York: A. S. Barnes, 1967.

Fast, Irene. *Gender Identity: A Differentiation Model*. Hillsdale, N.J.: The Analytic Press, 1984.

Faure, Elie. *Fonction du cinéma: De la cinéplastique à son destin social*. Paris: Librairie Plon, 1953.

Fenin, George N., and William K. Everson. *The Western: From Silents to Cinerama*. New York: Orion Press, 1962.

Fischer, Lucy. "Mama's Boy: Filial Hysteria in *White Heat*." *Screening the Male: Exploring Masculinities in Hollywood Cinema*. Ed. Steven Cohan and Ina Rae Hawk. London and New York: Routledge, 1993.

Fisher, James. *Spencer Tracy: A Bio-Bibliography*. Westport, Conn.: Greenwood Press, 1994.

Fisher, Joe. "Clark Gable's Balls: Real Men Never Lose Their Teeth." *You Tarzan: Masculinity, Movies, and Men*. Ed. Pat Kirkham and Janet Thumim. New York: St. Martin's Press, 1993.

Fogel, Gerald I., Frederick M. Lane, and Robert S. Liebert, eds. *The Psychology of Men: New Psychoanalytic Perspectives*. New York: Basic Books, 1986.

Folsom, James K., ed. *The Western*. Englewood Cliffs, N.J.: Prentice-Hall, Inc., 1979.

Ford, Charles. *Histoire du Western*. Paris: Pierre Horay, 1964.

Franklin, Joe. *Classics of the Silent Screen*. New York: The Citadel Press, 1960.

French, Philip. *Westerns: Aspects of a Movie Genre*. New York: Oxford University Press, 1977.

Freud, Sigmund. *Jokes and Their Relation to the Unconscious*. New York: Norton, 1963.

Gable, Kathleen. *Clark Gable: A Personal Portrait*. Englewood Cliffs, N.J.: Prentice-Hall, Inc., 1961.

Gallagher, Tag. *John Ford: The Man and His Films*. Berkeley: University of California Press, 1986.

Gehring, Wes D. *Charlie Chaplin: A Bio-Bibliography*. Westport, Conn.: Greenwood Press, 1983.

———. *Screwball Comedy: Defining a Film Genre*. Ball State Monograph, 31. Muncie, Ind.: Ball State University Press, 1983.

Gelmis, Joseph. *The Film Director as Superstar*. Garden City, N.Y.: Doubleday and Co., 1970.

Girgus, Sam B. *The Films of Woody Allen*. New York: Cambridge University Press, 1993.

Glatzer, Richard, and John Raeburn, eds. *Frank Capra: The Man and His Films*. Ann Arbor: Ann Arbor Paperbacks, 1975.

Godowski, Dagmar. *First Person Plural*. New York: Viking Press, 1958.

Goodman, Ezra. *Bogey: The Good-Bad Guy*. New York: Lyle Stuart, 1965.

Gramont, Sanche de. *The French*. New York: G. P. Putnam, 1969.

Gruber, Frank. *Zane Grey: A Biography*. New York: World, 1970.

Hall, Judith A., and Amy G. Halberstadt. *The Psychology of Gender: Advances through Meta-Analysis*. Ed. Janet Shibley Hyde and Marcia C. Linn. Baltimore: Johns Hopkins University Press, 1986.

Handel, Leo A. *Hollywood Looks at Its Audience: A Report of Film Audience Research*. Urbana: University of Illinois Press, 1950.

Hansen, Miriam. "Pleasure, Ambivalence, Identification: Valentino and Female Spectatorship." *Cinema Journal* 24, no. 4 (summer 1986): 6–28.

Hart, Daniel A. *Becoming Men: The Development of Aspirations, Values, and Adaptation Styles*. New York and London: Plenum Press, 1992.

Hart, William S. *My Life East and West*. New York: Benjamin Blom, 1968.

Harvey, James. *Romantic Comedy in Hollywood from Lubitsch to Sturges*. New York: Alfred A. Knopf, 1987.

Haskell, Molly. *From Reverence to Rape: The Treatment of Women in the Movies*. New York: Holt, Rinehart and Winston, Inc., 1974.

Hearn, Jeff, and David Morgan, eds. *Men, Masculinities and Social Theory*. London: Unwin Hyman, 1990.

Hellman, Geoffrey T. "Thinker in Hollywood." *The New Yorker,* 24 February 1940: 23–28.

Henderson, Brian. "Romantic Comedy Today: Semi-Tough or Impossible?" *Film Quarterly* (summer 1978): 49–56.

Hirsch, Foster. *Love, Sex, Death, and the Meaning of Life: Woody Allen's Comedy*. New York: McGraw-Hill Book Co., 1981.

Hitt, Jim. *The American West from Fiction into Film*. Jefferson, N.C.: McFarland and Co., 1990.

Hobbes, Thomas. "Human Nature." *Human Nature and De Corpore Politico.* New York: Oxford University Press, 1994.

Holley, Val. *James Dean: The Biography.* New York: St. Martin's Press, 1995.

Huff, Theodore. *Charlie Chaplin.* New York: Henry Schuman, 1951.

Hutchinson, W. H. "Virgins, Villains and Varmints." *The Western.* Ed. James K. Folsom. Pp. 31–49. Englewood Cliffs, N.J.: Prentice-Hall, Inc., 1979.

Hyde, Janet Shibley. "Gender Differences in Aggression." *The Psychology of Gender: Advances through Meta-Analysis.* Ed. Janet Shibley Hyde and Marcia C. Linn. Pp. 51–66. Baltimore: Johns Hopkins University Press, 1986.

Jacobs, Lewis. *The Rise of the American Film.* New York: Harcourt, Brace and Co., 1939.

Jarvie, Ian C. *Movies and Society.* New York: Basic Books, Inc., 1970.

Jeffords, Susan. *Hard Bodies: Hollywood Masculinity in the Reagan Era.* New Brunswick, N.J.: Rutgers University Press, 1994.

Jones, Howard Mumford. *O Strange New World. American Culture: The Formative Years.* New York: Viking Press, 1964.

Jung, Carl G. *The Mother Complex.* Vol. 9 of *Collected Works.* Princeton: Princeton University Press, 1957–67.

———. *Symbols of Transformation.* Vol. 5 of *Collected Works.* Princeton: Princeton University Press, 1957–67.

Kael, Pauline. *Going Steady.* Boston: Little, Brown and Co., 1970.

———. *Hooked.* New York: E. P. Dutton, 1989.

———. *I Lost It at the Movies.* Boston: Little, Brown and Co., 1965.

Kaminsky, Stuart M. *Coop: The Life and Legend of Gary Cooper.* New York: St. Martin's Press, 1980.

Kaplan, E. Ann. *Women and Film: Both Sides of the Camera.* New York: Methuen, 1983.

Kauffmann, Stanley. *Figures of Light: Film Criticism and Comment.* New York: Harper and Row, 1971.

Kinne, Thomas J. *Elemente Jüdischer Tradition im Werk Woody Allens.* Frankfurt am Main: Lang, 1996.

Kirkham, Pat, and Janet Thumim, eds. *Me Jane: Masculinity, Movies, and Women.* New York: St. Martin's Press, 1995.

———. *You Tarzan: Masculinity, Movies, and Men.* New York: St. Martin's Press, 1993.

Kreidl, John Francis. *Nicholas Ray.* Boston: Twayne Publishers, 1977.

Kuhn, Annette. *The Power of the Image: Essays on Representation and Sexuality.* London: Routledge and Kegan Paul, 1985.

Lax, Eric. *Woody Allen: A Biography.* New York: Knopf, 1991.

Lehman, Peter. *Running Scared: Masculinity and the Representation of the American Male Body.* Philadelphia: Temple University Press, 1993.

———. *Women's Pictures: Feminism and Cinema.* London: Routledge and Kegan Paul, 1982.

Lenihan, John H. *Showdown: Confronting Modern America in the Western Film*. Urbana: University of Illinois Press, 1980.

Leprohon, Pierre. *Charles Chaplin*. Paris: Nouvelles Editions Debresse, 1957.

Leutrat, Jean-Louis. *L'Alliance brisée: Le Western des années 1920*. Lyon: Presses Universitaires de Lyon, 1985.

Lynn, Kenneth S. *Charlie Chaplin and His Times*. New York: Simon and Schuster, 1997.

Machover Reinisch, June, Leonard A. Rosenblum, and Stephanie A. Sanders. *Masculinity/Femininity: Basic Perspectives*. New York: Oxford University Press, 1987.

Macklin, F. A. "Benjamin Will Survive." *Film Heritage* 4, no. 1 (fall 1968): 1–6.

Maland, Charles J. *Chaplin and American Culture: The Evolution of a Star Image*. Princeton: Princeton University Press, 1989.

———. *Frank Capra*. Boston: Twayne Publishers, 1995.

Manso, Peter. *Brando: The Biography*. New York: Hyperion, 1994.

Marañón, Gregorio. *Don Juan et le Don Juanisme*. Trans. Marie Berthe Lacombe. Paris: Gallimard, 1967.

Martin, Marcel. *Charlie Chaplin*. Paris: Seghers, 1966.

Mast, Gerald. *The Comic Mind: Comedy and the Movies*. New York: Bobbs Merrill, 1973.

———. *A Short History of the Movies*. Chicago: University of Chicago Press, 1981.

Mayne, Judith. *Kino and the Woman Question*. Columbus: Ohio State University Press, 1989.

———. *The Woman at the Keyhole: Feminism and Women's Cinema*. Bloomington and Indianapolis: Indiana University Press, 1990.

McBride, Joseph, and Michael Wilmington. *John Ford*. New York: Da Capo Press, 1975.

McCabe, John. *Cagney*. New York: Knopf, 1997.

McCann, Graham. *Cary Grant: A Class Apart*. New York: Columbia University Press, 1997.

———. *Rebel Males: Clift, Brando and Dean*. London: Hamish Hamilton, 1991.

McCarty, Clifford. *Bogey: The Films of Humphrey Bogart*. New York: The Citadel Press, 1965.

McGilligan, Patrick. *Cagney: The Actor as Auteur*. New York: A. S. Barnes and Co., 1975.

Mellen, Joan. *Big Bad Wolves: Masculinity in the American Film*. New York: Pantheon Books, 1977.

Metz, Christian. *Film Language: A Semiotics of the Cinema*. Trans. Michael Taylor. New York: Oxford University Press, 1974.

———. *The Imaginary Signifier: Psychoanalysis and the Cinema*. Trans. Celia Britton. Bloomington and Indianapolis: Indiana University Press, 1982.

———. *Language and Cinema*. Trans. Donna Jean Umiker-Sebeok. The Hague: Mouton, 1974.

Meyers, Jeffrey. *Bogart: A Life in Hollywood.* Boston: Houghton Mifflin, 1997.

Miles, Rosalind. *The Rites of Man: Love, Sex and Death in the Making of the Male.* London: Grafton Books, 1991.

Mitry, Jean. *Charlot et la fabulation chaplinesque.* Paris: Editions Universitaires, 1957.

Molyneaux, Gerard. *James Stewart: A Bio-Bibliography.* Westport, Conn.: Greenwood Press, 1992.

Morella, Joe, and Edward Z. Epstein. *Rebels: The Rebel Hero in Films.* New York: The Citadel Press, 1971.

Morin, Edgar. *Le Cinéma ou L'Homme imaginaire.* Paris: Editions de Minuit, 1956.

———. *The Stars.* Trans. Richard Howard. New York: Grove Press, 1960.

Mulvey, Laura. "Visual Pleasure and Narrrative Cinema." *Screen* 16, no. 3 (autumn 1975).

Nichols, Mary P. *Reconstructing Woody Allen: Art, Love, and Life in the Films of Woody Allen.* Lanham, Md.: Rowman and Littlefield, 1998.

Nysenholc, Adolphe. *L'Age d'or du comique: Sémiologie de Charlot.* Brussels: Presses de l'Université de Bruxelles, 1979.

Oberfirst, Robert. *Rudolph Valentino: The Man behind the Myth.* New York: The Citadel Press, 1962.

Olivier, Christiane. *Jocasta's Children: The Imprint of the Mother.* New York: Routledge, 1989.

Parish, James Robert, and Alvin H. Marill. *The Cinema of Edward G. Robinson.* New York: A. S. Barnes and Co., 1972.

Pettigrew, Terence. *Raising Hell: The Rebel in the Movies.* Bromley, Kent: Columbus Books, 1986.

Poague, Leland A. *The Cinema of Frank Capra.* New York: A. S. Barnes, 1975.

Potter, David M. *People of Plenty: Economic Abundance and the American Character.* Chicago: University of Chicago Press, 1954.

Raushenbush, Burns. "Broadway Danny Rose." *Cineaste* 13, no. 3 (1984): 40–42.

Reinisch, Machover, Leonard A. Rosenblum, and Stephanie A. Sanders, eds. *Masculinity/Femininity: Basic Perspectives.* New York: Oxford University Press, 1987.

Rich, Frank. "The Misfortune of Mike Nichols: Notes on the Making of a Bad Film." *The New York Times,* 11 July 1975.

———. "Woody Allen Wipes the Smile off His Face." *Esquire,* May 1977: 72–76, 148–49.

Richards, Barry. "Masculinity, Identification, and Political Culture." *Men, Masculinities and Social Theory.* Ed. Jeff Hearn and David Morgan. Pp. 160–69. London: Unwin Hyman, 1990.

Rieupeyrout, Jean-Louis. *Le Western.* Paris: Editions du Cerf, 1953.

Riggin, Judith M. *John Wayne: A Bio-Bibliography.* Westport Conn.: Greenwood Press, 1992.

Roberts, Randy, and James S. Olsen. *John Wayne: American*. New York: Free Press, 1995.

Robinson, Edward G., with Leonard Spigelgass. *All My Yesterdays: An Autobiography*. New York: Hawthorn Books, 1973.

Ropars, Marie-Claire. "Fonction de la métaphore dans 'Octobre' d'Eisenstein." *Littérature* 11 (October 1973).

Rose, Jacqueline. *Sexuality in the Field of Vision*. London: Verso, 1986.

Rowe, Kathleen. "Melodrama and Men in Post-Classical Romantic Comedy." *Me Jane: Masculinity, Movies, and Women*. Ed. Pat Kirkham and Janet Thumim. Pp. 184–93. New York: St. Martin's Press, 1995.

Roy, Jean. *Pour John Ford*. Paris: Les Editions du Cerf, 1976.

Ruddy, Jonah, and Jonathan Hill. *The Bogey Man: Portrait of a Legend*. London: Souvenir Press, 1965.

Sadoul, Georges. *Histoire générale du cinéma*. 7 vols. Paris: Denoël, 1946–54.

Samuels, Charles. *The King: A Biography of Clark Gable*. New York: Coward-McCann, Inc., 1961.

Sandburg, Carl. *The Letters of Carl Sandburg*. Ed. Herbert Mitgang. New York: Harcourt, Brace and World, 1968.

Sarris, Andrew. *The American Cinema: Directions and Directors*. Chicago: University of Chicago Press, 1985.

———. *The John Ford Movie Mystery*. London: Secker and Warburg, 1976.

Schickel, Richard. *Brando: A Life in Our Times*. New York: Atheneum, 1991.

———, ed. *The Men Who Made the Movies*. New York: Atheneum, 1975.

Schuth, H. Wayne. *Mike Nichols*. Boston: Twayne Publishers, 1978.

Sennett, Ted. *Lunatics and Lovers: A Tribute to the Giddy and Glittering Era of the Screen's "Screwball" and Romantic Comedies*. New Rochelle, N.Y.: Arlington House, 1973.

Shibley Hyde, Janet, and Marcia C. Linn, eds. *The Psychology of Gender: Advances through Meta-Analysis*. Baltimore: Johns Hopkins University Press, 1986.

Shipman, David. *Brando*. New York: Doubleday and Co., 1974.

Shulman, Irving. *Valentino*. New York: Trident Press, 1967.

Silverman, Kaja. *The Acoustic Mirror: The Female Voice in Psychoanalysis and Cinema*. Bloomington and Indiana: Indiana University Press, 1988.

———. *The Subject of Semiotics*. New York: Oxford University Press, 1983.

Sinclair, Andrew. *John Ford*. New York: The Dial Press/James Wade, 1979.

Sklar, Robert. *City Boys: Cagney, Bogart, Garfield*. Princeton: Princeton University Press, 1992.

Sperber, A. M., and Eric Lax. *Bogart*. New York: William Morrow and Co., 1997.

Stebbins, Robert. "Mr. Capra Goes to Town." *Frank Capra: The Man and His Films*. Ed. Richard Glatzer and John Raeburn. Pp. 117–20. Ann Arbor: Ann Arbor Paperbacks, 1975.

Stowell, Peter. *John Ford*. Boston: Twayne Publishers, 1986.

Studlar, Gaylyn. "Valentino, 'Optic Intoxication,' and Dance Madness." *Screening the Male: Exploring Masculinities in Hollywood Cinema*. Ed. Steven Cohan and Ina Rae Hawk. Pp. 23–45. London and New York: Routledge, 1993.

Swindell, Larry. *Charles Boyer: The Reluctant Lover.* Garden City, N.Y.: Doubleday and Co., 1983.

———. *The Last Hero: A Biography of Gary Cooper.* New York: Doubleday and Co., 1980.

———. *Spencer Tracy: A Biography.* New York: The World Publishing Co., 1969.

Thomas, Alison. "The Significance of Gender Politics in Men's Accounts of Their 'Gender Identity.'" *Men, Masculinities and Social Theory.* Ed. Jeff Hearn and David Morgan. Pp. 143–59. London: Unwin Hyman, 1990.

Thomas, Bob. *Marlon: Portrait of the Rebel as an Artist.* New York: Random House, 1973.

Thompson, Kristin, and David Bordwell. *Film History: An Introduction.* New York: McGraw-Hill, Inc., 1994.

Tompkins, Jane P. *West of Everything: The Inner Life of Westerns.* New York: Oxford University Press, 1992.

Tornabene, Lyn. *Long Live the King: A Biography of Clark Gable.* New York: G. P. Putnam's Sons, 1976.

Turow, Lester C. *The Zero-Sum Society: Distribution and the Possibilities for Economic Change.* New York: Penguin Books, 1981.

Tyler, Parker. *Chaplin, Last of the Clowns.* New York: Vanguard Press, 1948.

Walker, Alexander. *Rudolph Valentino.* New York: Penguin Books, 1977.

Warren, Doug, with James Cagney. *Cagney: The Authorized Biography.* New York: St. Martin's Press, 1983.

Warshow, Robert. *The Immediate Experience: Movies, Comics, Theatre and Other Aspects of Popular Culture.* Garden City, N.Y.: Doubleday and Co., 1962.

Wayne, Jane Ellen. *Gable's Women.* New York: Prentice-Hall, 1987.

Webb, Charles R. *The Graduate.* New York: The New American Library, 1963.

Wendell, Barrett. *The France of Today.* New York: Charles Scribner's Sons, 1907.

Williams, Chester. *Gable.* New York: Fleet Press Corporation, 1968.

Wilson, Robert, ed. *The Film Criticism of Otis Ferguson.* Philadelphia: Temple University Press, 1971.

Yacowar, Maurice. *Loser Take All: The Comic Art of Woody Allen.* New York: Frederick Ungar Publishing Co., 1979.

Yorburg, Betty. *Sexual Identity: Sex Roles and Social Change.* New York: John Wiley and Sons, 1974.

INDEX

About the Author

David I. Grossvogel is the Goldwin Smith Professor Emeritus of comparative literature and romance studies at Cornell University. He received his B.A. from the University of California at Berkeley and his M.A. and Ph.D. from Columbia University. He is the author of numerous publications on modern European literature and, especially, the theater. After founding *Diacritics*, the journal that fostered postmodern criticism in this country and was among the first to promote serious film analysis within the academy, he extended his interest in popular literature, writing, among others, books on the mystery genre, Ann Landers, and *TV Guide*.

ALVERNO COLLEGE LIBRARY

2 5050 00906425 0

10-12-2020

791.43
G878

REMOVED FROM THE
ALVERNO COLLEGE LIBRARY

Alverno College Library
Milwaukee, WI

DEMCO